William Henry Platt

The Philosophy of the Supernatural

William Henry Platt

The Philosophy of the Supernatural

ISBN/EAN: 9783337080266

Printed in Europe, USA, Canada, Australia, Japan

Cover: Foto ©Thomas Meinert / pixelio.de

More available books at **www.hansebooks.com**

The Bishop Paddock Lectures, 1886

THE

PHILOSOPHY

OF

THE SUPERNATURAL

BY

W. H. PLATT, D. D., LL. D.

RECTOR OF ST. PAUL'S CHURCH

ROCHESTER, N. Y.

———— · ————

NEW YORK

E. P. DUTTON & COMPANY

31 WEST TWENTY-THIRD ST.

1886.

THE BISHOP PADDOCK LECTURES.

In the summer of the year 1880, GEORGE A. JARVIS of Brooklyn, N. Y., moved by his sense of the great good which might thereby accrue to the cause of CHRIST and to the Church, of which he was an ever grateful member, gave to the General Theological Seminary of the Protestant Episcopal Church certain securities exceeding in value eleven thousand dollars for the foundation and maintenance of a Lectureship in said Seminary.

Out of love to a former Pastor and enduring friend, the Rt. Rev. Benjamin Henry Paddock, D.D., Bishop of Massachusetts, he named his Foundation "THE BISHOP PADDOCK LECTURESHIP."

The deed of trust declares that:

" *The subjects* of the Lectures shall be such as appertain to the defence of the religion of JESUS CHRIST, as revealed in the *Holy Bible* and illustrated in the *Book of Common Prayer* against the varying errors of the day, whether materialistic, rationalistic, or professedly religious, and also to its defence and confirmation in respect of such central truths as the *Trinity*, the *Atonement*, *Justification* and the *Inspiration of the Word of God* and of such central facts as the *Church's Divine Order and Sacraments*, her historical *Reformation* and her rights and powers as a pure and National Church. *And* other subjects may be chosen if unanimously approved by the Board of Appointment as being both timely and also within the true intent of this Lectureship."

Under the appointment of the Board created by the Trust, viz., the Dean of the General Theological Seminary and the Bishops respectively of Massachusetts, Connecticut, and Long Island, the Rev. W. H. Platt, D.D., LL. D., Rector of St. Paul's Church, Rochester, N. Y., delivered the Lectures for the year 1886, contained in this volume.

WORKS BY THE SAME AUTHOR.

NOTE.

The Lecturer is unable, in publishing these lectures, to reproduce the popular form of illustrations, that were allowable in the freedom of their extemporaneous delivery. His further revision of them has been impossible under the pressure of unassisted daily Lenten services and lectures, both in and out of his own parish. It is his hope, at no very distant day, to be able to give his subject a more extended and critical discussion; but, lest the realization of that hope should be unexpectedly delayed, immediate use has been made of such supplemental matter from his other lectures, essays and books, whether published or unpublished, as was thought to complete and strengthen his present argument. With the most careful proof-reading possible under the circumstances, the author discovers errors which every scholar will readily correct for himself.

W. H. P.

Easter Monday,
  Rochester, 1886.

ANALYSIS OF CONTENTS.

ERRATA.

Page 15—Second line from top, read the word *Inscrutable* for "Inscrutable."

Page 34—Fourteenth line from bottom, read *then* for "the."

Page 40—Sixth line from bottom, omit "But that is impossible."

Page 47—Fifth line from top, omit "We derive only power."

Page 49—Second line from bottom, read *noumenal* for "nomenal."

Page 63—Eleventh line from bottom, read *Though* for "As."

Page 105—Top line, read *Ethics is law* for "No ethics is law."

Page 107—Top line, read *effects* for "effect"

Page 129—Thirteenth line from top, insert *which* after "that."

Page 169—Top line, read *for* for "to."

Page 176—Put (*c*) in brackets for (e).

Page 278—Second line from top, read *1 & 2* for "142."

Page 320—Omit *equally*, in seventh line from bottom.

Page 321—Transpose *not* before "that," in fourth line from bottom.

LECTURE 1.

SUPERNATURAL POWER.

The Philosophy of the Supernatural is the deduction of supernatural principles from an induction of natural facts.

We can better hope to define supernature, when we have first defined nature. Nature is all that it can prove itself to be, and Supernature is all that nature is not, and which it cannot prove itself to be. Nature is the derived; supernature is the underived. Supernature is that which has always been; nature is that which has not always been. My object is to show that,

1. *Nature cannot be separated from Supernature*, the stream from the fountain, the human from the superhuman. Infinite, supernatural Power manifests finite methods. Nature, a part, makes the induction of supernature the whole. As a belief in supernature is intuitive to the human mind, we have not so much to prove supernature, as to disprove the arguments of those who deny it. In doing the latter, we confirm the former.

How shall we prove this? Shall we assume the supernatural, and reason, *a priori*, down to nature, or shall we begin at the admitted observable facts of nature, and reason *a posteriori* up to supernature? There are what we call natural *facts*, things done rather than things existing, which we can test by the scales, the scalpel, the retort, and the crucible. Let us, then, begin our study with the verifiable observations of the *facts* of nature. Subject and object are related as parent and child; one is derived from the other; and any philosophy of the relative that ignores either subject or object—cause or effect—noumenon or phenomenon—is incomplete as a philosophy. When told that facts are related by certain laws, the demand is irrepressible, that we go further, and account for the laws, and for their Law-giver. The loyalty of the human intellect to itself will never evade, nor permit any line of thinking calling itself philosophy or science, to evade a complete answer to the questions it may raise. We study matter for an objective base to a subjective theology.

Nothing is beyond supernatural purpose and power. Nature but photographs the map in the supernatural mind. Method is a working plan of Power. And here we notice the distinction between Power and Force, and between creation and causation. That which is Power to the philosophers is Force to the scientists. All new things as the first atom of any kind and the first organisms, are creations by Power as power; all chemical or mechanical uses of these atoms are causations by Power called Force. Power as Force has a direct causative method or plan of application; first, when it *chemically combines* inorganic matter, and secondly, when it *mechanically moves* inorganic matter. After God, as an originating Power, manifested matter, whether manifesting himself as matter, as some Pantheists say, or creating it when there was nothing, He proceeded to construct it into to forms and functions, creating or residing in it, as chemical combinations, mechanical motion, and vital force.   To find the Factor, let us begin with the facts.   To do this, let us imagine ourselves standing, for a moment, on the bank of a river.   In its depths are fish.   On the bank are trees.   We have water without life, trees with life, fish with life and intelligence, and we ourselves have conscious thought. Some one power is doing several different things. Every object is covered by the method of the universe, whatever the method is.   In the water, we see a direct method of extrinsic power, creating atoms of oxygen and hydrogen, and as force causing them to become, with an unsuspended causation, the inorganic substance of water.   In the organic trees, and in the fish, and in man, we see an additional, indirect method of extrinsic power, committing to the mystery of heredity the transmission of life.   Analyze one drop of water from the river, and we see it to be a fact, that

(a)   *Matter is chemically combined.*

The drop of water is the product of chemic affinity. But what is chemic affinity ?   Is it blind, unintelligent, aimless, impersonal ?   Belonging to the inorganic department of nature, one drop does not beget another ; but each for itself, underived from any other drop, must have just so many parts of oxygen, and just so many parts of hydrogen, and be the immediate causative combination of the original creative Power. No one drop by inheritance can help another. They must not only be causatively put together, but they must be causatively held together. Continued existence is continued creation. The mystery of combination is not in the oxygen alone, nor in the hydrogen alone, nor in both unless the proportions are exact. Fifteen parts of oxygen by weight will not combine into water with three parts of hydrogen. Creative power fixes its own conditions, if conditions it must have. The proportions must be sixteen of one and two of the other; neither more nor less. Even then, *how* is it that these gasses become water? Why do not these conditions produce ink, or wine, or milk, instead of mere water? No substance chemically definable has any attribute of life. Its atoms may be called dead. Who can explain the mystery?

We know that the sun's rays, acting upon the green surface of leaves over our heads, decompose the carbonic dioxide, fix the carbon, and set free the oxygen; but *how* is *this* done? How did the sun's rays get their power? We answer, by some creative will.

We know that chlorate of potash when heated alone, will explode like gunpowder; and yet we know that when this potash is heated in the presence of a little black oxide of manganese, it gasifies in perfect quietness and safety, and the manganese remains unchanged. To call this result a *catalysis* of the element, names, but does not explain it. How or by what *power* does the manganese hold the heated potash in subjection? By some creative will. How do similar molecules of gold or salt *cohere*, dissimilar

molecules of granite or gunpowder only *adhere?*
The same will is the only explanation. How is it
that by slowly heating with a certain proportion of
the oil of vitriol, diluted largely with water, common
sawdust, paper, and old rags even, have the properties of sugar? The power of the change is in this
same creative will. By what power does fire burn,
medicines affect disease, or any and all other chemic
changes take place? We know what occurs, but *how?*
And still more, *why*—for what end—are these changes
made?

Again, in this water, as in everything, from a grain
of sand to worlds and systems of worlds, we see it to
be a fact that,

(*b*) *Matter is mechanically moved.*

What is mechanic force? Is that, too, blind, aimless, unintelligent, and impersonal? Water goes up
in the trees, and down in the river. Why does the
same fluid move in these opposite directions? One
force overcomes another force. We say that water
rises in the trees by capillary attraction, and flows
down the channel by the attraction of gravitation,
and the fish swim up the stream by will-power, in
spite of gravitation. Unless will is law, fish swim up
the stream without law and against law. Are these
names of two different forces, or of one and the same
force, moving water in different directions? What
is gravitation? Is it intelligent or unintelligent?
Whatever it is, it is the all-embracing power of the
universe, holding all to one centre. But what is that
centre? And further, we see it to be a fact that

(c)   *Matter is vitally organized.*

What is *vital* cause or force? In these trees beneath which we pause, are atoms of carbon, hydrogen, and nitrogen, organized by some cause called LIFE. *What is life?* Let those who claim to explain the wonders of nature, explain life. How does any organism cure its wounds? How does the seed form, and the bud open, and the flower form and paint itself, and the fruit come to its ripened use?

Again, while we are looking at the work of some one Power masked in the atoms, and in the motion of the water, and in the growth and structure of the trees, we see in our own reflections upon these wonders, *a conscious cause or force.* How do we think, and *how do we think about our thoughts?* We are conscious that we are conscious. Do atoms think? If so, atoms of what? What class of atoms are so endowed, and who endowed them? Do they think separately, in composition, or when compounded?

2.   *Fact implies a factor* as much as the deed a doer; the thing made the maker; as much as a first implies a second, or the second the first; and if we deny a factor to a fact, the doer to the deed, a creator to creation, or a cause to an effect, we must remould all present thought and language.

But from facts we must form some notion of the Factor—from the seen we must form a conception of the Unseen—from phenomena we must form some opinion as to the Noumenon. For illustration; when we see a convex bullet we know that it came out of a concave mould.

We have said that every fact must have a Factor, and the Factor must be supernatural to a natural fact. These terms, fact and factor, strongly express creation and a Creator. Mr. Spencer calls the Factor of facts a Power; but right here the question is, is the force of the Factor extrinsic or intrinsic to the fact? Sometimes Mr. Spencer writes as though he thought the Power was extrinsic. He says, " We are obliged to regard every phenomenon as the manifestation of some Power by which we are acted *upon*." (F. P. § 27 *Ib.* §§ 28, 194.)

Nothing but will is automatic. Everything is either pushed or pulled along. Whatever evolution there may be, it is but the reaction of involution. For instance, the intrinsic energy of foliation returns the extrinsic Power of the chemistry of the Sun. Power ebbs and flows. Unless this Power be idle, all must also admit that this Power unlimited in time and space, manifests facts limited in time and space. Positive philosophy may arbitrarily limit itself to a study of facts—of phenomena—of effects—in a word, of the Object; but the intelligence of mankind will require a system of such pretension, to find a law-giver for its laws — causes for its effects — noumenon for its phenomena—a Subject for its Object. Facts must be traced back to facts, *ad infinitum*, to a Factor, in order to construct complete science. Science is more than a catalogue of facts. Facts are objective to subject-ive Power. And here we reach the distinction be-tween philosophy and science; philosophy studies the subjective Power, and science the objective facts as a method of all that is before the mind.

3. *Factor implies Power.* The Infinite Factor appears in the finite fact. The known fact reveals that unknown Factor, which in both Scripture and science, is called Power. St. Paul says, " the invisible things of Him from the creation of the world are clearly seen, being understood by the things that are made, even His eternal Power and Godhead." As the cause is greater than the effect—as the producer is before the produced—as that which is, came from that which was before—as the doer is greater than the deed—so the factor is greater than the fact, the Power is greater than its manifestation.

Prof. Fiske says: " There exists a power, to which no limit in time or space is conceivable, of which all phenomena, as presented in consciousness, are manifestations, but which we can know only through these manifestations. Here is a formula legitimately obtained by the employment of scientific methods, as the results of subjective analysis on the one hand, and of objective analysis on the other hand. Yet this formula, which presents itself as the final outcome of a purely scientific inquiry, expresses also the fundamental truth of theism—the truth by which religious feeling is justified. The existence of God—the Supreme truth asserted alike by Christianity and by inferior historic religion—is asserted with equal emphasis by that cosmic philosophy which seeks its data in science alone. * * * Though science may destroy mythology, it can never destroy religion ; and to the astronomer of the future, as well as the psalmist of old, the heavens will declare the glory of God." (Outlines of Cosmic Philosophy, 2 vol., p. 417.)

What is this Power, and what can we know of it?
Mr. Spencer says, " The consciousness of an Inscrutable Power manifested to us through all phenomena,
has been growing ever clearer ; and must eventually
be freed from imperfections. The certainty that on
the one hand such a Power exists, while on the other
hand its nature transcends intuition and is beyond
imagination, is the certainty towards which intelligence has from the first been progressing. To this
conclusion Science inevitably arrives as it reaches its
confines ; while to this conclusion Religion is irresistibly driven by criticism. And satisfying, as it does,
the demands of the most rigorous logic, at the same
time that it gives the religious sentiment the wid-
est possible sphere of action, it is the conclusion
we are bound to accept without reserve or qualifica-
tion. (F. P., § 31.)"

But this Inscrutable Power is so much a power of
not-nature, that we have the authority of Mr. Spencer himself for saying that,

4. *This power is supernatural.* What is supernature? This question is answered when we know what
nature is. Supernature is that which nature is not,
and for which nature cannot account. As the factor is
greater than the fact, so if the fact is natural, the
factor must be supernatural.

The two conclusions of Mr. Spencer are: first, that
nature and supernature are dual and not the same ;
and, second, that the ultimate genesis of nature is in
supernature—in other words, supernature begins all,
and manifests itself in a method of natural facts. No
greater inequality could be admitted, than that admit-

ted, but not defined, by Mr. Spencer. The difference, as just said, is in kind, not degree. One is what the other appoints, but cannot be what the other is. Supernature implies all possible inequality over nature in duration, essence, power and place. If supernature is eternal, nature must be temporal; if supernature is Being, nature must be manifestation; if supernature is omnipresent, nature must be local; if supernature is omniscient, nature must be nescient; if supernature is conscious, nature must be unconscious; Man is supernatural so far as he is supernaturally conscious, as were the Prophets and the Apostles; if supernature is power, nature must be only method. The *plan* of nature is supernatural to nature.

Material science, as science, could not possibly admit more to religion, than has been admitted by Mr. Spencer. Having traced, though to a limited extent, the methods of supernatural power, to the uttermost limits of its manifestation called nature, science must leave religion to follow on with its worship, of all that is beyond. Nature is but the method of supernature, and this method only is subject to scientific study. Religion is for the supernatural power behind the method. Science may study what supernature *does;* religion bows before what supernature *is.* Here, then, we have the two sides of the universe, nature and supernature; and the two studies, science and religion. Science ought not to question the beliefs of religion in that where it has no knowledge; and religion ought to rejoice for all knowledge of nature furnished by science, enlarging its conceptions of supernature.

So far as the modern theory of evolution is proved, it proves all that need be proved, as to the existence and attributes of the supernatural—of God. According to its logic of necessary progress, if God did not make nature, nature has made God. This is proved by the supernatural evolution of nature, or by the natural evolution of supernature. To begin is to create ; to continue is to evolve.

Did supernature evolve nature, or nature, supernature? In the supernatural evolution of nature, the less is from the greater, or the part from the whole. In the natural evolution of supernature, the greater is from the less or the whole from a part. Evolution is a method of unbroken, progressive creation. Direct or indirect creation is every moment, everywhere, in everything. Creation begins and continues the universe. Evolution, if anything, is an intelligent method of carrying on what intelligent power originally created. Our reasoning, whether from supernature to nature, or from nature to supernature, is both *a priori* and *a posteriori*. Supernature as an origin, leads us, *a priori*, to nature as a product ; and nature as a product leads us back, *a posteriori*, to supernature as an origin. So, nature as a cause, leads us *a priori* to supernature as an effect ; and nature as an effect, leads us back *a posteriori* to supernature as a cause. In either look, the Present is a historian of the Past, and a Prophet of the Future. If we cannot see that supernature has minimized itself to nature, we must admit, that in the necessity of eternal progress, nature must maximize itself to supernature.

" As to the students of science, occupied as such

are with established truths," continues Herbert Spencer, " and accustomed to regard things not already known as things hereafter to be discovered, they are liable to forget that information, however extensive it may become, can never satisfy inquiry. Positive knowledge does not, and never can, fill the whole region of possible thought. At the utmost reach of discovery there arises, and must ever arise, the question—What lies beyond? As it is impossible to think of a limit to space so as to exclude the idea of space lying outside that limit; so we cannot conceive of any explanation profound enough to exclude the question—What is the explanation of the explanation? Regarding science as a gradual increasing sphere, we may say, that every addition to its surface does but bring it into wider contact with surrounding nescience." (F. P. § 4.)

If asked what is supernature, I reply by asking what is nature? Is Power *over* nature natural or supernatural *to* nature? If nature is an explanation of all things, supernature is that explanation of the explanation which answers Mr. Spencer's question. In the dual existence of the universe, St. Paul says, " The invisible things of Him from the creation of the world are clearly seen, being understood by the things that are made, even his eternal power and godhead; so that they are without excuse." (Rom. i., 20.) Thought becomes visible. Power takes method. Mind is supernatural to the matter it proves to exist. To deny the supernatural assumes that the natural is both admitted and comprehended. But, if only the comprehensible is the natural, then nothing is the natural. If all is supernatural which is incomprehensible, then all is supernatural; for while we can apprehend some of the naked facts of matter, we cannot comprehend why the facts are facts—we can comprehend nothing. The supernatural is the incomprehensible part of the comprehensible; it is that which we do not understand in that which we think we do understand; it is the unknown part of the known. Supernature is the invisible and intelligent Power behind the visible and unintelligent Form. As every concavity must enclose a convexity, and every convexity be enclosed in a concavity—as nothing can contain, surround, or embrace itself, so the finite must be within the circle of the infinite—nature must be contained in some supernatural container, call it supernature or what you may. As between nature and supernature, one is as incomprehensible as the other—in fact, they are different names for the same existence, considered from different sides of the universe. One considers God in what He *is*, and the other in what he *does*. As from the South Pole to the North Pole it is all the way north, or as from the North Pole to the South Pole it is all the way south; so from supernatural existence to natural phenomena, it is all supernatural, and from natural phenomena to supernatural existence it is all natural. Is the movement from supernature down to nature or from nature up to supernature? The supernatural is the subjective side of objective nature; the natural is the objective side of subjective supernature. As the invisible fountain prolongs itself into the river, so supernature flows out into visible existence, called nature. Supernature, *Natura Naturans*, is always producing and is never produced; Nature, *Natura Naturata*, is always produced, and is never producing. But we cannot tell where supernature ends and where nature begins; for, in a sense, each is the other. There is subjective identity and objective difference. As said before, all is supernatural or above nature for which nature cannot account, such as its own origin and development, it is that by which nature is nature. Strictly speaking, however, to separate nature from supernature, other than verbally, is to separate the inseparable Creator and creation. Nature can no more separate itself from supernature than a cube can separate itself from its own outside. Nature and supernature have a common centre in a supreme, omnipresent, omnipotent Will, personal or impersonal.

The doctrine that supernature produces nature is the theistic logic of the whole producing a part; but the doctrine that nature, the part that was, produces the whole that is, is logically, pantheism.

The Factor that could make a part of nature could make the whole; and the Factor that could make the whole of nature, must be supernature. If words have any meaning, the finite is not the infinite, the fact is not the Factor, nor is the Factor the fact. Therefore, a natural fact implies a supernatural Factor. The manifesting thought must be supernatural to the manifested thing. In theistic evolution, mind manifests its own matter; in atheistic evolution, matter manifests its own mind. In this system the doctrine is, that the universe is the manifestation of a Power that transcends our knowledge. This Power is otherwise called the " Inscrutiable Cause," " Immanent Force," " The Unknowable Reality," " The Unknowable Cause, Power or Force." (F. P., § 62.) With these phrases begin and end all that agnostic evolution has to say about the origin of the universe. Indeed evolutionists cannot deny that facts have a Factor ; but who or what that Factor is, whether personal or impersonal, intelligent or unintelligent, evolution is silent. That Factor, to say the least, is a Power.

To say that all things are manifestations of a Power that transcends our knowledge, is to say, that what the manifesting Power is, the manifested thing is not ; and therefore, as just said, if one is natural, the other must be supernatural. Nature is the comprehensible side of the supernatural, and the supernatural is the incomprehensible side of the natural.

" Though the Absolute cannot in any manner or degree be known, in the strict sense of knowing, yet we find that its positive existence is a necessary doctrine of consciousness ; that so long as consciousness continues, we cannot for an instance rid it of this doctrine ; and that thus the belief which this doctrine constitutes has a higher warrant than any other whatever." (F. P., § 27.)

Does the bullet make its own mould ? Does the star evolve its own atmosphere? and prescribe its own orbit and place ? That the Supernatural is something that the natural is not, and by which the natural is natural, is admitted by Mr. Spencer when he says (F. P. § 30) " The progress of intelligence has throughout been dual. Though it has not seemed so to those who made it, every step in advance has been a step towards both the natural and the supernatural. The better interpretation of each phenomena has been, on the one hand, the rejection of a cause that was relatively conceivable in its nature, but unknown in the order of its actions, and, on the other hand, the adoption of a cause that was known in the order of its action, but relatively inconceivable in its nature. The first advance out of universal fetichism, manifestly involved the conception of agencies less assimilable to the familiar agencies of men and animals, and therefore less understood ; while at the same time, such newly conceived agencies, in so far as they were distinguished by their uniform effects, were better understood than those they replaced. All subsequent advances display the same double result. Every deeper and more general power arrived at as a cause of phenomena, has been at once less comprehensible than the special ones it superseded, in the sense being less definitely representable in thought ; while it has been more comprehensible in the sense that its actions have been more completely predicable. The progress has thus been as much towards the establishment of a positively unknown as towards the establishment of a positive known. Though as knowledge approaches its culmination, every unaccountable and seemingly supernatural fact is brought into the category of facts that are accountable and natural ; yet, at the same time, all accountable or natural facts are proved to be, in their ultimate genesis, unaccountable and supernatural."

Whether this directly results from creation, evolu-

tion or emanation, nature is not supernature, the fact
is not the Factor, the subject is not the Object, evolution is not the evolver. The Supernatural Factor,
is that incomprehensible Power in every fact which
the fact itself is not, and by which the fact is a fact.

We are told that nature includes all things; but if
" all things are manifestations of a Power that transcends our knowledge; then Power was before that
manifestation of Power we call nature; and what the
power is, the manifestation is not; yet if the Power
is Supernatural, the manifestation must be Supernatural. Power did or did not exhaust itself in nature.
If Power did exhaust itself in nature, then nature as a
whole, includes all Power; but how can Power manifest anything further when it is itself included in all
things? The effect cannot manifest its own cause.
Can the circumference manifest itself as the centre
and cease to be the circumference? What becomes
of the centre when the circumference is gone, and
what becomes of the circumference when the centre
is gone? If Supernature could have form, it would
be as unlike nature as the form of the concave mould
is from its reversed form in the convex bullet, and the
form of the die in the form of the coin; and in the
unity of both one is the complement of the other.
There can be no concavity without a convexity, nor
any convexity without a concavity. Even so does
God the infinite Spirit, " without body, parts, or passion, reverse Himself in the form of finite matter, in
the visible part of the invisible whole, and in animal
passions. As it is a contradiction to say that anything
is, and at the same time is not, so the impersonal forms

2

which we do know, cannot be the personal Power which we do not know but which can be proved. The infinite may create the finite, but the infinite cannot be the finite. These skeptics tell us that the Power that produces all things is unknowable; and yet they claim to know it so far as to say, that it is not our God. If it is unknowable to them, how can they say what it is—whether it is or is not our God.

Look through your window in the Spring time, and see nature develop a plan of Power. Each leaf, and bud seems to know when to come, what form to take, and when its form and function are complete does not fail or forget to repeat itself. What does all this? All admit Power. Who can doubt this superhuman intelligence when it sublimely surpasses all that human intelligence has ever done? It works to a plan incomprehensible to highest created thought. Evolution proper, like the Kaleidoscope, progressively changes but never repeats. If heredity in organic nature is a fact in evolution, it is a repeating fact, unlike all other evolution.

In materialism, or the Matter-System, eternal matter is all; in idealism, or the Mind-System, eternal mind is all; in evolution, or the Power-System, eternal power is all. In evolution so-called, there is both a Power, a Process and a Method. Supernature is this Power and Nature is the Method. The Supernatural Power, both abstract as Power and concrete as a Factor, is that by which everything is anything, and Nature the method, called Evolution, is the way of this Supernatural Power, by which everything is anything. For the present, we do not characterize this

Power as either personal or impersonal. All of Evolution that is not correlation, if such there can be, is simply a natural process or method of Supernatural Power.

If nature is a manifestation of supernatural power, how far is nature supernatural? From a supernatural fountain must flow a supernatural stream. As water will rise to the level of its fountain, it would seem that all manifestations called nature would be as supernatural as the manifesting Power.

5. *Supernatural Power is a manifesting Power.* Mr. Spencer says, "all things are manifestations of a Power that transcends our knowledge." Manifestations prove manifesting Power. These manifestations are either creations, causations, or derivations. Creative manifestations are manifestations of new things by Power as Power; causative manifestations are different uses by Power as Force, of things already created; derivative manifestations are hereditary manifestations by Power as genetic Function. In inorganic manifestations, or of things without life, Power manifests each individual as an individual, but not one from another; in organic manifestations, or of things with life, Power manifests one thing from another, in hereditary succession. In causative manifestations, unlike is from unlike; in derivative manifestations like is from like; in both, the less is from the greater, not the greater from the less—that is, the Power is greater than its manifestation—the effect is less than the cause, the derived is less than the underived. What does causative manifestations in nature prove as to the manifesting Power above nature?

They prove that all phenomena without life, are
caused by extrinsic, not derived by intrinsic power;
and that all phenomena with life are derived by in-
intrinsic, not caused by extrinsic power. Any way,
the Power is greater than its manifestation; or, which
is the same thing, the manifestation is less than its
manifesting Power.

(*a*) In causative manifestations, the manifested
atoms are unlike the manifesting Power; the effect is
unlike the cause— the thunder is unlike the lightning
— the bugle is unlike the blast — the oxygen that
consumes the carbon is unlike fire. What is cause?
Cause is Power at work. That is the true cause or
Power of the universe, which most intelligently accounts for the universe: a conscious cause, or Power,
most intelligently accounts for the universe: therefore, a conscious cause, or Power, is the true cause,
or Power, of the universe. Some agnostics prefer
the terms power and manifestation, to the old terms
of cause and effect; but the meaning of both pairs of
correlatives is the same. The bridge between unlimited consciousness of the Power, or cause, and the
manifestation of the limited consciousness of persons
and the absence of consciousness in limited things,
is in the unity of all things. Somehow, all is one
and one is all. The logic of personal pantheism is
the logic of St. Paul's argument. An omnipresent
God is an omnipresent life, mind, will, consciousness, power, and person. Like knots in a skein of
thread, or ganglions in a system of nerves, there is
a uniting movement in the several constituents of
cause, when they come to us as *one* cause. This is so

in the conditions of life, but not so in life itself. Life is cause to itself, if cause there be. Creation, as distinguished from causation, begins exactly when Will acts—when the absolute manifests the relative—when Power manifests force. Causation, as distinguished from creation, begins when Will changes the relations of things, or when force, as distinguished from Power, acts. Just how or why manifestation follows Power, or object follows subject, or effect follows cause, or matter follows mind, or phenomena follows noumenon, is inexorably inscrutable to human intelligence. "There is here interposed," says Prof. Tyndal (on Virchow and Evolution, Pop. Sci., Jan., 187,), "a fissure over which the ladder of physical reasoning is incompetent to carry us." But Prof. T. goes to the wrong place to get across. The 'fissure' that is open at the top, needing a bridging ladder, is closed at the bottom, where no ladder could be used. Below visible division is invisible unity. The two walls of a fissure, like a re-entrant angle, end as they meet each other. One Power takes many forms. One line may be rounded into curves, or sharpened into angles. "We must, therefore, accept," says Prof. T., "the observed association as an empiricle fact, without being able to bring it under the yoke of *a priori* deduction." Between the subjective and the objective, he asks, "What is the causal connection?" and answers, "I do not see the connection, nor am I acquainted with anybody who does" (*Ib.*). But as just said, fact is none the less a fact, because it is incomprehensible. We may comprehend the What, but not comprehend the How or the Who.

Prof. Youmans says: "The tendency of inquiry is ever from the material toward the abstract, the ideal, the spiritual. The course of astronomical science has been on a vast scale to withdraw the attention from the material and sensible, and to fix it upon the invisible and supersensuous. It has shown that a pure principle forms the immaterial foundation of the universe. From the baldest material, we rise at last to a truth of the spiritual world, of so exalted an order that it has been said to connect the mind of man with the spirit of God." (Youmans' Introduction to Essays on the Correlation and Conservation of Force.)

Boscovitch held that what we call a material body, is nothing else than an aggregation of 'centres of force.' John S. Mill psychologized matter down to a "permanent possibility of sensations." But we must not here enter upon the question, what consciousness there is veiled in apparent unconsciousness, or how much mind there may be in matter.

Holding natural life to be a mode if not an emanation of supernatural life, we need not join issue with Prof. Tyndal when he says (Belfast Address): "that as he prolongs the vision backward across the boundary of experimental evidence, he discerns in that matter which we in our ignorance, and notwithstanding our reverence for its Creator, have covered with opprobrium, the promise and potency of every form and quality of life." If matter and material forces do not themselves see, there are omniscient eyes that see for them and in them. As we magnify nature, we glorify supernature.

If Francis Galton's statistics be true, not more than one scientist in ten takes the non-religious ground, and says that matter is factor and mind is fact. To escape the perplexity involved in the impotency of unintelligent matter, impersonal intelligence has been attributed to it ; giving to matter and mind different names for one and the same existence. But mind does not know itself to be matter, nor does matter know itself to be mind. But if matter and mind are one and the same, shall we call that oneness matter, or shall we call it mind ? If mind exists, we cannot say that the universe is all matter: and *e converso*, if matter exists, we cannot say that the universe is all mind, unless each is the other.

Prof. Hœckel says : " Under whatever form we may picture to ourselves the union of soul and body, of spirit and matter, it is still clear, on the theory of evolution, that all organic matter at least in general, is, in some sense possessed of psychic properties. In the first place the progress of microscopic research has shown that the elementary anatomic parts of organs—the cells—generally possess an individual psychic life." (Munich Address in Sup. Pop. Sci., Feb., 1878.) He speaks of "cell-soul" "soul of the atom," &c. Wallace (Nat. Sel. 363) says, "none of the properties of matter can be due to the atoms themselves, but only to the forces which emanate from the points in space indicated by the atomic centres, it is logical continually to diminish their size till they vanish, leaving only localized centres of force to represent them." All atoms are equal but unlike, and one atom cannot be the cause of another atom, nor can one atom be the effect of another atom. An atom of carbon cannot be the cause of another like atom of carbon.

It has been said that Nature is an endless series of efficient cause. This may be admitted, if an endless series of efficient mean a system of persistently creative pulsations, propagated and transmitted, as said before, like concentric waves, from one central, omniscient, omnipotent, omnipresent and omnific cause; but there can be no series to a succession of blind, original, different, independent, impersonal causes. There can be no universe, as the word imples, without a centre; and that centre must be one to which both the inorganic and the organic look for their law of harmonious adjustment and operation—a centre of sufficient intelligence, power, and energy.

The Power of the cause of things, is, in fact, inscrutable to man. Aristotle's four causes—the material, the formal, the efficient and the final—teach us nothing. *What* anything is, *how* it is, *whence* it is, or *why* it is, man does not know. Herbert Spencer, as we have seen, gives the last formula and conclusion of philosophic thought, when he says, " The axiomatic truth of physical science unavoidably postulate Absolute Being as the common basis." That was the opinion of Parmenides, 460 B. C. The word " cause,' however, was not used in speculative discourse, until the time of Augustine, 400 A. D. Before that time the Greeks used words signifying the principle or beginning of things; but no word like " cause" in the sense of power, which is now associated with the word " effect " as its correlative, was then used.

Causal power seems to be Will. As we trace all our *own* work to will, why not trace *all other* work to will? As far as we can see, power is in will, will is in personality, personality is in being : Coming downward, we have being, personality, power, will or law.

If the one omnipresent cause be Absolute Being, then what are called secondary causes are not strictly causes at all ; but are only the systematic. persistent energy of this Being. Causation is the energy of one, ever-expanding, inexhaustible unit of cause, not of many units. If Absolute Being be cause, then, as there cannot be more than one Absolute Being, there cannot be more than one cause. Cause is one as the sun ; effects are many as the rays.

It has been objected that religionists insist that nothing can exist without a cause, except a cause, and that this uncaused cause is God. It is contended that every cause must produce an effect, because until it does produce an effect, it is not a cause, and every effect must in its turn become a cause. Therefore, it it argued, that in the nature of things, there cannot be a last cause, for the reason that a so-called last cause would necessarily produce an effect, and that effect must necessarily become a cause. The converse of these propositions must be true. Every effect must have had a cause, and every cause must have had an effect. Therefore, there could have been no first cause. A first cause is just as impossible as a last effect."

But such logic is fatal ; for, if there be no first cause, there can be no first effect, and if there be no first effect, there can be no effect at all. If there be

any effect at all, there must be a first effect; and if
there be a first effect, there must be a first cause.
Why is cause a cause? May we not say that what is
called an *efficient* cause is the activity of that Power
by which everything is anything? and includes originating intelligence, originating power, and the originating act? That cannot be the cause of a thing
which has no knowledge how to cause, nor has the
power to cause. Every series has a beginning. If a
series of causes is what is called nature, then nature
symbolizing that series, had a beginning in some supernatural power beyond it.

But let us drop this play of correlative words about
cause and effect, and speak of God as a Power. What
is spoken of as first cause, I call an intelligent, self-
directing, omnipresent, personal Power, from which
all other power is derived, realizing a purpose, and
originating and sustaining all things. Absolute Being
or existence is uncaused. This efficient Power is altogether outside and before the whole chain of what
is called cause and effect; and, in this sense, we find
God everywhere in the universe, manifesting himself
as "an endless series of efficient causes." That power
which is found behind, around, above and in all things,
by whatever name we know it, is what religion adores
as an omnipresent, personal Will, or God. Before
leaving the subject of will-power as cause, let me
notice the proposition that "every effect must in turn
become a cause;" but it does not follow that every
cause must have first been an effect. If there is any
mental or moral freedom in the universe, Will is a
cause that never was an effect; and this will, whether

its action be ascertained by consciousness or by observation and the experiments in science, or by the history of men and nations, we say is the Will of God.

(*b*) In derivative manifestations, the first organism being created, the second is genetically derived from the first, like from like, roses from roses, fish from fish, birds from birds, men from men. The first organism, like the first atom, was created, not derived ; the second organism was derived from the first, not created. The noumenon creates and causes phenomena, and organism derives from organism. Derived nature inherits the power that created it, and transmits it as genetic Function. The nature of the parent is in the child, the nature of the seed is in the rose, and the nature of the rose is in the seed ; sweet waters are from sweet fountains, and bitter waters are from bitter fountains. In causation, the subsequent effect is unlike the antecedent cause, as the shadow is unlike the sun, or as pain is unlike the blow that causes it.

First, in derivative manifestations of like from like, life in manifestation is derived from an antecedent life in the manifesting Power. The one unlimited Power of life limits itself in the different manifestations of life in tree and bird and man. Spontaneous generation is not only not proved, but it is emphatically denied. As life is a fact, if it be not spontaneously generated, it must be either eternal, or supernaturally originated. If according to Mr. Spencer, there never has been an absolute commencement of anything, then human life must be eternal in eternal superhuman life. Some materialists have searched

and experimented in vain to find a material cause of
life ; but Mr. Spencer says " I do not believe in the
' spontaneous generation ' commonly alleged." * *
* " That creatures having *quite specific structures* are
evolved in the course of a few hours, without antece-
dents calculated to determine their specific forms, is
incredible. Not only the established truths of Biology, but the established truths of science in general,
negative the supposition that organisms having structures definite enough to identify as belonging to
known genera and species, can be produced in the
absence of germs derived from antecedent organisms of the same genera and species." (1 Bio. 480,
Appendix.) " Construed in terms of evolution, every
kind of being is conceived as a product of modifications wrought by insensible gradations on a pre-existing kind of being ; and this holds as fully of the supposed commencement of organic life, as of all subsequent developments of organic life." (1 Bio., p. 482.)

Prof. Tyndall, approving of Prof. Virchow's denial
of spontaneous generation, says (Sup. Pop. Sci.,
April, 1878, p. 511), " I share his opinion that the
theory of evolution in its complete form involves the
assumption, that at some period or other of the world's
history, there occurred what would now be called
' spontaneous generation.' I agree with him that "the
proofs of it are still wanting. Whoever recalls to
mind the lamentable failure of all the attempts made
very recently to discover a decided support for *gene-
ratio æquivoca* in the lower forms of transition from
the inorganic to the organic world, will feel it doubly
serious to demand that this theory, so utterly dis-

credited, should be in any way accepted as the basis of all our views of life." "I hold with Virchow, that the failures *have* been lamentable, that the doctrine *is* utterly discredited."

Prof. Tyndall says (*Ib.*), "No denier of the potency of matter could labor more strenuously than I have done, to demonstrate its impotence as regards spontaneous generation. While expressing, therefore, unshaken "belief" in that form of materialism to which I have already given utterance, I here affirm that no shred of trustworthy experimental testimony exists to prove that life, in our day, has ever appeared independently of antecedent life." This is derivation, and not causation. That object which is caused does not depend on an antecedent like object; but rather on an antecedent unlike power. Prof. Tyndall distinctly places the presence of life upon a derivation from antecedent life. Matter, without life, is first created and then causatively combined, not derived. In other words, all atoms are created; all combinations of atoms are caused. Where Power stops creating, it begins to cause. In matter with life, the matter is caused and the life is derived; hence while matter is from power, life is from that form of power known as life.

Prof. T. further says, (see "Vitality," Fragments, ed., 1878, p. 459): "In tracing these phenomena through all their modifications, the most advanced philosophers of the present day declare that they ultimately arrive at a single source of power, from which all vital energy is derived." As this derived energy is life, there must be life in the underived

Power.   The dependence of this derived, natural life on antecedent, supernatural life, determines the origin of all attributes of life, such as mind, will and consciousness.   Life everywhere is one and the same Power, derived or underived, manifested or unmanifested.

Second, Will in manifestation is derived from antecedent will in manifesting Power.   We are conscious of a will-power, though we may not be able to define it.   I open and close my hand, and learn that my will is power.   All that we *know* of our personal power is in our wills; and we know that will is power.   Power is manifested as conscious Will in man, and as unconscious Force in nature, both organic and inorganic.   And though, as Mr. Spencer says, (F. P., § 18), "the exercise of force is altogether unintelligible," and though we may say that the exercise of Will is also unintelligible, yet, we know that Will acts, and we know that Force acts; and both Will and Force are special names of a general power. Wallace says: "If, therefore, we have traced one force, however minute, to an origin in our Will, while we have no knowledge of any other primary cause of force, it does not seem an improbable conclusion that all force will be *Will-Force* and thus that the whole universe is not merely dependent on, but actually *is* the Will of higher intelligencies, or of One Supreme Intelligence."   (Natural Selection, p. 368, Sec. Ed.)   If Will is Force, and Force is Will, we readily agree with Mr. Spencer that "the creation of Force is as inconceivable as the creation of Matter," (1 Bro. § 112.)   Uncreated and unlimited Will-Power acts, and its act is Force. But this Will-Power Mr. S. emphatically denies, even in the face of the proof, by his own experience. He says, " In one case after another is abandoned that interpretation which ascribes phenomena to a Will analogous to the human Will, working by methods analogous to human methods," (1 Bio. § 111.) But, if we affirm the human will and methods, how can we deny the superhuman will and methods? Whence is the human if not from the superhuman? It cannot be from an origin less than human, for the cause is always greater than its effect. But, if we deny unlimited superhuman Will-Power in the universe, we must, in the face of our consciousness, it would seem, deny limited, human Will-Power in ourselves. If human Power is human Will, why should not superhuman Power be superhuman Will? The way of Will is the way of Power, and the way of Power, except as to miracles and special providences, is method; but that which to man is method is not method to supernatural Will itself. Will as Will is not necessarily bound by method. While we find uniformity of will in law, we need not be surprised to find multiformity of will in miracles and special providences. Above many forces is one Power, and that one Power is Will.

Mr. Spencer declares that " each further advance of knowledge confirms the belief in the unity of Nature (1 Bio. § 117.) But if one " Power unlimited in time and space" accounts for the universe, and that Power is Will, the unity of nature is in the unity of Will. The logic of evolution must be consistent.

We shall not always particularize whether we

speak of the omnific Power as becoming or as creating phenomena. The elastic word manifestation will
be used to mean the creation by Power, or the metamorphosis of Power. Which it is, is a secret with
omniscience. What matters it to us whether Power
becomes or creates impersonal things, so long as the
personality of that Power is infinite and omnipresent? That is a question for God Himself. This will
be discussed more fully when law is discussed.

Third, Mind in manifestation is derived from antecedent mind in manifesting Power. That which
controlls matter, as some understand matter, is not
matter, as gravitation, heat, etc. Dr. Carpenter says:
" The culminating point of man's intellectual interpretation of nature may be said to be his recognition
of the unity of power, of which her phenomena are
the diversified manifestations. Toward this all scientific inquiry now tends. For the convertibility of
the physical forces, the correlation of these with the
vital, and the intimacy of that *nexus* between mental
and bodily activity, which, explain as we may, cannot be denied, all lead upward toward one and the
same conclusions—the source of all power in Mind.
*   *   *   And thus, whilst the deep-seated instincts
of humanity, and the profoundest researches of philosophy alike point to the Mind as the one and only
source of power, it is the high prerogative of science
to demonstrate the unity of the power which is ope-
rating through the limitless extent and variety of
the universe, and to trace its continuity through the
vast series of ages that have been occupied in its evolution." (Carpenter's Mental Physiology, sec. 576.)

I think of a friend or an enemy, and my blood runs to or from my heart—I smile or I frown, as I love or as I hate, in spite of all will. Indeed, mind is a power of its own.

Fourth, conscious mind in manifestation is a gift from an antecedent, conscious mind in the manifesting Power. The superhuman set off something of itself in the human. We speak of the conscious and of the unconscious, or rather, as we should say, the not-conscious. We must remember that we are considering the consciousness or unconsciousness of unlimited and eternal Power, not of its manifestations; for they are not eternal. Some of the manifestations are conscious and some not-conscious. If unlimited Power was eternally not conscious, how did it manifest limited consciousness in man? If it were eternally conscious, how did it manifest the not-conscious in things? Always the unlike from unlike, is causative, carrying somewhat of the *power* of the antecedent into the subsequent; but the manifestation of the conscious from the conscious being like from like, is derivative, carrying somewhat of the unlimited *attributes* of the antecedent into the limited subsequent. The derivation of human consciousness from what we call superhuman unconsciousness, is impossible; for there is no unconscious Power, as such, for the conscious to be derived from. In itself, Power must be unchangeably conscious or unconscious, but it cannot he alternately one or the other. The unconscious is not an entity, but the absence of an entity. The positive,—consciousness,—cannot be derived from the negative, unconsciousness. From nothing, nothing is. Conscious Power knows how to manifest the unconscious; but an unconscious Power, if such a Power could be, would not know how to manifest the conscious. The greatest Power is in the greatest knowledge. We see, as a fact, that unlimited Power manifests conscious persons and things that are not conscious.

What is consciousness? Consciousness, as just said, is not only to think, but to think about our thought; not only to know, but to know that we know. The horse may think, but we have not discovered that he thinks about his thought, or that he knows that he knows.

Mr. Spencer says (Pop. Sci., Jan., 1884): "The power which manifests itself in consciousness is but a differently conditioned form of the power which manifests itself beyond consciousness." As human life is derived from underived superhuman life, so human consciousness is derived from underived superhuman consciousness. If Power includes its manifestations, the Power includes both conscious force and form that is not conscious; for matter is one and mind is the other. If Power is unconscious, it manifested consciousness in personal man; if it is conscious, it could not lose its consciousness when it manifested forms that were not conscious and matter that was not personal. We must distinguish between derivation when Power is an ancestor and imparts its own likeness, and causation, when Power, like the spider spinning from itself a web unlike itself, manifests or constructs things that are unlike itself. The unlimited Power that manifests all things is conscious; because unconsciousness, being the absence of consciousness, as cold is the absence of heat, is only a *negative condition*, and not power at all. As it is not power, it can be neither cause nor an effect: it cannot know anything, do anything, or be anything.

As we understand the theory of agnostic evolution, all things are eternally evolved from underived, necessary unity, or from underived necessary plurality. But nothing could be evolved from underived plurality, for plurality itself is evolved from underived unity; therefore underived unity excludes underived plurality. This underived unity was either consciously intelligent, or unconsciously unintelligent. If it were consciously intelligent, it knew how to manifest the unconsciously unintelligent; but if it were unconsciously unintelligent, it did not know how to manifest the consciously intelligent. Consciousness, whether derived or underived, is exclusively an individual intuition. There is nothing in the consciousness of one that could be in the consciousness of another. Unconsciousness, on the contrary, is a state common to different things, such as trees, seas, stones and stars, and there is nothing in the unconsciousness of the stars that is not in the unconsciousness of a stone. Indeed, unconsciousness is only the absence of consciousness. Exclusive attributes distinguish the underived absolute and eternal unit; consciousness is an exclusive attribute; therefore consciousness distinguished the underived absolute and eternal unit. The original, underived Unit was, therefore, exclusively conscious; for though this underived, absolute, conscious, superhuman Unit may manifest limited human, individual consciousness, it can never share its own consciousness. The power to be conscious may be derived, but not the contents of consciousness. If the original Unit was a Unit of will, of mind and of power, it was a conscious unit, and if conscious, it was personal, and if it were personal it was that supernature which we call God.

We started with an universally admitted power. Power is derived or underived. If it is derived it is not eternal; if it is eternal, it is underived. To apply this: we are persons; *personality is in consciousness;* consciousness is either derived or underived. Human consciousness cannot be underived, for, though immortal, it is not eternal; as it is not eternal it is derived. We could not derive our power of consciousness from any derived power of consciousness below us; we must, therefore, derive our power of consciousness from underived power of consciousness above us. If derived power of consciousness is derived personality, so underived power of consciousness is underived personality. The admission of a derived power of human consciousness admits an underived superhuman power of consciousness, from which was possible for it to be derived—that is, the derived implies the underived.

Mr. Spencer speaks of " the one absolute certainty, that he (man) is ever in the presence of an Infinite and Eternal Energy, from which all things proceed." (*Pop. Sci. M.*, Jan., 1884.) If this Eternal Energy from which we *proceed*, could send us forth with a knowledge of ourselves, has this Energy no knowledge of its *own* self? Like is from like.

Fifth, that conscious power called human personality is the manifestation of an antecedent conscious Power we call superhuman personality. Unconsciousness in nature is the absence of that antecedent consciousness in supernature, called impersonal. A negative is the absence of a positive.

Sir John F. W. Herschell says ("Popular Lectures," XII), "In the only case in which we are admitted into personal knowledge of the origin of force, we find it connected with volition, and by inevitable consequence with *motive and intellect*, and with all those attributes of mind in which personality consists * * * It matters not that we are ignorant of the mode in which this is performed. It suffices to bring the origination of dynamical power, to however small extent, within the domain of acknowledged personality. In that peculiar mental sensation, clear to the apprehension of every one who has ever performed a voluntary act, which is present at the instant when the determination to do a thing is carried out with the act of doing it, we have a consciousness of immediate and *personal causation* which cannot be disputed or ignored."

From the point of our own conscious, derived personal power, unconscious, impersonal, underived Power is unthinkable. Personality, as we have said, is but a name given to the cumulative attributes of life, will, intelligence and consciousness; just as we call the combination of oxygen and hydrogen, water, or as we call the roots, trunk, branches, top of a tree, a tree.

Consciousness and personality are one and the same. Consciousness that we have considered, covers the whole idea of personality that we are now considering. We but use a different word for the same idea. Consciousness is the one, highest human attribute ; and personality implies the sum of all the attributes of life, will, intelligence, and consciousness. There can be life, will, and intelligence, as in the horse, without consciousness ; but there cannot be consciousness, as in man, without life, will and intelligence.

The admission of science, as expressed by Prof. Tyndall and by Mr. Spencer, that life depends on antecedent life, carries with it the admission that life with will, intelligence and consciousness, depends on antecedent life, will, intelligence and consciousness ; and this is all that is meant by personality ; and all that is affirmed by religion. If human, conscious power, as the culmination of human intelligence, will, and life is dependent on antecedent superhuman conscious Power, intelligence, will and life, there need be no further proof that human personality is dependent on, and proves superhuman personality.

Consciousness, as the highest entity, is called personal, to distinguish it from a large class of unconscious things, classified as impersonal, because unconscious. These impersonal things are without life, as the stone ; or with life, as the tree ; or with life, will, and intelligence, as the horse. But, not thinking about his thoughts, so far as is known, or not knowing that he knows, the horse, with life, will and intelligence, but wanting consciousness, is not a person, but only a thing not-personal. Man, however, has not only life, will, intelligence, or thoughts, but he thinks about his thoughts — he knows that he knows — in other words, he is conscious, and therefore is a person. If life depends on antecedent life, *a fortiori,* conscious power depends on antecedent conscious

Power. Human consciousness develops as human
life develops. As the perfection of one, so is the perfection of the other. So that human consciousness or
personality proves superhuman consciousness or personality, if we accept, as valid, Prof. Tyndall's scientific denial of spontaneous generation as we have seen ;
and also his doctrine, that all life depends on antecedent life. Thus, human life has its antecedent in
superhuman life ; and, as human life has will, its antecedent superhuman life has will ; and, as human life
has intelligence, its antecedent superhuman life has
intelligence ; and, as human life is conscious, its antecedent, superhuman life is conscious. As human life
having these attributes of life, will, intelligence, and
consciousness, is called personal, so its antecedent
superhuman life, being the source of these attributes
in man, must be called personal.

Where there is no life, as is the case of the inorganic atom, there can be no derivation of like from
like ; but only a causation of unlike from unlike. One
lifeless atom is not derived from another lifeless atom,
but is caused by adequate Power ; but where there is
life, there is derivation either by direct emanation or
transmission from the infinite to the finite, or indirectly, like from like, by genetic function. Having
considered consciousness and unconsciousness as to
unlimited Power, let us now turn to the consideration
of consciousness and unconsciousness as attributes
respectively of limited persons and things. If the
antecedent of conscious person is conscious Power,
must the antecedent of unconscious things be an unconscious Power? By no means ; for,

(*c*) The order of manifestation, whether by causation or by derivation, is,

First, as something cannot come out of nothing, to magnify the effect is to maximize the cause : $8+2=10$. As you add to the subsequent you must add to the antecedent—the greater manifests the less ; in other words, Power is greater than its manifestations. The infinite Subject manifests the finite object — the Noumenon manifests the phenomenon. The circle includes its diameter, chords, and segments : a gallon measure is never from a pint cup : there must be a whole before there can be a part. This, of course, applies to unlimited Power and its limited manifestations. To unlimited Power itself, there is neither greater nor less. Unlimited Power is simply unlimited Power. From the conscious, derived power of life in man, we prove conscious, underived life as antecedent in unlimited Power. Power must come from Power. Could limited, human, conscious life, come from an unlimited, antecedent, superhuman, unconscious life ? We say, no ; for that superhuman, antecedent life on which Prof. T. says all subsequent human life depends, must be altogether conscious or altogether unconscious. If it is altogether unconscious, then this superhuman unconscious Power manifested human conscious power. The powerless could not manifest the powerful. But, that is impossible ; for as finite knowledge is supreme over infinite nescience, so a great effect could not come out of a less cause. But, suppose that human finite conscious power proves superhuman, infinite, conscious Power, there could not be infinite unconscious Power, for there cannot be two infinities. Did eternal and infinite consciousness come out of eternal and infinite unconsciousness? In the same abstract subject, unconsciousness is the absence of consciousness; and consciousness could not come out of its own absence.

The conscious Power, unlimited in time and space, that we claim to have proved, that knows everything, cannot be derived from itself as a Power unlimited in time and space in an unconscious state, that knows nothing. Assuming that conscious Power is supreme over an imaginary unconscious power, the one unlimited Power must be conscious, not only because, on lines of life, like is from like, as conscious human life from conscious superhuman life, but because, if conscious persons came from unconscious Power, whether as an effect from a cause, the derived from the underived, as a manifestation of Power, the effect would be greater than its cause— the derived would be greater than the underived— the manifestation would be greater than the manifesting Power. But to say that the derived is less than the underived, is axiomatic, and covers all facts. The manifestations are less than the manifesting Power—the limited than the unlimited—the particular than the universal—the unconscious than the conscious—the relative than the absolute. We see that unlimited Power limited its manifestation in the first atom, by withholding life and intelligence. But as a limited atom did not exhaust unlimited Power, so, unlimited Power manifested something more of itself when it organized the atoms by manifesting vegetable life. Still, Power was greater than its manifestations. Power manifested animal, individual life, will and intelligence. Still Power was greater than its manifestation. But, far more than all was Power greater than its manifestation, when, in man, it manifested life, will, intelligence and consciousness—in other words, when limited human life and consciousness was derived from unlimited superhuman life and consciousness. We are always going back to something greater than we know. The boundary of the Infinite ever recedes as we approach it. Thus the Eternal marks off segments of itself, and we call it Time. We look at the Infinite through a reversed telescope, and call it finite; but in all things and everywhere, Power is greater than its manifestations.

If we trace human life—intelligent, conscious volitional and personal—back along its endless line of antecedent life, must not its intelligence, will, consciousness, and personality go back all along the line with it? How, where, when, and why stop or separate them? Shall they be in the subsequent and not in the antecedent? in the derived greater than in the underived? Power is life and will and mind. Who can prove that gravitation and other forces in matter are not modes or movements of supernatural life, intelligence, and will of the one unlimited Power? This unlimited Power has both life and mind; for it is neither blind as a force, nor unintelligent in its method. If it were, its phenomena could not be scientifically studied. Gravitation is not blind, but always pulls directly as to mass and inversely as to the square of the distance. Nor is chemic affinity blind; for it never combines three parts by weight of oxygen to two parts of hydrogen when it produces water. Nor are the methods of Power blind;

for in evolution as defined by Mr. Spencer, matter integrates only as motion dissipates. What we call blind force sees its way free of all mistakes or irregularities. Life must be conscious to be human. If science will adhere to its emphatic denial of spontaneous generation and to its doctrine of the dependance of all life upon antecedent life, as formulated by Prof. Tyndall, we must come back to the old doctrine of the production of effects from causes, and see that all along lines of life, like is always from like. Life goes back to life, consciousness to consciousness, the personal to the personal, until lines of derivation vanish in the Infinite. As we have said one primary element like carbon or oxygen is not from another primary element. Neither element by itself is a cause or an effect. As unconsciousness is nothing but the absence of consciousness, and as impersonality is nothing but the absence of personality, so human personal power must come from superhuman personal Power; because as superhuman impersonal Power is merely the absence of superhuman personal power, superhuman personal power cannot be derived from its own absence. Unlimited Power is one; subtract its personal power, and there remains nothing. From nothing, nothing can come.

Neither the not-personal nor the not-conscious can be a factor or cause; for being nothing, they can do nothing. That which does, is that which is; but unconsciousness as such, and impersonality as such, are nothing; and the power of nothing is nothing. We prove the derivation of human conscinusness or personality from superhuman consciousness or personality upon the derivative principle of like from like, and upon the principle common to both derivative and causative manifestations, of the less from the greater—the less effect from the greater cause, or the less manifestation from the greater Power. Thus superhuman consciousness or personality is greater than human consciousness or personality and cannot be derived from it; and human consciousness or personality is greater than subhuman things that are not-conscious or not-personal and cannot be derived from them. The less, therefore, must come from the greater, and not the greater from the less.

Besides, as we have seen unconsciousness to be only the absence of consciousness, so impersonality is only the absence of personality; and we say here, as we said of consciousness, a present personality cannot come from a negation of personality — that is, positive personality cannot be derived from its negative, impersonality. A thing cannot be derived from that which is not. Unconsciousness, or impersonality are not entities, but only the negation, or absence of the entities, consciousness or personality. Conscious personality cannot be derived from unconscious impersonality; for the conscious personality would be a greater from a less.

The relation of evolution to religion is thus seen to depend upon the answer to the question: Is superhuman power personal or impersonal? If the power is impersonal, like impersonal power in the main spring of a watch, with the maker of the spring out of our mind, there would be but one mechanical method, and nothing for religion. But, if, as we see all around us, there is one free, superhuman Will, this is a God, with everything for religion. In the derivative continuity of heredity, like must be from like.

Derived human personality implies underived superhuman personality. Here the less is from the greater. Here the look is *a posteriori* from a personal man *back* to a personal God. A human personality as a present fact, proves a superhuman personality as a past Factor. We must suppose that man was created to be a genetic creator of men; for such he is now; and we must suppose that man was created to be what he is. There are no mistakes in nature. Generation is a human mode of creation, as creation is a superhuman mode of Power. If we are created, we can be personal like our Creator, if He so chooses; or, if we are generated, we *must* be personally like our ancestor, or like from like. We *are* persons, whether created or generated; and we must have a Creator or a Father.

Personal nature and not-personal nature are both facts; but it is personal nature only that knows anything of the not-personal nature; or, to state it otherwise, we cannot declare a thing to be unless it is known to be; therefore nature cannot be said to be impersonal unless there is a personal nature to know and say it. Impersonality converts or evolves itself into personality when it speaks of itself.

The personality of God is one of the vexed and obscure theological and philosophical points discussed by John Fiske in his book on the "Idea of God." "To every form of theism, as I have already urged, an anthropomorphic element is indispensable." He says, "It is quite true, on the other hand, that to ascribe what we know as human personality to the infinite Deity, straightway lands us in a contradiction, since personality without limit is inconceivable. But, on the other hand, it is no less true that the total elimination of anthropomorphism from the idea of God abolishes the idea itself. We do not approach the question in the spirit of those natural theologians who were so ready with their explanations of the Divine purposes. We are aware that 'we see as through a glass darkly,' and we do not expect to 'think God's thoughts after Him,' save in the crudest symbolic fashion. In dealing with the Infinite we are confessedly treating of that which transcends our powers of conception. Our ability to frame ideas is strictly limited by experience, and our experience does not furnish the materials for the idea of a personality which is not narrowly hemmed in by the inexorable barriers of circumstance. We therefore cannot conceive of such an idea. But it does not follow that there is no reality answering to what such an idea would be if it could be conceived. The test of inconceivability is only applicable to the world of phenomena from which our experience is gathered. It fails when applied to that which lies behind phenomena. I do not hold, for this reason, that we are justified in using such an expression as 'infinite personality' in a philosophical inquiry where clearness of thought and speech is above all things desirable. But I do hold, emphatically, that we are not debarred from ascribing a quasi psychical nature to the Deity simply because we can frame no proper conception of such a nature as absolute and infinite."

But we can conceive the idea of omnipresent personality as clearly as we can that of omnipresent space, or of Power; and one is no less incomprehensible than the other. Indeed, they are but names for one and the same Power. Power is omnipresent, so is Space, Time, life, mind, will, consciousness and personality, whether comprehensible or incomprehensible. We derive only power.

Mr. Spencer says (F. P., § 20), " The personality of which each is conscious, and of which the existence is to each a fact beyond all others the most certain, is yet a thing which cannot be truly known at all; knowledge of it is forbidden by the very nature of thought." So, the inference is, that as we cannot truly know ourselves, we cannot know the Power not-ourselves. But religion would be content to know this Power as well as we know ourselves. The unit that pluralizes is a unit of Power; and there is no power in the unconscious. From the one Power came many manifestations. In man, impersonal matter is manifested along with personal mind, and unconscious, impersonal force; such as animal heat, along with conscious, personal power, such as thought and will. If there is anything in the effect that is in the cause, then human personality, as an effect, is from superhuman personality as its cause. If it be insisted that impersonal matter and unconscious force are manifestations of an impersonal and unconscious Power, like from like, then it is claimed *a fortiori,* that conscious, personal human mind and will are manifestations of a conscious, personal superhuman mind and will. If the cause is greater than its effects — the underived greater than the derived — then human consciousness is from superhuman consciousness, and not from a non-existing superhuman, impersonal unconsciousness; for this would be to make the

cause less than the effect—indeed to have an effect
from no cause at all; for unconsciousness is only a
negative state, and not a power, and cannot be either
cause or effect. Unconsciousness, the negative of
consciousness, cannot be higher than the consciousness of which it is the negative. Thus the philosophical bridge between human personality and superhuman personality, is, first, in the admitted principle, that the cause is both simpler and greater than
the effect; and, second, in the proof of the unity of
natural force and supernatural Power, and in the dependence of life upon antecedent life — that is, of
natural life upon supernatural life. If this be not so,
we must altogether discard *a posteriori* reasoning.

As personal beings are from personal beings, so
personal being must be originally from personal
Being. Personality objective in human beings is
subjective personality in superhuman Power. Subjective Power manifests, or objectifies itself, in impersonal things and personal beings; the subjective is
known in the objective. If Power was first, and at
first Power was all, as said before, Power either created matter or materialized itself, for there is matter;
Power either created mind or mentalized itself, for
there is mind; Power either created life or vitalized
itself, for there is life; Power either created persons
or personalized itself, for there is personality. If, as
we have said, cause is greater than its effects, then
the cause of matter is greater than matter its effect;
the cause of life is greater than life its effect; the
cause of consciousness is greater than consciousness
its effect; the cause of human personality is greater
than human personality its effect. But only super-

human personality is greater than human personality. As positive personality from a negative impersonality, or, rather a thing present from itself absent, would be the greater from the less, which is impossible, so, the less is from the greater, when we say that,

Second, having seen that to magnify the effect is to maximize the cause, so, as nothing cannot produce something, to minify the cause is to minimize the effect : as $10 - 2 = 8$. As you subtract from the antecedent you subtract from the subsequent. Equals must be added to equals, or equals must be taken from equals, the less is manifested by the greater—that is, the manifestations of Power are less than the manifesting Power. If natural impersonality, as the negation or absence of personality in things is called, were derived from supernatural personality, such a derivation, if it were possible, would be consistent with the principle of the less from the greater. Keeping in mind, that what we call impersonality, whether human or superhuman, is only the negative or absence of personality, human or superhuman, we see that impersonality, whether human or superhuman, is only where personality is not Impersonality could not come from impersonality ; for, if impersonality — a negative — were to come from impersonality — another negative—it would be a negative from a negative : which is absurd.

As human personality is inherited from human personality as far back as human personality can be traced, is not human personality derived from superhuman personality, or phenomenal personality from nomenal personality ? The derivation of personality from impersonality, if it were possible, would have

4

to be strongly proved, in order to disprove the law
and fact of heredity of like from like; but, if like is
not from like, and personality is from impersonality,
then, in unlike from unlike, the Creator is impersonal
instead of personal, and agnosticism dreads an impersonal Power where religion worships a personal
God. But a conscious effect called personality, cannot come from an unconscious cause called impersonality, as the effect would be greater than the cause;
but a conscious cause does produce an unconscious
effect, and the effect is less than the cause. Unconsciousness, unknown to itself, is known only to consciousness.

Mr. Spencer says, "Some make the erroneous
assumption that the choice is between personality
and something lower than personality; whereas the
choice is rather between personality and something
higher. Is it not just possible that there is a mode of
being as much transcending intelligence and Will as
these transcend mechanical motion? It is true that
we are totally unable to conceive any such higher
being. But this is not a reason for questioning its
existence; it is rather the reverse. Have we not seen
how utterly incompetent our minds are to form even
an approach to a conception of that which underlies
all phenomena? Is it not proved that this incompetency is the incompetency of the conditioned to grasp
the unconditioned? Does it not follow that the ultimate cause cannot in any respect be conceived of by
us because it is in every respect greater than can be
conceived? And may we not therefore rightly re-
frain from assigning to it any attributes whatever,

on the ground that such attributes, derived as they must be, from our own natures, are not elevations. but degradations? Indeed it seems somewhat strange that men should suppose the highest worship to lie in assimilating the object of their worship to themselves." (F. P., § 31.)

But why not hope to assimilate ourselves below to an object of worship above? Of course, human personality is in his mind; but is not superhuman personality that very something higher than human personality, to which he alludes? What is personality? We talk about persons and things. What is the difference? That which is not one, is the other. Why is a man a person, and an intelligent brute, and unintelligent objects only things? As said before, the man thinks. The brute thinks. The man thinks about his thoughts, or is conscious. and *for that reason* is a person. The brute thinks, but does not think about his thoughts, or is not conscious. so far as we have ascertained, and *for that reason* is only a thing. We know nothing in nature higher than consciousness. But to repeat, if there is con sciousness above human consciousness, why should not such superhuman consciousness constitute superhuman personality, as human consciousness constitutes human personality? Is there any more reason for personality in nature than there is reason for it in supernature? If superhuman consciousness be admitted, or proved, why should superhuman personality be denied? Personality does not ascend from man to God, but descends from God to man. His personality is underived and infinite; our personality

is derived and finite. God is not like us; but we are
as shadows self-cast from God. He was not made in
our image, but we are made in His. Mr. Spencer
admits both nature and supernature. Which begets
the other? As the greater contains the less, so supernature contains and manifests nature. Therefore, if
God, supposing Him to be conscious, from having
given us consciousness, is not personal in His consciousness, we are not personal in our consciousness;
but as we are from Him, if our consciousness makes
us personal, why does not His consciousness make
Him personal? Is nature parent or child? Did the
universe begin in the finite, or in the infinite? If in
the finite, then our personality is at the angle whose
sides open out to the infinite. If man began in the
infinite, then man's personality is the vanishing point
of God's personality. It depends upon whether we
look into or out of the angle, as to whose personality
is before us. The method of nature, according to the
theory of atheistic evolution, has been from the impersonal to the personal; for personal man is here.
In the future progress of man, which evolution makes
inevitable, is our present human personality to go
forward to a superhuman personality or to a superhuman impersonality? Which exalts the more? We
must remember that, in evolution, "progress is not
an accident, but a necessity." (Spencer, Social Science, p. 78.) Mr. Spencer said that "it seems somewhat strange that men should suppose the highest
worship to lie in assimilating the object of their worship to themselves." But it is not strange that men
should suppose that the highest worship lies in as-

similating the object of their worship to themselves."
The struggle is to lift our personality towards His :
to get something exalting from him. We think him
perfect in that which we, are imperfect. We accept
our personality as a profert of His personality. As
conscious intelligence constitutes us persons, we ascribe personality to Him from whom these and all
things come to us. Religion worships the parental
Being, whether personal or impersonal ; but constituted as we are, we cannot worship or feel accountable to a mere abstraction—an impersonal, blind, unintelligent Power. We are accustomed to associate
authority with personality, and to look to this Super-
nal Power as "touched with a feeling of our infirm-
ity." Beyond this question of worship, the personality of Power, is a mere idle inquiry to religion.

Has science more reason to impersonalize force, in
the face of our personal force, that religion has to
personalize it? Indeed, science can neither affirm
its impersonality nor deny its personality, as it confesses its entire ignorance of the whole subject.
Upon this question, the true scientific attitude of science is ignorant silence.

If human personality is derived, it must be, on the
principle of like from like, from a superhuman personality. If human personality is not derived by evolution it must be produced by original creation ; and
creation implies a creator.

If human personality be not derived from superhuman personality, it could not be derived from superhuman impersonality ; for the greater would be
from the less, and a thing present from itself absent.

If the eternal is one, and Personality and impersonality are not two eternal and different things, which
is from the other?   A few atheistic scientists assume
the impersonality, while the many theistic scientists
claim to *prove* the personality of the Factor of all
facts, by the very facts themselves.

Evolution claims that the eternal and universal instability of the homogeneous ever seeking an impossible equilibrium, produces the heterogeneous—something unlike itself.   How, then, does it account for
the law of heredity, of like from like?   The principles are directly contradictory, and so far as one is
true the other must be untrue, unless unified in a supernatural Factor.   To give up the differentiation of
the heterogeneous from the homogeneous, gives up
the whole theory of evolution for one of creation
where things originate in a Power unlike themselves
and to adhere to it, gives up the whole theory of
heredity, or of like from like.   Did human personality come from superhuman impersonality under the
law of heterogeneity from homogeneity, or did it come
from superhuman personality under the hereditary
law of like from like?   If it began under the law of
unlikeness, how did it get under the law of likeness?

Now, in the universe there is personal nature, and
there is impersonal nature;   but one is not the other.
Impersonal nature cannot do what personal nature
does, and personal nature cannot be what impersonal
nature is.   If, upon the principle of unlikeness, as between the mould and the bullet, or the coin and the
die, personal nature came from impersonal nature,
then, upon the same principle of unlikeness, imper-

sonal nature came from personal nature. But if, upon the principle of like from like, impersonal nature came from impersonal nature, then, as said a few pages back, upon the same principle, personal nature in man came from a higer personal nature in God.

Evolutionary changes from uniformity to multi-formity, in all things without life, as from minerals to vegetables, are creative, not genetic ; and the advance is *per saltum*, by extrinsic power. Heredity alone is directly genetic, and indirectly creative. All un-mixed matter, such as oxygen and hydrogen, is both homogeneous and inert. To these homogeneous gases, some extrinsic power first gives instability, by over-coming their inertia ; and then, by dissipating their motion, integrates them into heterogeneous water. In more technical phraseology, extrinsic power for these, and all other elements of matter, directly cre-ates the instability of the homogeneous ; and, indi-rectly, through the instability of the homogeneous, the same extrinsic power creates the heterogeneous. The same intrinsic power creatively dissipates motion, and, through the dissipation of motion, the same ex-trinsic power integrates matter. Extrinsic power, known as a single cause, creates a multiplicity of ef-fects. Extrinsic power, out of incoherence creates coherence ; and out of the infinite creates the definite. Here is a creative, not a genetic line of advance. *Hence, theistic evolution is simply a method of progress,* PER SALTUM, *by extrinsic creative power.*

Now, if the personality of this creative power be denied, its impersonality will be assumed ; and the same *necessity* of progress that moved impersonal nature on to personal nature in man, must move it on to a personal supernature in God. Here the *a priori* look is from a personal man on to a personal God.

The unintelligent impersonal necessity that did not know how to begin, does not know how to stop. If supernature did not originate nature, nature must originate supernature. In other words, if a personal God did not make impersonal nature, impersonal nature must make a personal God—there is a personal God at one end or the other of this line of evolution. The materialists insist upon the impersonality of the Factor of all facts ; and offer, in proof, two conflicting theories of nature.

The first theory claims that uniform law is the impersonal factor of all facts, like conditions producing like results. In this sense, law is only an impersonal method of impersonal power, and not the power itself. Method governs nothing and produces nothing. But, if we can judge as to what law is in nature without by the light of our own consciousness within, law is personal Will. This will may act with or without conditions; but, in itself, Will has no conditions. The method of law is only the uniformity of will, and its power is the diversity of will. In a word, can impersonal law account for the fact of human personality ?

The second theory of an impersonal Factor of all facts, including the fact of our personality, is that of impersonal evolution which we have been considering. Its leading idea is, that in the instability of the universe (called the instability of the homogeneous) things are agitated and changed into the condition we find them without the agency of a personal or even a supernatural Factor.

According to these two impersonal agencies, Law is a method of impersonal repetition, and Evolution is a method of impersonal development; but, if everything is repeated under law, then nothing is developed under evolution; and *vice versa*, if everything is developed under evolution, nothing is repeated under law. Both theories seem to be true but contradictory. But, evolution proves, as we have seen, a personal not an impersonal Factor.

The phenomena of the universe exhibits a fixed, mechanical method, and a free, voluntary method— fixed as in law, when, like a compass describing the same circle, like conditions always producing like results; and free, as in evolution, when, like the changes in the kaleidoscope, no combinations are ever repeated. The apparent contradictions of the universe all disappear under the management of a personal God. Law has a free Law-giver, and Evolution has a free Evolver.

If things are in the present as they have been in the past, then, the conscious (personal) is from the conscious (personal); but, if things in the present are not as they have been in the past, and the conscious comes from the unconscious—that is, things present come from themselves absent (as the unconscious is only the absence of the conscious)—when did things change, and what power changed them? and was it intrinsic or extrinsic?

It is said that consciousness affirms personalty, but cannot cognize it—think of it—formulate it, or make it, in logical order, the starting point of knowledge of anything outside or above itself. But consciousness *is* personality. Personality is *consciousness* and nothing more. What is knowledge? Knowledge is of two kinds, that of the ego, and that of the non-ego. Knowledge of the ego is consciousness, and is *sui generis*—it is the highest kind of knowledge, without either subject or object. We do not agree with Mansel when he says of consciousness; " that it is only possible in the form of a *relation.* There must be a subject, or person conscious, and an object, or thing of which he is conscious. There can be no consciousness without the union of these two factors; and, in that union, each exists only as it is related to the other. The subject is a subject, only so far as it is conscious of an object; the object is an object, only so far as it is apprehended by a subject: and the destruction of either is the destruction of consciousness itself." (Limits of Thought. Lect. III, p. 96.) Not at all. Just the reverse. There is information but no consciousness where there is subject and object. Consciousness is the knowledge of ourselves by ourselves. We are no subject, beause we need no object; and we have no object, because there is no subject. We ourselves, not as subject, know ourselves, but not as object. If we cannot say that the ego in itself is absolute, neither can we say that the ego in itself is relative. As in itself the ego is not relative, so, in itself, the ego can be neither subject nor object. There need be only ourselves to know ourselves; but to know others, there must be ourselves as subject in order to know others as objects. The conscious ego does not annihilate either subject or object, because as to it, there never has been either.

According to evolution, the unit that pluralizes is not a unit of matter, nor a unit of mind, nor a unit of Being, but it is a unit of Power. But, if Power be the *fons et origio*, it personalizes; for there are persons. Who makes One to be All — all matter, all mind, all Power—or Who makes All to be One—one matter, one mind, or one Power, as Hegel taught? It is evident that things are governed; but who governs? Nearly all systems of philosophy discuss only the methods, not the origins by Power. With these systems it is the having proved, the What, not the who or the why. Mr. Spencer, with whom evolution is only a process of power, says, " The universe is a manifestation of immanent force." Does the force manifest its own matter, or does matter manifest its own force.

When Mr. Spencer says that all things are manifestations of a Power that transcends our knowledge, he affirms with Hegel, that All are from One — that this One is Power—that this Power transcends our knowledge. According to this non-theistic evolution, all things, of course, include all inorganic and organic matter and forms — all thoughts and feelings — all tendencies and events — all experiences and destinies.

Does he mean by manifestations that what is here called creation, is by a Power *ab extra?* or does he mean that manifestation is what he calls Evolution, by Power *ab infra*, but which the Buddhist calls emanation?

Agnostic scientists are not agreed among themselves as to whether the manifesting Power is extrinsic or intrinsic. For instance, Mr. S. says, " we are obliged to regard every phenomenon as a manifestation of some Power by which we are acted *upon.*" (F. P., § 27.) And again: " The tendency to progress from homogeneity to heterogenity is not intrinsic but extrinsic." (Pop. Sci., Nov., 1880, p. 106.) From these statements we learn that Power is *ab extra.* But then Mr. Spencer seems to contradict himself when he says, " I recognize no forces within the organism or without the organism, but the variously-conditioned modes of the universal, immanent force; and the whole process of organic evolution is every-where attributed by me to the co-operation of its variously-conditioned modes, internal and external." (1 Biol., 491.) What then is the meaning of his doctrine, that all accountable and natural facts are proved to be in their ultimate genesis unaccountable and *supernatural?* Is this immanent force from whose modes, variously-conditioned, proceeds all organic evolution, natural or supernatural? If nature and supernature are not the same, to which belongs evolution?

Mr. Tyndall says, that " Science rejects the outside builder." (Pop. Sci., Jan., 1879, p. 274.) And, yet, what is not an outside builder to something else? The sun is an outside builder to all things; it paints the leaf, it perfumes the rose, it creates the wind, it

bridles the planets, it reveals and quickens and glorifies all. All external, controlling Power is supernatural to the nature which it controls. The sun is
supernatural to its planets. That external Power
which controls the sun in nature, is supernatural to
the sun, and so on back *ad infinitum.* We must either
deny all external control of anything in nature, or
admit a Power supernatural to nature, which controls. If all things in nature are the manifestations
of Power, then, unless Power and the manifestations
of Power are one and the same, unlimited Power
must be supernatural to its limited manifestations.

We may regard Power as the fountain of all forces.
Force is specialized Power. Specialized Power is
named differently according to different uses or manifestations. One manifestation of supernatural Power
is called the force of gravitation—another manifestation is called the force of heat—another is called the
force of electricity — another is called the force of
chemic affinity. The unit Power when pluralized and
as the latter incomprehensibility of God without
matter individualized in manifestation is called Force.

Two incomprehensibilities are propounded to account for the partially comprehended facts of nature.
One is the incomprehensibility of eternal matter without God, and the other is the incomprehensibility of
an eternal God without matter. The Theist holds that
a personal God created matter out of nothing ; while
the pantheist holds that an impersonal God converted
himself into matter—in other words he contends that
if there is a God, there is no matter, and if there is
matter, there is no God. Which is the greater in-

comprehensibility? We must stand by facts as we ascertain them.

Unintelligent, impersonal evolution is like a blind painter, working upon creations he cannot see, or like an insane logician wandering after reasons he does not comprehend. Such evolution is impossible. We cannot see that which does not exist. If we see reason in nature there must be reason in nature. If we see a plan, then there is a plan. Nature without a plan is more incomprehensible than nature with a plan. We cannot deny what we see. We cannot deny what we prove; we cannot prove that which does not exist. Reason cannot deny the reason that reason sees. If mind is an effect, it is the effect of some greater Mind or cause. One great cause differentiates into many minor effects. The many parts imply the one whole—Division implies unity. The special derivation implies an underived generality. One Power makes many manifestations; such as the power to live, the power to will, the power to think, the power to be conscious, or, which is the same thing, the power to be personal. We repeat, if there is reason or intelligence in nature, then unintelligent evolution is impossible. Unintelligent evolution is a blind process, and not an intelligent method. Whatever it is, it is an eternal necessity in which there is no creation because everything is eternal, and nothing is new.

Where we find anything, we find some mystery of Power, which, in itself, the thing is not—a something of the supernatural, for which, supernature personalized, the word God is the symbol. Religion simply adores the Personal Presence of whatever is admitted to be at the background of the universe, whether it be called law, cause, force or being. And a personal omnipresence is no more incomprehensible than an impersonal omnipresence. Nature is the known method of self-revealed Supernatural Power. To deny the Power is to deny the method.

Some deny that there is any Supernatural Person or personal God, because there is evil in the world. But whether Supernature is personal or impersonal, evil is not its work; for nothing that is supernatural can be evil. Some supernatural Power commands man to do or not to do certain things, and urges motives for the one and against the other. The sovereignty of God (using that term as the symbol of a supernatural person) includes man's freedom; or rather God as a sovereign act, made man free. As evil, in the sense of sin is the act of will, so individual evil is the act of individual will. Human evil began, continues and ends with the human will. When the human will shall fully obey the superhuman will, all evil will cease. As there can be no science of Being (God), yet there is a science of the method of God in matter. The difference between science and religion is, that science is limited to the part, and religion extends to the conceivable whole.

If we have reached, logically, the proof of a supernatural Person whom we call God, as a verbal symbol of Power, is it illogical to affirm that God, as unembodied power, may be, if He so please, the God of embodied, or Incarnate Goodness, whom we call Christ? If God is manifested Power in his imper-

sonal Works, why should He not be manifest Love,
in His Personal Son? Indeed, the one is no more
incomprehensible than the other.

7. *The supernatural Power is one Power.* The manifesting Power is one—monistic; not two—dualistic;
nor many—pluralistic. There can be no quality or
plurality of Time, Space, Power, or eternal duration.
We have said that supernatural evolution is infinite
Power manifesting a finite Method ; but the Power
and a Method are relatively one as the substance and
the shadow are one. God *is* all, or God *creates* all.
The Power to be a thing is the power to create it.
Of the two incomprehensibilities, it is more unthinkable that God should be a bird, a bug or a stone, than
that he should create them. He can *be* that which
He does not choose to *create*, and He can create that
which he does not choose to be. The secret of
which, is with Him.

As we understand the theory of agnostic evolution,
all things are eternally evolved from underived necessary unity, or from underived necessary plurality.
But nothing could be evolved from underived plurality, for plurality itself was evolved from the underived unity ; therefore underived unity excludes underived plurality.

8. *Supernatural Power is one Being.* Herbert Spencer says, " The axiomatic truths of physical science,
unavoidably postulate Absolute Being as their common basis.   *   *   *   We cannot construct a theory
of internal phenomena without postulating Absolute
Being ; and unless we postulate Absolute Being, or
Being which persists, we cannot construct a theory

of external phenomena." (F. P. ch. vi, sec. 60, edition of 1875.)

" Our knowledge of noumenal existence," says Herbert Spencer, *Prin. Psy.*, " has a certainty which our knowledge of phenomenal existence cannot approach." (See Cazelles, 31.)

August Comte, near the beginning of this century, got up a Religion of Humanity. George Lewes, his biographer, at the conclusion of his book says: " Indisposed as I am to occupy any of the few remaining pages with criticism, I cannot forbear pointing out one immense omission. It makes religion purely and simply what has hitherto been designated morals. In thus limiting religion to the relations in which we stand towards one another, and towards humanity, Comte leaves an important element aside; for, even upon his own showing, humanity can only be the Supreme Being of our world—it cannot be the Supreme being of the universe. To limit the universe to our planet is to take a rustic, untraveled view of this great subject. If in this, our terrestrial sojourn, all we can distinctly know must be limited to the sphere of our planet; nevertheless, even here, we, standing on this ball of earth and looking into the infinitude of which we know it to be but an atom, must irresistibly feel and know that the humanity worshiped here cannot extend its dominion there. I say, therefore, that supposing our relations towards humanity may one day be systematized into a distinct cultus, and made a religion; and supposing, further, our whole practical priesthood be limited to it, there must still remain for us, outlying this terrestrial

5

sphere, the other sphere named infinite; into which our eager and aspiring thoughts will wander, carrying with them, as ever, the obedient emotions of love and awe; so that beside the religion of humanity, there must be a religion of the universe; besides the conception of humanity we need the conception of a God, as the infinite of life; from whom the universe proceeds, not in alien indifference, not in estranged subjection, but in the fullness of abounding power, as the incarnation of resistless activity."

And now, having proved by the facts of science, as we claim, that there is a supernatural Factor for all natural facts—that such supernatural Factor is not only a Power but a Being—not only a Being but a Person, we claim that such supernatural Power—Being—Person, is what we mean by the word God, or the Good One.

A hole in the ocean fills up as fast as we make it. The stone that Sisyphus rolled up the hill, ever rolled back upon him. The incomprehensible ever increases with the increased comprehension of the incomprehensible. As the incomprehensible becomes less the comprehensible becomes just so much greater. What we lose on one side we gain on the other. Has the atheist no other hope of annihilating God, than that of his boast of comprehending the incomprehensible? After comprehending all that we can, that which remains incomprehensible will be enough for our God. When we have apprehended that the solar system is held together by what is called gravitation, still we have not comprehended incomprehensible gravitation. Though we may comprehend a few facts, we are utterly unable to comprehend a single cause. The wisdom of man is foolishness to God. The higher we rise, the wider is the view. As we advance, the horizon before us recedes, and behind us it follows. The God of a savage is a Fetish; the God of an Isaiah, or a Newton, is an Infinite Being.

Hereafter we shall use, *ad libitum* , the word God, interchangeably with the word Power, as a verbal symbol of the supernatural. Let us now study its ways or methods of manifestation.

> From supernature, nature came ;
> The two are one, or both the same.
> For each is part of each the whole,
> As each is all of each the soul.
> Yet bird and man and jewelled sod
> Are God-made things that are not God.
> The star is not the leafy tree,
> Nor e'er can each the other be.
> Still earth and sky and central sun,
> Though all from God, in God are one.
> Each sound and form, and throbbing star,
> Of thought eternal, fragments are.
> The finite proves the Infinite,
> As night reveals the hidden light.

LECTURE II.

METHODS OF SUPERNATURAL POWER.

There is further proof of supernatural Power in the methods of its manifestation. What Power does proves what Power is; even as the tree is known by its fruits. Power may manifest itself directly in things without life, and indirectly in things with life. Power may manifest itself uniformly as in what is called natural law, or multiformly, as in creation and generation. Power begins or creates things, continues or generates things, exchanges or correlates things. Sometimes the manifestation or way of Power is a method, sometimes it is a process and sometimes it is neither a method nor a process. Method is a plan or uniform habit of Power. As human Power is human Will, so we may conclude that superhuman Power is superhuman Will. Thus we say that a plan, a way, a habit, of Power, is a plan, a way, a habit, of Will—of one Will, whatever its methods. Will, human or superhuman, or subhuman, is behind everything done in the universe. Where superhuman will stops, the human or subhuman goes on.

1. *Method as related to Miracles.* There are, however, special manifestations of Will Power that exhibit no method, such as miracles and providence. Miracles are sporadic acts of Power. After God's Will became known as matter, as cause, as force, as life, as providence, as law, as command, when it did some special thing, it was known as a miracle. A miracle is a fact. The first of everything was a miracle—the first atom, the first seed, the first insect. God is the worker of superhuman miracles as man is of human miracles. Nature is a miracle of supernature.

A superhuman miracle is a fact, as the creation of the world, and all that is in it ; and a human miracle is a fact, as every act of the human Will. We say this, because every act is a miracle which is not under law, and no Will, human or superhuman, is under law. All Will is a law unto itself. Even superhuman Will may speak to, but not coerce human Will, without destroying it. There is everywhere, and in everything, nothing but a miracle. Law is the miracle of miracles. The first drop of water produced was a miracle ; nor did it cease to be a miracle when the second was produced.

All original and unrepeated acts are miracles ; all acts are original and unrepeated : therefore all acts are miracles. To repeat is to do the *same* thing ; but while similar things are done, the *same* thing can not be done twice. If to overcome law is a miracle, then any one may perform a miracle. When it is said that the universe is governed by law, of course it is meant that every atom, motion, and change of every kind, is governed by law. Raise your hand and let it fall again to the side! So. When your hand, which hung at your side under the law of gravitation, was raised by your Will, was it raised by law or not? If it was raised by your Will in spite of law, your Will overcame the law, and is a miracle. If Will is not law, then it is stronger than law, and law does not govern the universe, for it does govern Will. That governs the universe, as we have said, which governs natural law. In the case before us, Will governs law, and therefore Will governs the universe—indeed, Will is law. If Will governs the universe, then there may be answers to prayer, special providences, and miracles, or anything and everything that Supreme Will may choose to do.

But right here is a difficulty, not in the sufficiency of proof, but in the prejudice, or prepossession of the mind, to which it is submitted. Everything is doubtful to a doubting mind. All proof, whether of one kind or another, must be submitted to minds of pre-conceived notions of some sort—minds with a theistic or an atheistic bias—and these proofs are sufficient or insufficient, according to the bias. To an atheist, miracles are impossible, because he believes in no God to work them. In denying a God, he denies all a God can do. In other words, admitting a God, we can account for all things ; in denying a God, we can account for nothing.

A supernatural Being can do supernatural things. But to believe in a truth, we must be in sympathy with it ; or at least not in antipathy to it. As before said, all is doubtful to a doubting mind. While preposses-

sion is not proof, prejudice is not refutation. The
mind without a God, e. g., denying a God, sees a
universe without a God. But a mind having God
within, e. g., in its faith, sees all things live, move,
and have their being in God. Law, force, miracle
and cause are different names for Will. As we
widen the field of law, we multiply the number of
miracles ; for miracles are not the exception to law,
but law is the uniformity or system of miracles. Law,
as the assumed invariability of will, is essentially and
possibly, variable. Law-phenomena and miracle-phe-
nomena, are both will-phenomena. A equals X plus
Y. In other words, law and miracle, cause and
force, make the sum of will ; but *to this will, there is
no law and no miracle.* One volition is as natural as
another ; is as much a law as another ; and is as much
a miracle as another. If asked what is a miracle, I
ask, what is law ? Miracles are defined when law is
explained ; when law is explained, miracles are
proved. Miracles have hitherto been put upon the
defensive ; but the time has come, for the more philosophical understanding of truth, to put law upon
explanation. That is miracle in nature which is
alone in nature. Each of the three Kingdoms, mineral, animal, vegetable, is alone in the universe ; and
each to every other Kingdom, is a Wonder—a Miracle. Law is the greatest miracle of God. To say
that law is in the fact of like results from like conditions, is to state merely a fact, not to give a principle ;
a result, not an effect ; a method, not a power ; a sequence, not a consequence. According to some,
notion of the change of condition changes the law.

Miracles may work by conditions as well as law. In law the conditions are repeated ; in miracles they are not repeated. Put the possibility of miracles in the change of conditions, if that will help the matter. Give to law its conditions, and to a miracle its conditions. Nothing is impossible with God.

It is said "the elevation of a body in the air by the force of the arm, is a counteraction of the law of gravitation, but it is a counteraction of it by another law as natural as the law of gravity. The fact, therefore, is in conformity with the laws of nature. But if the same body is raised in the air without any application of known force, it is not a fact in conformity with natural law." But when the arm raises a stone in the air, it is not the arm, but the will of the man that raises it ; and the will is a known force. Is not that will a netural law—all the natural law there is ? If so, may not the will of another raise it ? If a will can raise it, what is it that pulls it down, but the will of some other ? If some other will pulls it down, may not the will of that other raise it up ? When a man raises a stone in the air, his will overcomes the will of some invisible person that pulls it down. If the will of a finite person raises, may not the will of an infinite person pull down ? God's will manifests itself twice as much in two ounces as it does in one.

When science explains a law, theology will explain miracles. To account for law is to account for miracles. Law is essentially what miracles are, and nothing more ; and miracles are essentially what law is, and nothing less. The mistake has been in putting miracles upon proof, instead of putting law upon

explanation. Miracles are not the exception to law ;
but law is the uniformity of the miraculous Power.
Law is the totality of miracles. But law and miracles are essentially the acts of one and the same
Absolute Will. The will of God has general manifestations called laws, special manifestations called
miracles. But there was a miracle before there was
law, just as the end of a line is before its prolonga-
tion. The first thing in the universe was a miracle—
a something done antecedent to all conditions—an
act of Absolute Will.

An uniform repetition of those miracles or acts of
the will, are the laws of nature. But the special was
before the general—indeed the general was only
many specials in succession. Nature is but the visible shapes of will—some special as in miracles, and
some general and uniform, as in what are called laws.
Both miracle and law mean nature, and nature means
Absolute Will. Therefore, the explanation of miracle
is identical with the explanation of law. Miracle
does not suspend, violate or withdraw itself as an
exception to the law-order of nature; for law being
the uniform willing, or volition of the Absolute Will,
cannot suspend, violate, or except itself. One act of
will does not suspend another act of will ; nor does
one act of will violate another act of will ; nor is one
act of will an exception to other acts of the same
will. Will is will, and that is all there is about it.
When law is accounted for essentially, then miracles
are accounted for rationally.

2. *Method as related to providence.* The universe is
under the control of Will, direct or indirect, or under

necessity. If all things are under the control of Will, nothing is necessary, or if under necessity nothing is free, and nothing can be right or wrong. If conduct can be morally right or wrong, Supreme Will controls all, and providence is both possible and probable. So that the question is not, can there be a providence? but, as Supreme Will controls all, the question is, what is not a providence? Here too we see the possibility of answer to prayer. If unlimited Power is unlimited Will, prayer may be answered, and no law broken; for law is will, as we now proceed to show.

3. *Method as related to Law.* In what is called natural law, supernatural Will Power manifests uniformity rather than method. Law is Will; Will is one as the sun, law many as the rays. As every ray is all sun, so every law is all Will. In other words, as the sun and its rays, so is Will and laws. Natural law is supernatural Will, uniform as we think law to be. Will is not only Power—personal power—but Will is law-power.

The law of human, individual and collective, conduct is superhuman Will, stereotyped in the inevitable state of society. That is natural law which is best under natural circumstances. Circumstances over which we do not have control reveal the law of conduct over which we do have control.

If the universe is governed by law, it is governed by Will; for, as said before, if Will is not law, then the motion of my hand which is governed by my Will, is not governed by law, and so the whole universe, of which my hand is a part, is not governed by law. So far as law is uniform, it is the uniformity of Will. Supreme Will prescribes its own supreme conditions, supreme operations, and supreme aims. Law is Will, uniform as we see it. Natural law, as contrasted with civil law, is supernatural Will, uniform in natural order.

But law creates nothing, therefore if law is only a fact, it governs nothing; for fact belongs to method and not to power; and while power governs everything, method governs nothing. What is method? Method is a way of power, and may be uniform or multiform. As in initial creation of the inorganic, in progressive creation called evolution, and in special creation called miracles, omnipresent Will observes a self-prescribed method of special diversity in a general system of uniformity, doing different, original, creative things, with or without conditions; so in Law, the same omnipresent Will observes a self-prescribed method of general uniformity in special diversity; doing, uniform things under uniform conditions, governing, under a method of uniformity, a universe it had created by its power, under a method of diversity. The scientific notion of law is in its apparent uniformity. I say its *apparent* uniformity, because, as Prof. Jevons says, " Law is not inconsistent with extreme diversity."

According to Mill, " the expression ' law of nature,' *means* nothing but the uniformities which exist among natural phenomena."

The essence of law is in the will behind the uniformity. Even Mr. Mill admits that " the expression ' law of nature,' is generally used by scientific men as a sort of tacit reference to the original sense of the word *law*, the expression of the will of a superior; the superior, in this instance, being the Ruler of the Universe." If law is will, then uniformity of law is but a method or uniformity of will. Laws are as uniform as the purpose of the law-giver. The purposes of law, and the purposes of even miracles, are purposes of one and the same will; and therefore, as actions of the will, there can be nothing in law so fixed that a miracle would conflict with it. One volition of the will cannot conflict with another volition of the same will. Difference is not conflict.

It has been said that force cannot exist apart from matter; and that matter exists only in connection with force. As to saying that matter exists only in connection with force, matter becomes less and less material as you reach the immaterial force with which it is instinct. The constant tendency of science is to idealize or immaterialize matter. Omnipresent force is omnipresent will. Will is manifested as gravitation, and *is* gravitation; it is manifested as chemical affinity, and *is* chemical affinity; it is manifested in the interchange of all the energies of nature, and *is* those energies. God's will as heat becomes God's will as electricity; and God's will as electricity becomes God's will as heat, and God is all in all. God's will is uniform in God's uniform purpose. Science studies this uniformity in matter, and calls it law, whereas it is only a method. God is omnipresent as will, as force, as providence. Usual acts of will are called laws; unusual acts are called miracles. But to Him, the volitions of his will are not known as usual or unusual ; He neither looks forward nor backward ; all is one eternal NOW. To Him all present acts or phenomena are alike creative. As there is no past time to God, there is no past creation to Him. Creation is perpetual. To continue is to create—continuation is only prolonged creation. A growing tree is a growing creation ; every second, is a new creation. That which seems to come to us by the uniformity of law, is an instantaneous creation as God's will. He knows no law or creation apart from His will.

As we have said, God created some things without individual wills, and some things with individual wills. To things without wills of their own, as minerals and vegetables, He addressed no command, as they had neither intelligence nor power to obey or disobey them. He imposed upon them, consequently, no moral accountability, but He, Himself, dwelt in them as their will. What we call the mechanical forces of gravitation, heat, electricity, and the forces of chemical affinity, and the vital force of germination and growth, are but names we give to God at work. They are not so much manifestations of His will, as they are His will itself. Where uniformity is the uniformity of Absolute Will—uniformity is a fact or method, but not an essence.

" Theological philosophy supposes everything to be governed by *will*, and that phenomena are, therefore, variable, at least virtually. The *positive philosophy*, on the contrary, conceive them to be subject to invariable laws, which permit us to predict with absolute precision." Between these two accounts of things, there is said to be an utter incompatibility. Suppose

we admit the existence of these uniform laws, whose
operations we may predict with absolute precision, so
far as they portend to matter.   Does that forbid them
to be will—uniform will?   May not this uniformity
be self-prescribed by will?   Uniformity is not the
essence of law, but its method.   Positive philosophy
does not investigate that essence.   It cannot deny
that uniform laws may be uniform will.   It says that
it knows not what it is that is uniform ; only that
something is uniform ; whether it is will, or whatever
it may be.   Positive philosophy confines its researches
to the *fact*, and does not investigate the *cause* of uniformity.   Facts belong to methods, not powers.   But
may not will in nature choose to be uniform (in nature,
at least) to us?   There are two facts in nature—unintelligent, unconscious, impersonal matter, and intelligent, conscious, personal being.   Science is impatient that religion should teach that nature rests upon
supernature—the objective upon the subjective—impersonal facts upon a personal Factor.

Nature is multiformity in uniformity.   Distance
blends the uneven into the even, the variable into the
invariable ; and that which is invariable to us, is
variable to Him, and the reverse.   Science must
study what it calls the variable, as in the wills of all
animal natures, or confess its impotence as a knowledge of the uppermost lines of nature.   When we
pass from matter to human conduct, human will is
the most obtrusive of all facts in human nature.   If
supernatural will be too variable to be studied by
science, so, *a fortiori*, must be the will of all below
the supernatural.   Is man without law because he

has a will? Will is variable or invariable, as it
chooses to be. As said before, supreme will is invariable, when it has an invariable purpose; though
with the Almighty, there " is no variableness, neither
shadow of turning." " I am the Lord, I change not;
therefore ye sons of Jacob are not consumed." Science cannot prove that variableness is more a char-
acteristic of will than invariableness. It is claimed
that the laws of nature may be scientifically observed and ascertained because of their invariability;
but that does not prove that they are not acts of will,
unless it can be proved that acts of will are invariably
variable, which is absurd. The power to be variable
is one thing, and the exercise of it another. The
existence of will cannot be denied. If nature can be
invariable without intelligent will, as some contend,
it is likely to be more variable with the intelligent
will, for which is here contended? The simple difference is this; some see that what they call the laws
of nature are invariable, but neither know nor inquire
why they are so. Others see the laws of nature to
be equally invariable, and believe them to be the
energies of the possibly variable will of God. To
these they have a personal origin; to those others an
impersonal one. Some study and trust them as the
invariable facts of an impersonal nature; others study
and reverence them as the invariable decisions of a
Personal God. They attribute them to a person, because they are acts like those of a person. They are
as invariable to theology, as they are to science.
What is called unchangeable nature, is but unchanged
will. But let us bear in mind, that unchangeable

will need not always do the same thing. An unchangeable will may do different and progressive
things, as in all evolution. It may do similar things,
under what we may call laws, and it may do many dissimilar things we may call miracles. But as acts of
will, each is independent, and in no sense violative of
other acts of will. The directing and effective energy
of the universe, which is a great fact in God, is inces-
santly willing different things. *If the theory of evolution be valid as a process or method of God's will, then, of
course, that will is invariably variable.* The invariable
or uniform is stationary ; the variable is the progressive. The incessant development of the homogeneous into the heterogeneous, of species into varieties,
has a persistent method of will ever varying its work.
No miracle is more a departure from uniformity than
the ever changing variations of species and individuals. These are, in fact, miracles, if law is uniform. In a word, *evolution is a process* of miracles. In
evolution, all is instability, change, creative, and miraculous. If law is a method of stability and not in
the power of will, then there is no law, if evolution
be true ; for, as seen in inorganic evolution, all is instability, and *per saltum.* Development is variation.

In the law theory, the conditions and results are
ever alike ; in the evolution theory, conditions and
results are ever unlike. In law, nature never extends,
but always repeats ; in evolution, nature never repeats, but always progresses. One theory, as an
exclusive theory, contradicts the other. If one is
exclusively true, the other must be false. It is alone
in the absolute will of an Absolute Being, that the

mystery and conflict of causation, law, evolution, miracle and providence, can be accounted for and harmonized, as diverse methods of one manifesting Power. With a divine Will as the unity of all things. the evolution system may be true as a *will-method* of progressive instability, and the law-system may be true as a *will-method* of conservative stability. Absolute Will can do either, both, or neither. Law is a Will-power working to a plan, with a method of diversity; miracle is Will-power working specially to a purpose without a method of any kind. Law is nothing but a method, and governs nothing; and not the power behind all methods, governing everything. Why is it that like conditions produce like results? Materialism does not explain.

We have said that originating power is one, and its methods are two, both multiform and uniform. They are also both free and fixed. Power is its own measure of freedom. The method of power is free because the power is free to produce dissimilar things, such as minerals, vegetables and animals. It is also fixed in the instrumentalities by which it produces similar things, such as moulds for similar bullets as before shown, and dies for similar coin. But the instrument is always in the hand of the instrument maker. Nature never gets away from supernature, but is the miracle of the supernatural. Supernature and nature are two realities of One Being—I do not say of one Person. There never was a bullet without a mould — never a coin without a coiner. The *fons et origo* of moulds and bullets, and of die and coin, is the conception of the One Mind, omnipresent

6

in the universe. The originating thought is the intrinsic energy continuing down all lines of derivation, but one bullet is not derived from another bullet. In the concavity of the mould it shaped the convexity of each bullet. Pieces of coin correspond, not to each other, but to their common die; and the die transmits, without repetition, to each, the one original thought of its maker. Two pieces of coin from the same die are not two thoughts, but are two facts of the one thought fixed in the die. The same mould may repeat the form and multiply bullets, but never repeat the same bullet. Even the act of moulding is never the same act, for the bullet is never the same. Every bullet is an original product of the one common mould; a creation, not an inheritance, or a derivation.

With the second drop of water was revealed a mental method of creative repetitions. Original power created the first drop, and original power created the second, similar drop. Their similarity was but the act of the originating mind, imitating its own work. This imitativeness may be free, or it may be fixed. The individual pieces of similar coin come from a method of repetition fixed in the die. This die repeats coin as the like conditions repeat like results.

As an illustration of the consistency of law and miracle in Will, suppose an invisible expert were to roll in succession, a million or more marbles, on a certain line, between certain hours of the day; all who observe it would conclude that it is a fact, and that in the fact is a law, that round pieces of stone, between certain hours of the day, would roll successively on a certain line. There would be, to the observer, a certain uniformity, and the condition of certain hours, would invariably attend the phenomena. But how would the facts be to the expert himself? To him, each marble would roll as impelled and directed by a distinct act of his will. There would be no uniformity to him, for each act would be original and independent of every other act, and uniformity can be predicated only of repeated and dependent acts.

To God there is neither uniformity nor necessity : and even to the observer, *uniformity is only a method* not a power. But suppose that this expert, upon the asking, and apparently without intermitting his usual roll of marbles along the given line, should throw a marble now and then, to a boy in some window above him? Such an act would be neither a violation of, nor a departure from, nor an exception to, the million of marbles rolled as described. Each act of throwing the occasional marble to the boy, would be original and independent, and as natural as any and all the other acts of his will ; for one act of will is as natural as another. *With God there is no distinction between natural and supernatural ; and miracle is as natural as law.* He does not know one act of His will as miracle, and other acts as laws. In the will of God there is enough uniformity of the method of law, and enough variation for the theory of evolution. If it be insisted that will is too variable for law, what must be said as to the variability of that uniformity called evolution? Variation is essential to evolution. All change from genus into species, and of species into individuals, is just so far a departure from uniformity, and so form the jurisdiction of what is called law.

God's will, as said before, in inorganic things is known as chemical affinity and gravitation : in organic matter, His will is known as life ; in lower animals, His will is known as instinct ; but to a man, God addresses his will as command or moral law, and looks to conduct. It is the will of God that some of His creatures should have wills of their own. Some of these subordinate wills, as in the case of brutes, were merely self-preserving wills, and morally irresponsible; and, as to them, He included His will in their instincts. As to man, it was God's will that man should have the will of reflective intelligence of His own, and He expressed His will to the will of man, in commands. In this, man became a responsible and moral being. If our wills were not given to us by some other will, then, contrary to the doctrine that like begets like, and that nature makes no leaps, we should get our wills from that which had no wills to give. We might as well expect to see a horse born from a fish. We see, on the contrary, will derived from will, all around us, in the phenomena of heredity. As Shakespeare puts the doctrine, " there's a Divinity that shapes our ends, rough hew them how we will." To a certain extent, we go where we will on this globe ; and yet, some superior will takes the globe, with all on it, where we do not will to go. Just as in the case of one carrying a vase of fish ; each fish swims around according to its own individual will ; but the will of another carries the vase and the fish in spite of its will, where that other will pleases. The two orders of will conflict, but each is free.

We have described the method, and have been silent as to the power of law. The power to walk is one thing, and the method or way of walking, as fast or slow, constantly or occasionally, uniformly or diversely, is another thing. Now, like results from like conditions, is a method of uniformity ; but there must be some power to make the results uniformly follow like conditions.

Blackstone says : " As man depends absolutely on his Maker for everything, it is necessary that he should, in all points, conform to his Maker's will. This will of his Maker is called the law of nature." God's will pervades the universe and energizes matter. The universe is both the fact, and a method of God's will—its materialization. So far as we can form an opinion on this subject, will is the centre of power. Will creates will. The Creator wills that some of His creatures shall have will of their own. As said before, when Will combines matter, moves matter, or vitalizes matter, it is called FORCE.

In other words, Will may be creative in cause, invariable in law, creatively variable in evolution, and special in miracle ; but, if evolution and law, as well as miracle, be not exponents of Will, and either be exclusively true, the other two are false. If the old notion of the absolute inflexibility of law be true, there can be no progress of evolution and no isolated miracle ; or, if either of these be true, as a power or as method, there can be no inflexibility of law. All may be true as the acts of absolute Will ; for the absolute Will of an Absolute Being may do things apparently contradictory to finite intelligence, but perfectly consistent to infinite intelligence. In tracing all phenomena back to Will, we reach a sufficient reason, accounting for everything; but in setting up any one atheistical system as exclusive, the facts of the universe become too conflicting, and we cannot account satisfactorily for anything.

To say that this universe, including all substance, systems of phenomena, force, motion, feelings, and results, is governed by law, is to say that all these are governed by Will; for Will is law. For illustration: as the idea of the universe covers all motions, whatever is moved, is moved by law: my hand is moved; therefore my hand is moved by law. Again, whatever moves my hand is law: my Will moves my hand; therefore my will is law. Now, if the law-power which moves my hand is human Will, why is not the law-power which moves the stars, super-human Will? Supreme Will is supreme law. This Will is one as the sun; law many as the rays; as every ray is all sun, so every law is all Will. If *will* is law-power, law-power can have no fixed conditions; for will can have none. But if the will-power which moves my hand is not law-power, then the universe is not governed by law; for the motion of my hand, governed by my will, is not so governed. As just said, if any law-power is will-power, why is not all law will? And *e converso*, if any will is law, why is not all will law within its sphere?

But, if the universe is governed by law, the government is personal, not impersonal; for government is a personal function, and law implies a personal law-giver.

In *matter*, that part of the universe with no intrinsic will traceable by us, there is extrinsic personal Will-power, called gravitation ; and there is the *method* in which all objects near the surface of the earth, for instance, are drawn towards its centre, with a force, directly as to mass and inversely as to the square of the distance. In the government of this matter-part of the universe there is an inevitable *must*—it cannot do otherwise than it does.

In *mind*, that part of the universe where there are intelligent things called brutes and intelligent persons called men, the case is different. They have intrinsic wills subject to a supreme extrinsic Will. Law with the brutes is the extrinsic Will of their Maker, intrinsic in them as instinct. God fixes the intelligence of the bee who builds its cells in exactest hexagons, by making the eyes of the bees in a group of hexagons. The lines of the eyes give the lines of the cells. This instinct or fixed intelligence is their law. As to man, his Maker's superhuman intelligence appeals to man's human intelligence by commands, motives, prophecies, and by providential events. Here the idea is the moral *should*, not the physical *must*, as in matter. If we describe law as a method of like results from like conditions, and yet remain silent as to the power or cause by which like as from like we might as well speak of the engine and be silent as to the motive power by which the engine is operative : What is the power on the other side of phenomena, by which phenomena are phenomena ?

We are confidently told that law is on this side of

phenomena, not on the other. But while the *method* of law is on this side, the *power* of law is on the other. The shadow on this side of the earth is cast by sunlight on the other. If there be no *noumenon*, there can be no *phenomenon*. But in refining law down to a method, we intensify the inquiry into the power behind the method. Turn which way we will,—doubt, deny, profane the Supernatural—omnipresent omnipotence envelopes and arrests us. We cannot have a method of facts without a power to realize the method. All the phantoms of science fall back into the Eternal Being.

Necessity is inconsistent with the government of law. We are told that the universe is *governed* by law, but if everything is *necessary*, then nothing can be governed; and, if everything is governed, then nothing is necessary. If it is meant that everything is necessary, and nothing is a creation, then, I ask, is the intelligence which we predicate as the necessity of everything, a necessary intelligence? Do we necessarily know that everything is necessary? If we necessarily know this, why do not all necessarily know the same thing? Are the religious doubts of one necessary, and is the religious belief of another necessary? In a word, do all who hate, necessarily hate; and do all who love, necessarily love? Are all dishonest people necessarily dishonest, and all honest people necessarily honest? If all the evil conduct of men is necessary, and has no creator in the man himself, why hold him responsible? Was it necessary for the Egyptians to enslave the Israelites? or for the Jews to have polygamy? Where does necessity end and where creation, or liberty and responsibility, begin? If that which necessarily exists be necessarily unintelligent, then it is necessarily ignorant and ought to be silent.

But necessity is only a method of self-prescribed uniformity of Will. Prof. Huxley says, " If there be a physical necessity, it is that a stone unsupported must fall to the ground. But what is really all we know about this phenomena? Simply that in all human experience, stones have fallen to the ground under these conditions; that we have not the smallest reason for believing that any stone so circumstanced will not fall to the ground; and that we have, on the contrary, every reason to believe that it will so fall. It is very convenient to indicate that all the conditions of belief have been fulfilled in this case, by calling the statement that unsupported stones will fall to the ground, a 'law of nature.' But when, as commonly happens, we change *will* into *must*, we introduce an idea of necessity, which most assuredly does not lie in the observed facts, and that have no warranty that I can discover elsewhere. For my part, I utterly repudiate and anathematize the intruder. Fact I know and law I know, but what is this *necessity* save an empty shadow of my own mind's throwing?" Mr. John Stuart Mill's idea of necessity is " That word in its other acceptations involves much more than mere uniformity of sequence; it implies irresistibleness. Applied to the will, it only reasons that the given cause will be followed by the effect subject to all possibilities of counter action by other causes; but in common use it stands for the opera-

tion of those causes exclusively which are supposed
too powerful to be counteracted at all. * * * Any
given effect is only necessary provided that the
causes tending to produce it are not controll."
(" Logic " Bk. vi., ch. 2., § 3.)

Admit that ill consequences uniformily follow actions classed as evil, because of those consequences.
Is that uniformity preventable or not preventable?
If preventable, the idea of uniformity does not exclude remedial or interrupting factors. In other
words, causes called evil may be naturally or supernaturally resisted ; as in the case of one natural law
preventing the operation of another natural law. If
nothing can prevent certain consequences from following certain actions, there must be some irresisti-
ble power to make it certain ; and this brings us back
to the remark, that power measures necessity, and
the necessity of results is in the power to necessitate
results. There is more necessity for power in necessity than in all else. The difference between a system of necessity in nature, and of an economy of
grace, is that in an economy of grace the great
Ruler publishes laws that are holy, just and good,
and prescribes the consequences of persistent disobedience. But he ever holds the conduct and
the consequences, as he does all else, in his all-wise
control. He is merciful and forgiving, where a God
might well claim to be merciful. Knowing that it is
a fearful thing to fall into the hands of the living God,
we are sure that no mercy included in the religious
system of conduct and consequences ever encour-
aged wrong doing. That is, which we observe to be ;

but there is no necessity that it should be as it is. There is necessarily no necessity in anything. All is as God wills it; and will to be will, must not be under any necessity. *There is no necessity above God, compelling Him to make anything necessary below him.* That which is called necessity to men is no necessity to God.

But whatever law may be essentially, and to us, it is no law to the lawgiver. He makes no law for Himself; and His will being law itself, is bound by no law. Supreme law cannot bind Supreme law. As he that makes anything must himself exist before the thing which he makes, so must the lawgiver exist before the law is given. Nothing can bind the Binder. Nothing can be more omnipotent than omnipotence. That which is a rule to man is will, but it is not a rule to God. Below Him all is as He pleases, whether it be uniform or not uniform, connected or disconnected; whether we call it law or miracle.

Nature is the code of the supernatural. Supernatural Power behind the stars, and system of stars, is, alike, the moral authority of social as of material systems, and of confederate systems. As law is like a royal coin, precious and current, whether expressed in material symbols or prescribed in rules of human conduct, so the Will manifesting the material and moral systems is one and the same. The unity of law is the unity of Will. To understand the highest generalizations of either the material or moral system of law, we must understand the highest generalizations of both; exactly as we understand one we shall understand the other. Therefore, with our eyes fixed upon the uniform manifestations of will in the laws of matter, as admitted in recent thought, let us study in the revelations of the material and visible, the nature of will in the moral and the invisible. Leaving theories to shape themselves, let us go directly to the facts of the universe. If nature is one the evolution of the supernatural will as law must be one; and what is found authoritative in the material, will not be contradicted in the moral. As the radii of a circle have the same centre, and as the two equal angles at the base of an isosceles triangle have the same vertex, so we may expect the laws of matter and morality to focalize in the same will, and manifest their presence by the same operative method. If the laws of matter multiply effects and segregate phenomena, so the laws of morality multiply results. As harmony is the result of compulsory obedience in matter, so it is of voluntary obedience in morality. The evolutionary laws of integration, environment, propagation, growth and correlation are the same in both. Supernatural unity of material and moral law is seen in the unity of essence, the unity of sanctions and the unity of manifestations.

Blackstone says that "law depends not upon *our approbations*, but upon the *maker's will*." If Blackstone be correct, law is neither a cause nor an effect, but, as a volition, is *sui generis*. Statute law is the will of the legislature. International law is the will of the nations. The law for the servant is the will of the master. In ultimate generalization, we may say that all law is will. It is in this sense of

will, that we everywhere use the word law. The
supreme will is the supreme law. Laws, as forces of
will, may be distinct as the waves, but they are in
essence one, as the sea. Law is the universal nature
of things, relations, and actions: It is not made, but
it exists. There is as much law at one time as another. There was no more or other law at the time
of Justinian than at the time of the XII Tables.
There were more prohibitions, but not more law ;
for universal reason neither increases nor diminishes.
When man is commanded not to steal, no new law is
made. Honesty is the law—dishonesty its violation.
Law is in doing or being; not in not doing or not
being. Prohibitions may indicate or reveal law, but
they are not laws. They only forbid the breaking of
law. Prohibition implies the law. As society grows
older, it gains, through religion or mere human reason, what the law of universal reason is, and declares
prohibitions against its violation. So the enlighten-
ment of the world enables it to discover what the
nature of things requires or necessitates, and also to
prohibit its disregard. The affirmation of law implies
a prohibition of its violation, and the prohibition of
an act implies the law threatened to be broken.
Thou shalt not steal implies the right of property
and possession of a thing. The correlative of
every affirmation of law is the negation of its violation, and the reverse. As the convex side of every
curved line has, on the obverse, a side of correlative
concavity, so every law has a correlative warning or
prohibition not to violate it. The law of gravitation
is in the falling tower, not in the notice to keep from

under it. Law is in the ownership of land, not in the posted warnings not to trespass on it. Law is executory, not prohibitory. The multiplicity of prohibitions do not multiply laws: They at most suggest what the law is whose violation is forbidden.

For this reason, the growth of codes, as that of Justinian, does not indicate the growth of law, but the growth of its violations to be prevented. So the maximum of law, as it is called, is the maximum of its violation. The multiplicity of rules of morality indicates a multiplicity of immoral customs. Rules of morality multiply as principles of morality are broken. We must distinguish between legal rules which are logic, and the principle of legal principles which is natural or universal reason. The law of right conduct of men is the same as the law of gravitation of matter; for both are will. Gravitation holds matter to centres and systems of centres, producing the harmony of circular motion; so the laws of moral conduct hold men, races, and nations to social centres and systems of centres, producing domestic, municipal, and international order and harmony.

Look at the consequences of the *disobedience of matter.* "If," says Hooker, "nature should intermit her course, and leave altogether, though it were but for awhile, the observation of her own laws; if those principal and mother elements of the world, whereof all things in this lower world are made, should lose the qualities which now they have; if the frame of that heavenly arch erected over our heads should loosen and dissolve itself; if celestial spheres should

forget their wonted motions, and by irregular volu-
bility turn themselves any way as it might happen;
if the prince of the lights of heaven, which as a giant
doth run his universal course, should, as it were,
through a languishing faintness, begin to stand and
rest himself; if the moon should wander from her
beaten way, the times and seasons of the year blend
themselves by disordered and confused mixtures, and
the winds breathe out their last gasp, the clouds
yield no rain, the earth be defeated of heavenly influence, the fruits of the earth pine away, as children
at the withered breast of their mother, no longer able
to yield them relief, what would become of man
himself, whom these things now do all serve? See
we not plainly that obedience of creatures unto the
law of nature is the stay of the whole world?"

The consequences of *disobedience* are not different
in *morality*, but infinitely more dreadful. If in moral
life every man should disregard every right of his
fellow-man; and if every husband and wife should
violate every law of their relation, and every parent
and child be unnatural to each other; if every master
should oppress and not pay the wages of the servant,
and every servant disobey and rob his master; if
every government should seek to crush its citizens,
and all the citizens constantly war upon the government; if every man were to treat every contract as
a baseless promise; if no man had an admitted right
to live, to own lands and chattels—in a word, if there
were no obedience, and every man were a law unto
himself, would not social chaos and reconstruction
come as certainly from disobedience in morality, as

chaos and reconstruction would come from disobedience in matter? The same will is behind all. The
threads of all laws are gathered into the same hand.
Nature rejoices in such principal things as the ocean
and the sun, where the many look to the one. Centripetalism is the law for both atoms and men.

The uniformity of effects shows unity of cause.
The uniformity of phenomena is the exponent of the
unity of law. This unity is in the analogy that moral
laws are as self-assertive as those we call inorganic
or material, and can no more be broken with im-
punity than they ; for, we repeat, they both are the
expression of one will. All wrong is indelible ; and,
in a system of mere material law, disobedience is
neither forgotten nor forgiven ; for there can be no
disobedience as such. But moral responsibility transcends knowledge. Its limitations wander through
a moral economy of the ages, untraceable to finite
intelligence. A cause is an immortal thing. A wrong
is an ever parturient womb, like that of Milton's hag
at the gates of hell, from which a life-repeating
progeny comes, to curse and die. A felony is social
suicide. Every act has its equivalence in either compensations for suffering virtue and acts of kindness,
in reparations for moral injuries, or retributions for
injustice. But we have no telescope with which to
look on to the hidden end. Be sure your wrong-
doing will find you out and drive you into a corner.
" 'Tis the eternal law that where guilt is, sorrow shall
answer it."

Nature neither sleeps nor dies ; for supernature
never sleeps or dies. For every injury she returns a

blow. As you twist the twig, so must run the sap of
the tree. All beginnings are solemn, but bad ones
" cast their shadows before." Punishment may seem
to be postponed ; but, as in the constitution of man,
matter and morality are each the avenging Nemesis
of the wrongs of the other -punishment is sure to
come.

As to the special ground of essential right, it is
eternally omnipresent, and let us see what method,
if any, material science furnishes to ascertain the
fact of law. Can we use, in reasoning about
morals, the principles used in reasoning about
matter; and, by induction in morals as well as in
matter, discover any one principle upon which all
material and moral phenomena rest? Does not the
universality of law necessitate the unity of law ? If
it can be seen that a *tree* and a *system of morals* are
made upon the same principles, we can well believe
in a one Law-giver, and in the unity of His will as
laws. Similarity will be lost in identity, and parallels
will meet in infinity. This identity of principle of
all phenomena, material and moral, is seen in universal organizations, universal development, universal
individualization. This is evolution, and pertains to
the method, not the cause of manifestations. The
cause lies out of sight. Herbert Spencer calls it
" The Unknowable." We can know *what* law is, but
not *why.*

The supernatural unity of will in law is seen in the
unity of all evolution. The necessities for abstract
unity of law compel the venture upon most abstract
generalizations. But we shall be more than repaid

7

for such dry investigations and discussions if we find
the unity we seek. Unity is an essential quality.
Circumferences must have centres. From the one
all lines converge, and from the other all lines diverge. There can be no diversity without a correlative unity. Plato says that all unity tends to plurality, and all plurality ends in unity. As the
engineer must know the unity of his machine, as
well as the diversity of the several parts, in order to
manage its tremendous power, so the lawyer must
know law in the unity of its principles, as well as the
plurality of its rules, in order to know his ground.

Laws are not made, but they appear as there is
need. Like the " ever-becoming " of Heraclitus, law
is. " Mankind's notions of right are generally founded upon prescription."[a] " Roman law grew out of
the varied experience and the practiced forethought
of a great people, and which provided naturally and
easily for the numberless questions of human life and
intercourse."[b] " The study of a great variety of nations shows that none of the conditions essential to
the existence of men in a social order can be said to
have been at any time artificially made for them by
any prophet or law-giver. The utmost that legislators can effect is to modify, to improve, to purify existing systems and institutions. To none of them,
that we know of in history, was it given to find a void
which he could fill with a theory of his own inven-
tion. Laws are not made, but grow. Even now, in
our time of restless and over-prolific parliamentary

(a) Hallam's Mid. Ages, 337.   (b) Church's Mid. Ages, 53.

law-making, new laws mark only the endeavors of legislators to find the forms in which the general feeling of justice is to be expressed, or in which new wants, felt by the community, are to be satisfied under public authority."[a] And in order not to conflict or fail, they must come from one will. Law, to be law, is infallibly wise.

The evolution of matter, the evolution of morals, or rather the evolution of the knowledge of morals, or law, and the evolution of character, show that the laws of all phenomena, both material and social, are the same. Though evolution, as a theory, received the assent, qualified or unqualified, of many, if not a majority, of the thoughtful minds of the age; yet, before we can use it in the study of ethics or character, we must ascertain more definitely what it means.

The word evolution expresses for science what the word progress formerly did for society. Both words cover the idea of traceable derivation or development, not of causation. To evolve is not to cause. As a philosophy of the beginning of things, like other schemes, evolution is useless. In the language of Herbert Spencer, its great teacher: " Evolution, under its simplest and most general aspect, is the integration of matter, and the concomitant dissipation of motion." What is meant by "integration of matter," and how does that principle in material phenomena help us to understand the nature of ethical principles? As nature can not obey contradic-

---

[a] Ihne's Early Rome, ch. IV.

tory commands, the unity of law is a necessity. Accordingly we see all phenomena have the same method of manifestation from the many to the few, from the incoherent to the coherent, and from the homogeneous to the heterogeneous.

In the integration of matter the law is either that of chemical affinity or of mechanical force. When the cream gathers on the surface of milk; when straws and litter in the current become collected in an eddy; when boiling syrup crystallizes into sugar; when a crowd gathers in the street; when various religious opinions cease discussion, and assent to a creed; when political parties stop agitation, and agree upon a platform; when many things in action become one in repose; all division of labor, all committee work in legislative bodies, all specialties in skill, all variant moral notions formed into rules of conduct—all this is *integration*, or the first step in *evolution*. The exploring star-gazer, who, in imagination, sees the worlds come out of the initial mist enveloping the beginning of all things, beholds integration upon integration—the mist, the sphere, the system of spheres, and system of systems. The great law is exemplified in the rose bush of your garden. It is an organization of special elements, developing into structure, beauty, and sweetness. It is Will taking organic order. For further illustration, take a given volume of oxygen and twice that volume of hydrogen. Bring these together and you have water; which is distinctly neither gas, yet chemically both. The hydrogen in it will no longer burn, nor will its oxygen any longer promote combustion. Neither gas can then obey its own distinctive laws. When water was produced it brought its own law with it. Indeed, as the laws of a thing are in the thing itself, so a drop of water bears in its sphere a whole code of the laws of matter.

Ethical law observes the same method. Moral thoughts integrate into moral convictions, and convictions into laws, and laws into systems, and systems into codes. New laws are in new relations. The law does not anticipate the relation, but the relation *exhibits* the law. The law of evolution takes hold of the *life within nature* itself, and correlation manifests the movement of that life in its *relations* without.

Suppose that only two men existed in the whole world, and each dwelt in a separate island. Whatever may be said of their rights when apart, bring them together and each becomes to the other a possible wrong-doer; and, as to the other, each has rights. Chrysippus said, " Men exist for each other."[a] As the hydrogen and oxygen together make something that neither is by itself, so these two persons, when associated, develop a law of property and of person that neither needed by himself. The two coming together make a relation, and the relation is its own law.[b]

If there were but one person in all the world, the law of that one would be absolute selfishness. His ownership and possession would be exclusive — at least undisputed. All the sunlight would be his, all

(a) [Zeller on Stoicism, 312.] Protagoras said, " Relations are for all."

(b) Paulus, Digest, Lib. 1, Tit. 1–3; 1 Lecky E. M. 313.

the hills and valleys, all the springs and rivers, all the gold and silver, the cattle upon the thousand hills, all the trees and fruits, would be his. But the appearance of a second person would be another unit of selfishness, and if there was of any one thing only enough for one, and both sought it, there would be a conflict, in which the stronger would prevail. Each would be supreme to himself, but not to the other. But harmony requires law that shall be supreme over both.

One law ties many different things together, and one method of law is the same as to matter and mind. If one thing could exist by itself, it would be powerless. One atom without another atom amounts to nothing.[a] The end of essential morality is one of self-preservation, the survival of the fittest, or the perpetuation of that which has been begun. For illustration, when the second man appeared, the producing power cannot be supposed to have worked in the dark, or in vain. The producing power is also the preserving or continuing power. Therefore, that is right to be done by either or both of the two which will best preserve the two. This is not the ancient doctrine of *Summum Bonum*, because that looked to results that could not be estimated alike by all. The scope was too wide and remote for any one. But the law of harmony, discoverable by each one, was a law practicable to each one. But essential law is not more a law of harmony than a

---

(a) " Nothing in this world is single,
All things by a law divine
In one another's being mingle."

law of preservation; and the question is, what exists
to be preserved. For instance, when two men looked
each other in the face for the first time, what were
they to each other? Both had a right to live. Were
they strangers, enemies, or brothers? Or, when man
and woman met for the first time, did they meet with
permanent or transient interest in each other? Did
they meet as merely lower animals, or were they
social beings of a progressive destiny? The law is
according to the answer to these questions. That
only is done which is well done, and what is done is
to be preserved.

As everything in the universe seeks its own perfection, so groups of things seek to create something
that each is not, and which shall be higher than all.
For instance, a tree is a compound. From the earth
comes one agent, from the air another, and from
the water another, and all these work together
for the good of every other thing, and for their own
glory. The one tree integrated, or evolved, out of
these several crude elements, becomes a marvel of
order and beauty. It is what none of the elements
could be by itself, and only appeared when they combined. Thus, integration, or initial evolution, is a
way of creation. Antagonism subsides, discussion
between individuals ceases, agreement is reached.
The solidification of the diffuse, the fixedness of the
elastic, the unification of the many, the repose of the
disturbed, the equilibrium of the unstable, is the
method of law—of development—whether in matter
or society. By the universal law of compensation,
what is lost in one direction is gained in another.

Hydrogen, in becoming a constituent of water, sur-
renders its volatility, and becomes a standard of
weight. Oxygen, to become water, ceases to promote combustion, but becomes active in extinguish-
ing it. The will of the many individuals becomes
the will of the one state. In a word, all things that
come together must leave something of themselves
in abeyance. All building, whether of worlds, of
law, or of character, is on the same principle by
which motion becomes organic rest; incoherence
becomes coherence, and the transient becomes the
permanent. This integrating principle has been
active from the beginning. As the gaseous form of
the earth lost its heat, it lost some of its motion.
Particles cohered or solidified; the crust thickened,
and effects multiplied upon effects, until chaos
evolved into order, and light came from sun and
star, and vegetal chemistry prepared food for thinking beast and conscious man.

What is law, and what are the ethics of law ? That
social condition which is best is ethics; and all ethics
is law. All so-called law-making is the codification
or integration of ethical ideas. Law is both an ethical principle and a logical rule. And yet the principle and the rule are not two distinct things, but
only different sides of the same thing. Moralists
ascertain and define the principle, legislatures prescribe, and courts announce the rule—in other words,
there is statutory morality, adjudicated morality, and
speculative morality. The principle is to the rule
what the soul is to the body, and without which the
body cannot be. *Cessante ratione, lex cessat.* Neither

the conscience nor the relations of society could long tolerate an immoral law. Indeed, an immoral law is not law, though it may be aquiesced in as law. Social necessity as law emphatically forbids anything *contra bonos mores.* Take the ethics out of law, and what have you left but a rule? Law and its maxims are adjudicated ethics, or abstract ethics converted into an authoritative rule of action. For the purpose of getting at this ethical principle or rightness in claims triable before the courts, are all the rules of evidence and all the forms of procedure. Ethics, or rightness, then, as the appointment of supernatural will, is the essence of law. In other words, law is only applied ethics.

In the law, moral principles, like sunlight on a rolling planet, rest upon and glorify whichever side comes up. The sun is ever the same, but the side of the planet next to it is ever changing. Rather, morality is to the law what sun is to the wheat; without the sun there is no wheat, and without morality there is no law. New events evolve new relations, and new relations bring their own moral principles, or laws, with them. Law is an optimist, and by dropping the obsolete and applying the new, ever seeks its own perfection. Rules of conduct scattered through the moral sentiments of mankind attract each other, and become a code. This is legal integration. Uncertainty, discussion, and conflicting opinion agree upon some formula to which applies the arbitrary doctrine of *Stare Decicis*—let the decisions stand; let something be settled. Society seeks to know the universal truths concerning itself, and to

announce them as authoritative rules of conduct.
The special is ever transmuting itself into the universal, and the universal into the special, and the temporal is ever moving on into the eternal. The law of this universe is improvement, not change for the sake of change.

The Jewish conscience, social habits, and theocratic polity integrated in the Ten Commandments or code of Moses. Greek wisdom, sentiment, and conviction integrated in the code of Solon. Roman law was first a family discipline; afterwards it integrated in the laws of the Twelve Tables, in the annual Edict of the Prætor, in the Responses of the Jurisconsults, in the codes of Gregory, Hermogenes, and Justinian. All codifications are integrations; and so universal is litigation, that codification upon codification is constantly made; nearly every dispute between man and man being now brought into court.

Here, the complexity of material causes and the complexity of moral causes are the same in some principle common to both. What is that principle? The integration of hydrogen and oxygen produce water, a substance that is neither, but chemically both. So in moral law. Two individuals, in associating, mingle their rights and form a third, including the individual rights of both, but exclusively the right of neither. The right of the two, when associated, is as much a new right as a drop of water is a new compound. The moral and the material chemistry is the same. But notice that I do not say that moral law is created by moral relations, only that it then appears. The unity of material and moral law is in the unity of plan, or, rather, the unity of all law is in the unity of the *idea* of all law. Matter integrates and makes the world of matter. Moral principles integrate and make the laws of conduct. The integration of one is one with the integration of the other.

But supplemental to this we see the unity of law in the further fact that all causes multiply their effects. Universally, the effect is more complex than the incomplex cause. Light a candle, and you have heat, light, carbonic acid, water, and divers colors. Throw a pebble in the ocean, and you move every drop in its awful fullness. Raise your hand or whisper a word, and you stir all the atmosphere that surrounds our globe. If law be a cause, we see the law of gravitation produce many effects in the water gathered in mountain-tops. As it gravitates down through the gorges, it gathers the materials for the masonry of its channel in the plains below. It abrades from the hillsides fragments of stone, picks up the sand and washes out the earth, carrying all in solution, until a less precipitous flow weakens its momentum. Then begins, from the one law of gravitation, a multiplying of effects, calling out other laws. Gravitation pulls down its heaviest material along the margin, where the current begins to weaken. The masonry here is wonderfully perfect. Every pebble is laid exactly where the strength of the future bank of the river will most need it. Pebble is laid on pebble for years, it may be for centuries—for nature keeps no chronology—until the waters have walled themselves in, leaving the plains on either side as a home for man.

The second effect of gravitation, as it pulls the waters down the mountain-side, after it has surrendered the pebble to form the wall of the bank, is to carry the lighter sand a little more to the side, and drop it behind the pebbles, as a parallel and supporting buttress.

The third effect is to carry the lighter soil still further back, and form a bank of earth behind both the former; thus building for itself its own pathway to the receiving sea. Here are different, but consistent effects from the same law.

Again, the sun shines on a field where both tares and wheat are sown. The same cause produces effects specifically different. It quickens both the the tares and the wheat.

Again, one grain of wheat will produce manifold other grains. This wheat becomes food; this food nourishes brain, this brain sustains the song of the poet, the eloquence of the orator, and the thought of the statesman. One case of infectious disease flies from man to man, until a dreadful epidemic lays towns, cities, and states in the grave. How trivial often the cause of disasters, and yet how multiplied the effects. From one little cell, life is said to continue itself through all living forms. From the monotony of the inorganic mineral arose the innumerable vegetable life, with its marvelous functions of inhalation and exhalation, the chemistry of its assimilative powers, its beautiful forms, and the utilities of its fibrous substances. With it man builds the palace and the ship, the temple of worship and the den of despair, the forum of the law and the throne of authority. Indeed, to specify the manifold effects of a cause would be to give a catalogue of the number and splendor of all phenomena—of heat, light, electricity; and of all forms, colors, sound, and motion.

As in matter, so in morals. Moral effects from moral causes are prodigiously multiplied. Mackintosh and Buckle would have us believe the contrary; but they lose sight of the fact that, while the theoretical morality of each man is left to self-culture and the teachings of religion and the philosophers, his practical morality, as it applies to his relations to his fellow-man, is taught him by municipal law and the courts; and there is nothing stationary in the teachings of these.

Society, as it grows older, and as new relations and questions arise, more and more prescribes and enforces moral conduct. In nothing does civilization show less stagnation and more advance, than in the growing perfection of its law; absorbing and adjudicating, from age to age, the moral sentiments of mankind. Rome is still potential through her system of civil morality as thought out by her jurisconsults and adjudicated by her prætors. Law being law only as it is morality, no one can say, in the presence of its voluminous body, that moral ideas are stationary. Account for it as you may, whether by the influence of great religious or general intellectual culture, thousands and tens of thousands of great lawyers are so many great moralists, and show that moral science is the true and ever enlarging basis of law and of a true civilization. The highest happiness of mankind lives along moral lines; and, as everything seeks its own perfection, so moral ideas must grow more and more enlightened and more universal.

To show how moral causes multiply moral effects, take any one act of life. On the making of a promissory note, the drawing of a bill of exchange, there arises, with and in the act, a whole volume of moral rules called laws. The principle of rightness at once regulates its parties, their competency, rights, duties, and obligations. The conscience of the law looks well to the value of its consideration. Then there is the moral obligation of its acceptance, or its protest for non-acceptance, if a bill of exchange. There is punishment for its forgery, and help in the event of its loss. If one receive a little package to carry for hire, instantly that act is covered by many laws looking to the rights of owners and the responsibility of the carrier. If you speak of another's fair fame, law warns you to guard your lips. If you build a house, the law makes it your castle, gives you certain rights of defense. Laws forbidding burglary and arson at once come to protect it.

There is a point of unity in all this in Will. The intention to go on and out of itself, is seen in an atom of matter and in a principle of morals. Each is instinct with the desire, so to speak, and is distinguished by the act, of imparting or giving itself away to something else. An atom is not an orphan, or friendless, or without the sympathy of other atoms. As the acorn produces many oaks, the fountain produces many streams, the sun gives out many rays, and from ancestors descend many heirs, so no right is solitary or barren; but rights beget rights, and duties beget duties. The law of ownership begets the law against trespass and against larceny. As no atom can be an outlaw, so law is multiplied as relations are multiplied. Indeed, the law of a thing is inseparable in the thing itself. As the universe is filled with things, so is it filled with law. Are not all these laws one, if their *idea* be *one?*

But still more do the principles of material science show their identity with moral principles in Will, is the fact and law of aggregation. We mean by aggregation, not the importance of many things abstractly by themselves, but the concrete importance of one thing as related to every other thing. In the material world every atom is a help to every other atom. Things are different; but they are dependent. Concord includes discords. There must be contrasts, as well as analogies. In colors. the mind could not endure monotony. Suppose there were but one color — everything were blue, yellow, or red — the universe would be intolerable. So in forms, the more varieties, the more individualities, the more pleasure we derive therefrom.

This is not a movement of antipathy, but of sympathy; not of aristocracy, but of fraternity; not of affinity, but of association. In integration, things are both related, combined and assimilated. In aggregation there is relation and mutual help. In material aggregation, like things go to like. *Similis simili gaudet.* The law here is sympathy, not affinity. The result is association, not a compound. Things are together, not one. It is not integration, but aggregation; not oneness, but unity. Antipathy for-

bids like things to become one with unlike. The
dove flies from the hawk; men and vipers cannot
sleep in the same bed. The wind lifts the chaff into
a cloud by itself, and leaves the wheat in a mass by
itself. Species stay with species, and genus with
genus. When unlike things attract each other, as
oxygen and hydrogen, by the creative or integrating
law of chemical affinity, they drop their individuality
and become something else. In aggregation, every
individual is distinct and separate in character, but
joined in purpose with something else.

The importance of any one law is seen in the con-
fusion that would result if other laws did not exist.
If laws arise, they must be interpreted and executed.
Each department is dependent on the other. The
executive is useless without the legislative, and the
legislative without the executive. It is useless to
declare a right unless it be protected and enforced.
The law of propriety necessitates the law of penal-
ties. The declaratory and the vindicatory are mutually dependent on each other.

The point of unity seen between material and
moral aggregation is in the fact of universal dependence and the law of universal help. Everything, as
we have said, depends upon every other thing, atom
upon atom, principle on principle, and all on something beyond them. Each link of the chain that
hangs must hang from the same thing. If everything is under any one thing, in that one thing is
unity. Helpfulness is omnipresent in matter, and
helpfulness is omnipresent in mind and morals, and
in the omnipresence of helpfulness is the unity of
material and moral laws.

LECTURE III.

METHOD OF CREATION.

The first lecture, after having proved supernatural Power, as is claimed, spoke of its manifestations as creative, causative and derivative. Causative and derivative manifestations were then considered ; we now come to the method of creative manifestations. Let us begin with

1. *The first atom or inorganic nature.* What is creation? That is uncreated which has always been, and that is created which has not always been. The creative method is, therefore, a way or method of newness ; and, in inorganic nature, it is seen in the first atom. The first atom is the crucial test of philosophical systems. Whence is this first atom? The first unexplained atom is the throne of a personal God, and the grave of an impersonal evolution. However much aside skeptical science may engage the attention of reason, reason demands that science shall come back and account for the first atom, or be silent when religion gives the answers that science cannot. As to this, reason will not tolerate the least evasion, equivocation, or omission. Skeptical science must begin at the beginning. THE FIRST ATOM ! whence is it?

8

Evolution, as a mere method of integrating matter, assumes the existence of matter, and does not open the question of its origin. But when Mr. Spencer announced evolution as eternal and universal, excluding the action of will and the work of creation, he antagonized the theistic philosophy, and the basis of all religion. Evolution as a mere method of Power, leaving to religion the deification of that power as a personal Being, was a harmless theory. But intentionally or unintentionally, Mr. Spencer attacks the very basis of religion, when he so impersonalizes Power as to leave to religion nothing to worship. For a person to worship a thing is debasing fetichism. The creative method of supernatural will is a way of newness—of originality—of production. Direct creation is of kinds or types; indirect or genetic creation is of individuals.

Mr. Spencer says: "A Power of which the nature remains forever inconceivable, and to which no limits in time or space can be imagined, works in us certain effects" (F. P., § 194). Again, "All things are manifestations of a Power that transcends our knowledge" (Ib. § 28). We have seen that the elastic word manifestation covers the ideas of causation and derivation, and we now proceed to show that its meaning is that of creation. Power and its manifestations are not two infinities. For Mr. Spencer asks, "How self-destructive is the assumption of two or more Infinities, is manifest on remembering that such Infinities, by limiting each other, would become finite" (F. P., § 24). But while we have not two Infinites, we do have one Power unlimited in time and space, with limited manifestations. We start with Power. Power is not its manifestation, nor is manifestation Power; but as the spider spins its web from itself, so supernatural Power manifests nature from itself. The first manifestation of Power was the first creation by Power of unlike from unlike. If Power is eternal, the manifestations of Power are not eternal. If the manifestations of Power are not eternal, shall we call them creations or evolutions? Theists call them the creations of a personal Being; atheists or agnostics call them the evolutions of impersonal Power. But they are one or the other. How shall we decide which? Mr. Spencer says "the affirmation of universal evolution is, in itself, the negation of the absolute commencement of anything." "The absolute commencement of organic life on the globe, * * * I distinctly deny" (1 Bio., 482). A commencement is all that is claimed, whether it be called absolute or relative. Mr. Spencer asks, "Is it supposed that a new organism when specially created, is created out of nothing? If so, there is a supposed creation of matter; and the creation of matter is inconceivable (1 Biol., § 112). Of course, in this as well as elsewhere, Mr. Spencer is planted directly against creation. But what is creation? Power is admitted, and its manifestations are admitted. If manifestations are not eternal as eternal Power, then they are commenced. According to Mr. Spencer, "evolution is always to be regarded as fundamentally an integration of matter and dissipation of motion." This integration is either of inorganic matter, or of organic matter. The evoluion of inorganic matter, Mr. Spencer passes without formal discussion. He says, parenthetically, in his preface to his treatise on First Principles, "in logical order should here come the application of these First Principles to Inorganic Nature. But this great division it is proposed to pass over; partly because even without it, the scheme is too extensive; and partly because the interpretation of organic nature, after the proposed method, is of more importance." This is, indeed, a vast and inexcusable leap: but thus to decapitate evolution, is to take the brains with its head. Mr. Spencer discusses organic nature, denying that he is compelled to assume a first organism; and in passing over inorganic nature, he escapes the necessity to account for a first atom. Certain it is, that in leaping over inorganic to organic nature, he assumes the existence of the inorganic nature when he makes it a basis of organic nature. A material atom is a fact, though hypothetical, and the question is, who is its factor? In passing over the inorganic, Mr. Spencer ignores the philosophical key of the philosophical arch.

Agnostic or atheistic evolution begins at the organic; but in accounting for that, it accounts for nothing else: but theistic evolution begins far back at the inorganic, and in accounting for that it accounts for all else. The Power that manifests an atom, manifests the universe. He ignores a personal Creator in admitting an impersonal Power; and in manifesting some of the organic manifestations, he passes over, as of less importance, the origin of the inorganic on which the organic rests. We propose to go from where Mr. Spencer begins in the organic back to the inorganic on which the organic rests His system of philosophy is like a house with an unknown foundation. He denies that he is a materialist, and yet he has built on inorganic matter and impersonal Power, for which he has not accounted. Agnostic science assumes, unless its eternity be assumed, that Power manifesting all things is impersonal. Mr. Spencer, in passing over unknowable matter in inorganic nature, cannot suppress an inquiry as to the Unknown Power behind the Unknown Reality of the symbol of matter. If the organic rests on the inorganic (see 1 Biol. § 14), what does the inorganic rest on? The human mind will not consent that Mr. Spencer may begin his agnostic philosophy where he pleases, and ignore, as less important, truths that explode its conclusions. Let us push this pseudo materialism beyond matter, to that on which matter rests. Mr. Spencer says that there is no matter, but that which we call matter is only a symbol of some Unknowable Reality. What is that? It is said to be impersonal and unintelligent; and right here is the issue. To know what this Unknowable Reality is, it would be more fundamental in that which aspires to be a philosophy, to go back from the line of causes in later phenomena as seen in organic nature to the First Cause in which they all began, beyond inorganic nature. We cannot understand secondary causes so long as we are utterly ignorant of the Cause of causes. It is not sufficient for this agnostic evolution to begin arbitrarily at the organic, and say that its foundation is the inorganic. True philosophy seeks to know what is the foundation of the foundation. Religion says to evolutionists you have admitted a Power unlimited in time and space; and it claims, from human personality, to have proved superhuman personality. The demand, therefore, will not be silenced, that evolutionists shall admit or deny the connection between this supernatural Power and inorganic nature, as well as with organic. Religion devoutly kneels before the Power in both organic and inorganic evolution; while science, as just said, keeps in view only the method of organic evolution, and ignores the method of inorganic origin and the Power behind both.

The creative principles necessary to inorganic evolution apply to organic evolution, but the genetic principles of organic evolution do not apply to inorganic evolution. It is only when Power has objectified itself in not only inorganic substance, but in organisms built on that substance, that formal consideration, certainly of organic evolution, begins. It is in the presence of life in organic evolution, for which the integration of matter and the dissipation of motion do not account, that evolution, seems only the equivalent of growth, and not at all like inorganic evolution; if such there be.

It was a method of Will-Power that manifestations should be new, whether by what is called creation or evolution; it was a method to continue types; it was a method that things and forces should be exchanged or correlated.

The elements, the seasons, the universe of worlds and systems of worlds manifest the phenomenal energies of this omnipresent Power. Manifestation is the word that covers all ideas of this activity, whether manifestation means creation, causation, derivation, correlation, generation or evolution. This power goes forth in some way. There is a manifestation that is creation.

Have the creative manifestations of supernatural Will-Power a chronology? The time consumed in supernatural manifestations is not prescribed. God is not slack as some men count slackness. With him one day is as a thousand years and a thousand years is as one day. As the era of supernatural Power is eternal, it keeps no record of time or of progress definite to man. To itself, eternity is one eternal Now. The human cannot chronologize the super-human or the natural the supernatural. As there is no time in eternity so there is no date to the eternal in the manifestations of the eternal.

It is said that " It is almost an absolute and de-monstrable certainty that the human race appeared on the earth long periods before there was any such chronology as the church has hitherto held." Noth-ing in science is more dogmatic than this. A few scientists hold up the little light they have to the scarp of hills heaved from the depths below, and say, as this mass has been forming so many years, there-fore the whole earth has been so many untold ages in its formation. All such calculations seem to be uncertain if you admit the instantaneous revolutions of catastrophies as factors. Shall we adopt the Uni-formity or the Catastrophic theory of the Cosmos? It is not important that we fix upon any period as the age of the world. The Bible says that " in the beginning God created the heavens and the earth," but does not say when that beginning was.. It has been said that the "chronology based upon the Sacred Scriptures, is acknowledged by the very men who made it to be uncertain." But is the chronology based upon science any more certain? The chronology of the Bible and of science are both equally uncertain. The point made here is, that the uncertain chronology of science shall not be used, in proving the chronology of the Bible to be uncertain, to prove that the Bible itself is therefore untrue. It is merely human opinion as to how old the world is, whether the calculation be made from the facts of the Bible or the facts of nature. Some few scientists rejoice that they have destroyed the Bible itself because they have destroyed a chronology which the Bible does not set up. God made the Bible, and man has read into it a chronology which God did not put into it.

But the material phenomena around us show the work of ages, and the work of special moments. We see the work of ages in the uniformity of the rocky formations; and we see the catastrophic work of dreadful moments, when the hills heaved up, the valleys dropped down, and the shallow waters gathered into deep seas. The catastrophic evidences of these great instantaneous convulsions, impress us more than all other facts in nature. That is, the fast movements of nature tell us more than the slow movements of nature. When we stand by the ocean shore and look off into its inscrutable depths, and remember that they were formed by one exertion of awful power, or stand upon the sublime summit of heaven-reaching mountains, and remember that in one instant of omnific energy, they arose as thrones of the Infinite, we see that nature does not always take eons of time to do her grandest work. We see how idle it is to assume that what we see was necessarily the slow work of Power. We see not only that nature *can* work prodigiously fast, but that she actually has worked prodigiously fast. All the proof we have, is of nature's fast work; while we have only conjecture that she has worked in the slow uniformity of ages. A few months only intervene between snow and flowers, between seed-time and harvest, between birth and burial. Think of the rapidity with which nature moves! Though we seem to stand still, yet, during the hour we shall, by revolution of the earth, be a thousand miles away from the point in space where we were when we entered this house; and, in our orbit around the sun, we shall be 68,000 miles away from where we were when we entered it. We move nineteen miles at every tick of the clock. The earth has to make, in one year, a distance of 545,000,-000 of miles. Sound travels over a thousand feet each second. Light flies 190,000 miles a second. Nature needs no million of ages to make so small an affair as this earth, unless she worked infinitely slower in the past than we know she works in the present (see F. P., § 17). Science must deny its own facts in order to deny the Bible account of creation.

If we start with Power, force must be another name for that Power itself, or force must be a creation of that power. We agree with the remark of Sir John F. W. Herschell, before quoted, that "in the only case in which we are admitted into personal knowledge of the origin of force, we find it connected with volition, and by inevitable consequence, with motive and intellect, and with all those attributes of mind in which personality consists." We start with Will. Will is force, force or Will is Power. From the consciousness of our own human will-power and its methods, we must infer a superhuman will-power and its methods. We have seen that the Power is one; we shall now see that the methods are many.

Personal, supernatural Power may manifest itself without means, *ex mero motu*, as seen in sporadic acts of Power called miracles and providence; or Power may prescribe to itself methods of means as seen in the method we are to discuss.

The method is either creative, as seen primarily in the atom of inorganic nature, where matter is begun; and in the first organism of organic nature; or the method is causative, as seen in inorganic relations where the elements of nature are combined or exchanged; or the method is derivative or genetic, as seen primarily in organic nature, where kind propagates its kind. Either method is as supernatural as its Power.

Mr. Spencer says that " we are obliged to regard every phenomenon as a manifestation of some Power by which we are acted upon " (F. P., § 27). But how does manifestation differ from creation? Does Power evolve itself, and from itself manifest or produce things not itself, as the spider does its web? That is, are these manifestations of Power its intrinsic transformations or its extrinsic creations? Does

manifestation mean transformation, transubstantia-
tion, transmutation, metamorphosis? Does manifestation imply that supernature naturalizes itself, or
that the subject objectifies itself, or that infinite mind
finitely contracts itself, or that the Creator creates
outside himself that which the Creator himself is not?

Materialists teach the eternity of matter, and of
course deny its creation; because, they say, that
something cannot be created out of nothing. Nothing,
in the sense of negation, can produce nothing. Whatever else may or may not be eternal, all admit that
Power is eternal. Even if Power and matter be co-
eternal, and concomitant, Power controls matter;
and, if Power controls matter, must it not have produced it? and is it not reasonable to conclude that
such a superior as Power must have produced such
an inferior as matter? Indeed, Mr. Spencer admits
this in saying, that "we are obliged to regard every
phenomenon as a manifestation of some Power."
This seems to amount either to impersonal Pantheism, in which all is an impersonal God or to admit
creation, in which a personal God creates all things.

An incomprehensibility is not solved by its denial
or by the affirmation of another incomprehensibility.
To say that something cannot be made out of nothing,
does not prove the eternity of matter. Both are
alike incomprehensible. We cannot conceive of
the eternity of matter, and yet Mr. Spencer says,
speaking of special creations, "It is supposed that a
new organism, when specially created, is created out
of nothing? If so, there is a supposed creation of
matter; and the creation of matter is inconceivable—

implies the establishment of a relation in thought between nothing and something—a relation of which one term is absent—an impossible relation." " The creation of force is just as inconceivable as the creation of matter " (1 Biol., § 112). Again he says, " All things are manifestations of a Power that transcends our knowledge and that which is not one is the other " (F. P., § 28).

As said before, the uncreated, as the eternal, is that which has always been ; the created is that which has not always been. Power has always been and is therefore uncreated. The manifestations of Power have not been always and are therefore creations. Matter is a manifestation of Power, or it is Power; but if matter is Power, then what is Power; if Power is matter, then what is matter? But as unlimited Power is infinite, and as there cannot be two infinities (F. P., § 24), so either matter is Power, or matter is finite, and if finite it is created. The doctrine is not that something was not made out of nothing; but when there was nothing but Being, something was made. It is impossible to conceive of the eternity either of impersonal matter, or of a personal God. The eternal—the Absolute—the Infinite —is the incomprehensible. We can know nothing about the eternity or the creation of matter; but little as to the personality or impersonality of Power; nor can we know any more as to what cause is, what law is, or what nature is. At best we see as through a glass, darkly, and know that there is an eternal Being. Where no opinion can be absolutely certain, we must take that view which leads to the best life,

and the most hopeful death. We think that a belief
in a personal God does this. How God is an omnipresent person—how intelligence and will can be
omnipresent—how God created matter when there
was nothing, or transformed himself into matter—all
this is utterly incomprehensible. But to set up matter and deny God, does not solve the mystery. The
eternity of matter and the denial of God are as great
a mystery as the eternity of God and the creation of
matter. As there cannot be two infinities, if matter
is eternal, God is not at all; if God is at all, matter
cannot be eternal.

We cannot, indeed, conceive of the creation of or
of the evolution of something out of nothing; but can
we say that there is nothing where there is Power?
Power must be something, or all manifestations of
Power would be manifestations of something by
nothing out of nothing, and this manifestation no less
in evolution than in creation; that is, there is no
more incomprehensibility in saying that something
was *created* out of nothing, than in saying that something was *evolved* out of nothing. But, as Power is
something, in denying the eternity of matter, we do
not affirm that it is produced out of nothing when
we say that it was produced out of Power. Matter
interprets Power, and matter is a substance from
Power. Does Power create matter by becoming
matter? that is, is not the Power to create matter the
Power to be matter itself? and the reverse.

In materialism, philosophy starts from the doctrine
of eternal matter; in idealism, it starts from the denial of matter; in theism, it starts from the belief in

an eternal person. The worship of eternal Power in an eternal Person, is religion. Everything according to evolution is the metamorphosis of personal or impersonal Power. When a certain manifestation of Power is present, we call it life; when there is no manifestation of the same Power, we call it death. That which is called cause does not produce that which is called effect; but both cause and effect are threaded, like beads, on the string of Power.

Continuity as a method of Power pertains only to the past and present, but not necessarily to the future; and is not between cause and effect, as such; but future continuity is in the persistence of the admitted Power by which the cause is cause, and by which the effect is effect. Cause and effect are but names given to successive phases, or phenomena of Power—noumenal Power. Cause is an energy of Power and effect is a result of Power. In a word, unthinkable Power produces thinkable things. A thing is that which is thinkable, and *no*thing is, not the non-existent, but merely that abstract existence, which is unthinkable. Think and thing are radically the same word, the verb ending in the sharp *k*, and the noun ending in the flat *g*. We think a thing in the same sense as we dream a dream, act an act, or do a deed. To say that *some*thing cannot be made out of *no*thing, is to say that the thinkable cannot be made out of the unthinkable; but thinkable something is from unthinkable Power.

What is thinkable? The unthinkable, in the sense of the non-existent, cannot be represented in thought. Mr. Herbert Spencer (F. P., § 29) says, " though the *law* of gravitation is within our mental grasp, it is impossible to realize in thought the *force* of gravitation. * * * In grouping particular relations of phenomena under laws, and these special laws under laws more and more general, is of necessity a progress to causes that are more and more abstract, and causes more and more abstract are of necessity causes less and less conceivable; since the formation of an abstract conception involves the dropping of certain concrete elements of thought. Hence the most abstract conception, to which science is ever slowly approaching, is one that merges into the inconceivable or unthinkable." If the inconceivable or unthinkable is *no*thing merely because it is unthinkable (which point of the unthinkable, science is ever slowly approaching), science is ever more and more proving that unthinkable *some*thing is made out of unthinkable *no*thing. Is *force no*thing because inconceivable or unthinkable? We may not be able to grasp in thought what we can logically prove to exist. Realities are none the less realities because incomprehensible or unthinkable; nearly all realities are incomprehensible. If all ultimates are nothing because unthinkable, as everything is made out of ultimates, so everything is made out of nothing. All modern thinkers admit the omnipresence of Power—parturient Power—manifested Power—inconceivable Power. But is Power nothing because inconceivable or unthinkable? If Power is a name of the negation called nothing, then all evolution of Power is something developed out of nothing,—in a word, that the thinkable something, called facts, are made out of unthinkable Power called nothing because unthinkable. But, if Power, though inconceivable or unthinkable, is something, then, as things are things, there are things thinkable and things unthinkable—things material and things immaterial—and things material are made out of things immaterial—tangible things out of intangible Power.

Mr. Spencer denies both the eternity of matter and the commencement of matter. In a communication in reply to a critic, written for the North American Review, dated London, December 5, 1868, and re-published in an appendix to the first volume of his Biology, he says: "that, however, which I regard as most reprehensible in his criticism is the way in which he persists in representing the *System of Philosophy* I am working out as a materialistic system. Already he has once before so represented it, and the injustice of so representing it has been pointed out. He knows that I have repeatedly and emphatically asserted that our conceptions of matter and motion are but *symbols* of an Unknowable Reality ; that this reality cannot be *that* which we symbolize it to be." (*Italics ours.*) If we understand him, that which we conceive of as matter is not matter, but only a symbol of an Unknowable Reality. Of course he can be no materialist, because he denies the very existence of matter. He would be called a Potentialist, if classified at all.

What, then, is this system of philosophy that is neither materialism, nor idealism, nor pantheism? As Mr. Spencer says, "the problem to be resolved is a problem of dynamics," he has given the name of

POWER to this Unknowable Reality behind the symbol of matter. In such a system Power as Power is neither matter, nor mind, nor being; but, as modes. Power might be, as it would seem, either or neither or both. Power is its own measure. Power is its own interpreter. Mr. Spencer does not say whether this Power is personal or impersonal.

If Mr. S. were a materialist, he would believe in the eternity of matter; but, though he does not believe in the eternity of matter, he does not believe in its creation; for that would be the commencement of matter. With him all that now is, is all that ever has been; and that ever will be, is all that now is. According to his theory, there could be no such commencement; for he says, as we have seen, that "the affirmation of universal evolution is in itself a negation of an absolute commencing of anything." That which has never commenced and is not eternal when all is eternal, is not at all. So, as matter is neither eternal nor has a commencement, there is no matter. And yet, he everywhere means by evolution the process which is always an integration of matter. If Mr. Spencer does not mean to assume matter, when he says that it integrates, he must go back and show how matter, before it integrates, came to be matter at all. If we understand Mr. Spencer, matter and motion are but symbols of an Unknowable Reality. Then, evolution is an integration of an Unknowable Reality with the concomitant dissipation of another Unknowable Reality. We know that this Reality is not that which we symbolize it to be. If Power materializes, and evolution is the integration of matter, the evolution is the integration of materialized Power — in other words, matter is only a form of Power.

We start with omnipresent, formless Power. In some way we must get from Power to Form. Omnipotence is parturient of all forms and substances; and the creation of something out of nothing is no more incomprehensible, than that Power should materialize itself, or that matter should be eternal, or that matter should mentalize itself. And, yet, some minds to whom two incomprehensibilities are equally difficult can bring themselves to accept one incomprehensibility and reject another. And yet that matter is a manifestation of Power, is more thinkable than the eternity of matter.

If evolution is the method of the universe, then it covers inorganic atoms; which must be creatively evolved, *ab extra*, or not be evolved at all; as each atom holds its own Power. One atom cannot evolve or manifest another atom. If, in universal evolution, there is no absolute commencement of anything, then the matter to be integrated in evolution is eternal and the process of evolution is eternal—that is, there must be an eternal evolution, by eternal Power, of eternal matter.

Religionists and some scientists are not agreed as to the manifestations of this Power. The former contend that Power commenced or created things; some of the latter contend that matter is eternal; others, such as Mr. Spencer, contend that matter was neither eternal nor created, but that there has been an eternal process or parturition—that what we call matter is not matter, but only a symbol of that which has ever been becoming matter. The distinct doctrine of those who believe in creation is, that what is now, once was not. The distinct doctrine of evolutionists is, that that which is, has ever been coming and will ever be going. But both agree in this—that the phenomena which are, whether by direct act of personal creation or by the eternal process of impersonal evolution, once were not, and if they once were not, we say they must be new. Thus, as the new is the created, the ever-becoming of impersonal evolution is ever the new of a ceaseless creation of personal Power.

We do not ask Power how it manifested, commenced, made or created things, whether out of itself or out of nothing. All-Power knows its own possibilities, so to speak, and can do all things. All manifestations of Power, as they are new in the universe, are creations in the universe, whatever we call these manifestations, whether evolution, emanation, creation, metamorphosis or generation.

Power was first, and, at first, Power was all. The first manifestation of Power was *form.* The first form was that of an atom, and the first atom was the first form. Form was not as old as Power, for form was a manifestation of Power. Eternal manifestation of eternal Power is utterly unthinkable. The first manifestation of Power was that activity of Power called creation. It was called creation because it commenced phenomena. Mr. Spencer denies this commencement. He says "the affirmation of universal evolution is, in itself, the negation of the absolute commencement of anything." As Mr. Spencer denies being a materialist, he denies the eternity of matter, and as he denies the absolute commencement of anything, whether a first atom or a first organism, he denies the creation of matter; so there is nothing left for him but to believe in the eternal *process*—the *ever becoming* of Heraclitus. But what is it that is ever becoming but never is? According to such teaching, as there is no matter or only the symbol of matter, Power must be the ever becoming of itself. But this will be more specially discussed in the lecture on evolution. But if Power is ever becoming, and never becomes matter, it must be because Power either cannot or will not become matter. To say that Power will not is, in will, to admit a personal factor, which is denied; and to say that it cannot, is to deny that it is Power, as affirmed. We therefore conclude that as Power is Power, it can materialize itself as matter, or, it can produce—manifest—create matter. Power is manifested as direct creation in the first atom and in the first organism; and as indirect creation in the second or inherited organism.

Right here, in the real or hypothetical atom of inorganic nature, is the battle ground of religion and science. If the theory of evolution is to give us light anywhere, it ought to give it here. Does evolution account for the first atom? On the contrary, it denies that there was a first atom. Agnostic if not atheistic evolutionists cannot admit a created atom; for that implies a creator. As they hold to an eternal Power, they deny eternal matter. But to say that matter is neither created nor eternal is to say, that while eternal Power is ever becoming matter, yet matter never is—that a materializing tendency is all. Thus evolution, like a blind bat flying in the dark between the two unknown walls of the inorganic and the organic, finds no outlet. Evolution, defined as the integration of matter and the dissipation of motion, confessedly passes over the inorganic atom to be integrated, and does not prove the mental and vital force in organic phenomena to which it is compelled to apply. The whole theory of atheistic evolution is buried in an unexplained atom. If Power is eternal, and all things, of course including atoms, are manifestations of this Power, then nothing but Power can be eternal, for things manifested cannot be as old as the manifesting Power.

Mr. Spencer says "a Power of which the nature remains forever inconceivable and to which no limits in time and space can be imagined, works in us certain effects." (F. P. § 194.) His expression elsewhere is, "all things are manifestations of a Power that transcends our knowledge." (F. P. § 27.) The manifestions of this Power are both inorganic nature, and things and persons with life. Creation is direct when Power produces that which Power is not—as the mould, the bullet; such as inorganic things or things without life—the first atom, the first molecule, the first mass. The created is the new—the original. Things are eternal, or they are begun. That which is not one, is the other. But Power unlimited in Time and Space is eternal, and never began, and all that is not eternal Power, when eternal Power was all, is begun. So, then, we start with Power—Will-

Power—personal or impersonal. As just said, Power was first ; and, at first, Power was all. What could be without Power ? To admit eternal Power is to admit that all else is at its sufferance. Whatever was second was a manifestation of the first ; and, if the first was supreme, it was eternal, and the second was not eternal ; and because it was not eternal, it was new ; and, because it was new, it was created.

Power being admitted to be the *fons et origo* of all things, all things must be either created by Power, caused by Power, or derived from Power. If all things are derived, then the principle of like from like prevails ; from Power only Power could be derived, conscious human beings from a conscious Superhuman Being, and impersonal things from impersonal, trees from trees, rocks from rocks, beast from beast. But, as we see, all manifestations of Power are not derivatives of like from like, and that Power must create or cause all manifestations of Power that Power is not. Derivation is for organic nature, and for the organic nature only. Inorganic nature is one unsuspended creation or the result of causation.

The underived is that which never commenced, as the derived is that which was commenced. To commence things is to create them, and that is underived and therefore uncreated which has always been. That is created which has not always been ; as when Power manifests itself, not as Power, but as Form, or as anything which Power is not. According to evolution, as Power only is eternal, it would seem to follow, that the manifestation of eternal Power, whether by what we call the process of evolution or by what we call the method of creation, cannot be eternal. Therefore, the manifestations of eternal Power may be either a process or method; yet, all new manifestations are logically proved to be methods of creative manifestations. The first grain, say of wheat, because the first grain of wheat was something that had never been before, was manifested creatively from Power; and the second grain of wheat was created genetically by Power from the first. If there is no absolute commencement of anything, then there is an eternal continuity of commencements; for the second genetic grain of wheat proves that there was a first created grain. The methods are cumulative. The creative method is derived from underived Power; and the genetic method is derived from the created. Everything is directly or indirectly created but uncreated Power. Creation is the addition of any *new* manifestation of unlimited Power. Power thus unlimited in Time and Space, manifests the addition of material, atomic elements, or of inorganic nature, and then the addition of organic nature. Each step is the addition of a new, and therefore a creative manifestation of original Power. *At all times, all but Power is new; and, therefore, all but power is created.* All manifestations, transformations, transmutations, metamorphoses, transubstantiations, or causations are creations, because they are new and not eternal; for nothing eternal is new, and nothing new is eternal. As all but Power is unstable, so instability of the homogeneous is new and, therefore a creation. The transformation of the homogeneous into the heterogeneous is the addition of a new and, therefore, a creative manifestation of Power. If all development is evolution, all addition is creation.

All manifestation is a creation, not an emanation? What is the difference? Emanation, as the word implies, is when Power (when Power was all) goes forth from itself as Power, whether that Power is called Power, force, or energy, such as gravitation, chemic affinity, and so on. Creation is when Power does not go forth from itself as Power, but when it manifests Form. Force is nothing new to Power, for it is Power itself; but Form is new to Power, for it is not Power. Power, therefore, creates when it manifests anything that Power is not, which is, therefore, something new; and while only omniscient can interpret omnipotence, yet it is certain as just said that All-Power can do all things.

The difference between creation, causation, and evolution is, that in inorganic nature the first is a creation, and the use that Power as force makes of that creation, is causation; and in organic nature the first of anything is a creation: the second of the same thing is a derivative or generative development from the first—or rather, evolution as defined, or described, is the process of culminative creation; whether of the origin of atoms, the relations of things, or the persistence of things. If all things are manifestations of a Power that transcends our knowledge, we ask again, what is the manifestation? Manifestation by Power is not the Power itself, and Power is not the manifestation. We must find *that first atom* in inorganic nature, in the creativeness of Power or in the eternity of all atoms, somewhere in eternal Power. If evolution is eternally creative, it is so in the passage of eternal Power into eternal atoms; and the passage of these atoms from a diffused to an aggregated state, is culminative evolution. The creative evolution of the atomic matter which Mr. Spencer does not define, must be prior to that correlative evolution of atomic matter which he does not define or describe.

Methods of uniformity advancing to multiformity, include all the facts of the universe, and cover lines of nature without life, and lines of nature with life. We have, therefore, two methods of manifestation: one, direct in either the creation or causation of all things, with and without life; and another indirect, in the generation or delegated creation of all things with life. It is a method of beginning things, and a method of continuing things. A drop of water illustrates the first, and a mustard-seed illustrates the second. Things without life are creatively begun, and creatively continued, and causatively combined. With the drop of water, unable to repeat itself, unbroken existence is unbroken creation. Things with life are creatively begun and genetically continued. With the mustard seed, the power of its direct creation remains in it as the power of its direct generation; but whatever is direct generation to nature, is indirect creation to supernature. Genetic power is creative power, delegative. Natural generation is supernatural creation, at second hand. If the maxim of human law—*qui facit per alium, facit per se*—what one does by another, he does by himself—could be applied to superhuman law, God himself would be said to *create* that which He appoints and empowers another to *generate*. Let us remember that we speak of nature as the method of supernature.

Things without life are extrinsically created; things with life are intrinsically generated. Mind presides ever the sphere of like things of life, where by fixed intelligence in lower spheres things propagate things like themselves, as oaks propagate oaks, and wheat propagates wheat. But in the sphere of unlike things without life, such as oxygen and hydrogen, all depends on extrinsic creation by free intelligence. Oxygen cannot create oxygen, nor hydrogen create hydrogen, nor can either by itself produce anything else. Water is neither one gas nor the other, but a creation based upon both. One drop of water does not generate another drop; but each drop is an original, and as to other drops, is an underived creation. The matter of the universe is an ever-continuing *creation :* its redistribution an ever-active causative *phenomena :* the life of the universe is an ever-continuing derivative *generation.* Therefore, as mind and matter are most unlike, if one is from the other, each is an original creation, and not as a derivative propagation : just as the spider creates but does not generate from itself its own web. Every new web is a new creation, and not a hereditary generation.

As that which does anything must know how to do what it does, universal mind must be the universal Factor, and all else are its facts. Science is limited

to these facts ; theology includes the facts, and by
these goes on to a knowledge of their personal
Factor.

If all things are manifestations of a Power that
transcends our knowledge, it is important to know
how much manifestation covers. The manifestation
of Power cannot be co-eternal with Power. But the
relation and the propagation of things are manifestations of Power. Things began in some way ; unless
it be true, as Mr. Spencer says, that " the affirmation
of universal evolution is in itself a negation of the
absolute commencement of anything." But, we shall
see, if there never was an absolute commencement of
anything, that it was because everything is to be regarded as possibly eternal in eternal Power.

But if eternal Power could evolve things, whether
eternal or not eternal, why could it not create things,
cause things or propagate things? If Power could
evolve a rattlesnake, why could not Power create
one ? Impersonal Pantheism is as incomprehensible
as impersonal creationism or impersonal evolution.
Unlimited Power is unlimited Power. Creation is a
limited act of unlimited Power; and admitting unlimited Power, evolution is as incomprehensible as
creation.

This confounds Phenomena with Noumenon ; for,
though Noumenon never was but always is, yet, to
say that there is no absolute commencement of anything, is to say that Phenomena are ever going on
without having ever started, for things do go on :
but as no Phenomena can go on that has not started ;
and as, according to Mr. Spencer, nothing has ever

started, so nothing is going on; that is, as organic nature never had an absolute commencement, it can have no actual continuation; which is absurd.

If there is anything new evolved in the universe, it has been creatively evolved. But, as materialistic evolutionists deny "the absolute commencement of anything," they deny the creative evolution of anything new. With them the new is essentially a phase of the old. Therefore, in such an eternal evolution, the old, as an eternal birth, is forever coming out of itself; but, in what is here called creative evolution, the new, as an eternal begetting, is forever coming out of Power. As the old is ever a genetic evolution, so the new is ever a creative evolution.

Power manifests all things; but does this Power manifest old things or new things? If manifested things are new, then Power is manifested either by the production of something out of nothing, or by the emanation of itself from itself; and one is as incomprehensible as the other. The Pleroma of the Buddhists emanates itself as things and re-absorbs itself as things. This is evolution. Buddhism teaches the fullness of Being, intelligent and impersonal; evolution teaches the fullness of Power, unintelligent and impersonal. Both are agnostic. The method of emanation is one and the same of all impersonal manifestations, whether of intelligent Being, as Buddhism, or of unintelligent Power, as in agnostic evolution.

But, if evolution is the integration of *matter*, whence came matter to be integrated? And how can the integration of matter create anything without life, as the inorganic, and especially of anything with life, as the organic? Is the integration of impersonal matter vitalizing and personalizing? Mr. S. admits that "the connection between the phenomenal order and the ontological order is forever inscrutable" (F. P., § 194). "So is the connection between the conditioned forms of being and the unconditioned forms of being forever inscrutable." And, yet, Mr. Spencer attempts to evolve an evolution of life. Evolution will do well enough when we get something to be evolved. But we shall continue to inquire whence came matter, and whence came the Power to integrate matter? How was the inertia of matter overcome, and when overcome, whence came the power to dissipate the motion, and restore inertia?

We are told that universal, immanent force integrates matter; but we again ask, whence is the force and whence is the matter? Mr. S. speaks of this force as Inscrutable Cause. If we understand Mr. Spencer, the universe is a manifestation of an immanent force. But in what was the force immanent before it manifested the universe in which to be immanent? Did the child manifest its own mother?

Power, supernatural and personal, without what may be called method, is directly creative when out of unity is produced plurality or out of uniformity is produced multiformity, or out of sameness is produced difference.

The inorganic is created, not evolved; for the evolved is eternal if at all; for, if Power manifests the inorganic, then the inorganic, as a manifestation, was not always, and so is not eternal. But if our argument has proved one supernatural, personal Power, unlimited in time and space, of course, all that is multiform, natural and limited must be its personal or its impersonal manifestations in time and space. All the manifestations of Power unlimited in time and space must be limited by Power in time and space; and that which is limited in time and space is not eternal, and that which is not eternal is not infinite, and that which is not infinite is finite.

As the organic and inorganic are manifestations, they are that which Power is not; and it is surprising that in a philosophy of First Principles Mr. Spencer passes over the evolution of the inorganic without discussion. If evolution is only the integration of matter, then there is no evolution of the organic. Organic evolution is a method of life within the inorganic. If organic nature finds its factor in life, or, if life finds its factor in organic nature in what does inorganic nature find its factor? Materialists assume the facts of nature and do not attempt to find a factor. Materialism is a mechanical and not a chemical system of matter. The carbon, oxygen, hydrogen and nitrogen in animal bodies may combine, but they never cease to be those elements. Combination does not destroy. Throughout nature, nothing ever changes its kind; nothing can become heterogeneous *to* itself. Combinations may change, but not the elements of combinations. Nature works over her old materials. Nature is the manifold expression of material elements and immaterial Power.

We must conclude with the materialists, either that matter is eternal; or with the theists, that Power created matter out of nothing ; or with the pantheists, that Power materialized or transmuted itself into matter—that is, that eternal matter is possible in eternal Power. If Power is all, then matter is only a mode of Power; if matter is all, then Power is only a mode of matter. Is matter and a mode of matter one and the same, in which the eternity of one is the eternity of the other?

The whole process of organic evolution is everywhere attributed by Mr. Spencer to the co-operation of the variously conditioned modes of this universal, immanent force, internal and external. That is, Power manifests itself. Now, is that manifestation of Power what is called creation or generation? Creation is something new. If Power is all, it must materialize, for there is matter. And is not the materialization of itself or the taking of form by Power something new, and so a creation? All admit. as we have seen, omnipresent Power. To theistic evolutionists that Power is a personal Creator ; to atheistic or agnostic evolutionists, who deny creation, that Power is impersonal, and manifests an impersonal evolution. But, if impersonal Power can evolve, why can it not create? Is Power unintelligent in evolution and intelligent in creation? Did not the Power that continues all things begin all things? To prove creation of the inorganic, organic evolution need not be denied. To prove evolution of organic nature, creation of the inorganic need not be denied. Creation of inorganic nature and the evolution of organic nature do not conflict. They are simply different stages of the same phenomena. The creation of the inorganic precedes the creation and the evolution of the organic. Those who deny creation seem to fear that unless matter be eternal, Power would be driven, so to speak, to create something out of nothing. But something is not made out of nothing, if matter is only a symbol of Power, unless Power is nothing. Those evolutionists who cannot say that matter is manifested Power, cannot say that it is anything else; for, it is claimed, that all things are manifestations of Power. Matter is only a manifestation of Power, unless matter is Power. But matter is said to be not Power, but only a symbol of Power. If a symbol, it is a manifestation, and if a manifestation of eternal Power, it is not eternal itself.

We have said that methods are sometimes creative and sometimes genetic. The creative method of supernatural Power is denied by Mr. Spencer when he says that "the affirmation of universal evolution is, in itself, a negation of the absolute commencement of anything" (1 Biology, 482, Letter to *N. A. Review*). That is to say, by theory, all evolutions are eternal—all things are evolutions—therefore all things are eternal; which is a *reductio ad absurdum*. Assuming the major premise, as before, let us rather say, whereas all new things are creations—all *changes are new* things—therefore, all changes are creations. Or, as all changes are creations—all new things are changes; therefore, all new things are creations. If the new is the created, then there is creation when, as the idealists say, supernature naturalizes, when the subject objectifies, when the mental materializes, when the homogeneous heterizes, when the indefinite becomes definite, when the incoherent becomes coherent—in short, when there is a new number, a new quality—a new quantity, or a new relation. Thus the averment of eternal evolution is illogical. But even according to this theory, only Power is eternal. Power had no absolute commencement; but all manifestations of Power when Power was all, whether creative or evolutionary, had a commencement. If manifestations of Power had no "absolute commencement," the manifestations of Power must be co-eternal with Power—that is, the child is as old as its parent; which is impossible.

An atom (inorganic matter) cannot be integrated in itself. Molecules of inorganic matter may be integrated as motion is dissipated—and molecules of inorganic matter may be disintegrated as motion is absorbed; but there can be no evolution of the inorganic atom itself. One element can never be changed into another element; oxygen can never be changed into carbon. Different elements must have a common factor or Power, because they cannot be evolved one from the other. But as elementary atoms can never be other than they are, there can be no transformation of the sameness of atoms into an impossible difference of atoms, and so no evolution of atomic matter.

Homogeneity means sameness of kind, and heterogeneity means difference of kind. Solid carbon is one kind of element and æriform oxygen is a different kind of element. If carbon is changed from a homogeneous state to a heterogeneous state, it must still be carbon, and not an element of another kind;

10

and so of every other primary element. The solid element of carbon cannot be gasified, nor can one gaseous element like oxygen be changed into another gaseous element like hydrogen. But if one *kind* is not transformed into *another kind*, there can be no evolution. What is meant by evolution is, the transformation of uniformity of organic phenomena into multiformity of organic phenomena, or of unity into plurality, as of one grain of wheat into many grains of wheat; but this is not a transformation of one *kind* into another *kind*, but a multiplication of the same kind. There may be homogeneity of a unit, but there can be no heterogeneity of the same unit, and so no evolution. The transformation of homogeneity into heterogeneity must be in the *same individual;* but that does not give transformation of one kind into another kind. Evolution, as defined, consisting of the transformation of the elements, is simply impossible. There must be creative lifting of the elements. There may be and is change—development—progress of the same organic individual, but no change of kind, organic or inorganic, and so no evolution of kind.

Strictly speaking the molecule only can be heterogeneous, and the atom only can be homogeneous, as an atom of carbon, or of hydrogen, or of oxygen; but it is a homogeneity that never can be heterogeneous. The atoms we mention can never be other than they are. If evolution depends on the transformation of the homogeneous into the heterogeneous, then evolution does not include any of the inorganic and primary elements admitted by science. The *relations* of these atoms may, indeed, be allotropically changed; but is evolution nothing but a change of relation? Is a relation homogeneity, or is relation heterogeneity? Is an atom homogeneous to a molecule, or is a molecule heterogeneous to an atom? If so, homogeneity and heterogeneity is not sameness or difference in *kind* but in quantity—in number—in relation. If then, there can be no evolution when there can be no transformation of the homogeneous into the heterogeneous, and if there can be no heterogeneity to the primary homogeneous elements, then there can be no evolution, as evolution is defined, of any part of the inorganic world; and Mr. Spencer was wise to pass over it to the evolution of organic natures, but it leaves unwritten a large and by far the most important part of his philosophy.

In passing over the application of his First Principles to the evolution of Inorganic Nature, Mr. Spencer leaves an unbridged chasm between evolutionary Power and Organic Nature, which, we must suppose, those First Principles would span, if applied. If all manifestation of Power is evolution, then, as we have just said, the method of evolution is creative in Inorganic Nature, and genetic in Organic Nature; for the methods of manifestation must differ as the manifested natures differ.

This supernatural method appears to be uniform in "the Constitution of things," where its grasp is only on what is said to be blind, impersonal, unconscious, inert, matter. The eternity of uncreated and and uncreating matter and force is as incomprehensible as the eternity of an uncreated and all-creating

God. Is mind the product of matter, or is matter the product of mind? Matter, as some think of it, cannot answer the question. Gain is a fact, and in that fact is a law of nature, to hold all gains. Now, mind made matter, and not matter mind; because, if mind materialized, it took on original form, or length, breadth and thickness, and this was a gain in the universe; but if matter mentalized, it dropped length, breadth and thickness, and this would have been a loss in the universe, and so an impossibility. Matter knows nothing of its own essence, origin or history, any more than the paper knows the origin of the poem or history written on its surface. But, if matter has existed from all eternity, has nothing but such matter so existed? The eternity of matter does not disprove the mind of God. As mind is no less real than matter, if matter only be real and eternal, then matter is mind unto itself. But matter does not know itself to be mind, nor does mind know itself to be matter. Matter cannot be said to be until it is known to be; but matter cannot be known to be until there is mind to know it. Rather, when matter was known to be there was mind to know it. In other words, matter is altogether unknown unless known to mind. As mind knows nothing older than itself, matter is not known to be older than mind.

If matter is eternally all, and being is not eternal, how is it that there are beings at all? It is a law that like produces like, but what is there alike in matter and being, that matter should beget being? If matter might propagate matter, how can matter propagate mind? If matter is the mother, and mind is the child, it is indeed a strange, unnatural moment when the child openes its conscious eyes upon the form of its unconscious mother. Can mind be the chance product of matter? If mind be the product of chance, then what is by design? Can unintelligent chance produce a designing thing? Does matter work by design or by chance? If it work by chance, it produces designing mind; if it work by design, then is it not God? But if being be eternally all, and matter is not eternal, then what is that which we call matter? Is it Being materialized? Is matter only an idea? We must think of being as a mode of matter, or of matter as a mode or as a creation of being. Both exist. How did omniscience get that control of matter which it now has? Did matter create or evolve mind as its own master, and did it, in mind, dig its own grave? Did matter surrender or delegate to mind, its own child, the control of its movements?

We do not know what matter is, nor what absolute being is; nor whether being can become matter, or matter can become being. The Scriptures teach that " in the beginning God created the heavens and the earth;" but whether creation means that Absolute Being originated matter, or that he materializes and manifests something of himself as matter, no human mind can know. How far is the creator identical with his creation? Is the web a part of the spider? Does heredity make parent and child one? Can God make himself something that he is not? If not, must not that which we call matter be really a metamorphosis of the Being—another name for a

manifestation—God himself? As God cannot separate or divide himself into parts, it would seem, to
short-sighted mortals, that all is God, and God is all.
Who can deny a personal and creative pantheism?
We can neither affirm nor deny that God may become what we call matter, for we know not what
God may choose to do with himself. To God that
is a God, nothing is impossible. Are we individualities of God? Can a conscious Being so abdicate
himself as to become an unconscious thing? It is
more probable that God should convert himself into
a serpent, than that he should create a serpent? Is
not metamorphosis as incomprehensible as creation?
Indeed, how do metamorphosis and creation differ?
But Absolute Being, creation, matter, are all alike
incomprehensible.

So far as our minds can grasp and state their relations, we may say, that, in the necessary unity of all
things, this Absolute Being manifested himself both
in unconscious things and in conscious persons, the
highest personality being Christ. When his will is
creatively manifested in, if not as substance, it is
known as matter: when as chemic force that will
combines this matter, or when as mechanical force, it
moves, or as vital force it organizes this matter, it is
known as cause or force. When the Absolute Being
manages this matter in a way that seems special to
us, we think of him as a worker of miracles. When
he manifests himself as a conscious person, we call
him the Father of man ("for in him we live, move,
and have our being"). When he addresses himself
to man as an intelligent, moral, and therefore account-

able being, his will is known as moral law. Paul
says that there are diversities of gifts, but the same
Spirit.   And there are differences of administrations,
but the same Lord.   And there are diversities of
operations, but there is the same God, which worketh
all in all.   All is a something from, if not of, God's
personality.   So that, to get God out of religion, you
must first get him out of nature, by getting rid of
matter, and by getting rid of his creative energies
included in the idea of cause, known as force, law,
life ; for these are manifestations of Absolute Being,
or facts of his intelligence and power—modes or out-
comes of his personality.

We hold that, as God is spirit, we cannot think of
matter as God ; and yet we cannot think of anything
as apart from God.   His infinity and omnipresence
would seem to displace matter, if spirit can be said
to displace substance.   The difference between this
doctrine of *omnipresent and omniscient personal will,*
efficient rather than immanent, and the ancient notion
of *anima mundi,* or soul of the world, and Shopen-
hauer's impersonal, unintelligent, blind Will, is just
the difference between God and no God.   Does God
create the matter-forces and then retire and leave
them to go on without him, or *is He personally those
forces themselves ?*   No mortal can tell which.   Can
we not say that we see the efficient worker immanent
in the effected work ?   St. Paul says, " God worketh
all in all."   But " God is a spirit, and we must worship him in spirit and in truth."   Science must be
silent when faith distinguishes between God and
matter.   God may incarnate himself, but *if God ma-*

terializes himself, he forbids us to worship the divine materialization. We must honor matter, not knowing how divine it may be. We may all say to each other, as the Angel said to Moses at the Burning Bush, " Put off thy shoes from off thy feet, for the place whereon thou standest is holy ground." Nor was Prof. Tyndall so very profane when he said that " matter had the promise and potency of every form and quality of life."

Taking the eternity of God as a hypothetical standpoint of thought, there is seen to be from Him an ever-increasing materialized emergence—God's thought beaming visible. We cannot deny that there is a God by making matter everything ; for that which is matter to you is Absolute Being to Spencer, Will to Wallace, Mind to Carpenter, Pure Principal to Youmans, Power to Fiske, Spirit to Paul, and God to the Angels. Matter is a form of spirit. The visible side of matter is next to man, and the invisible side next to all above man. Still, whatever God may be to his matter, or whatever matter may be to its God, to *us* mind is not matter, nor is matter mind. We cannot deny the duality, but in the perspective of thought, God is the unit of both. He is the centre of that life which permeates the universe. We can think of eternal Being or existence, but we cannot think of an eternal thing or of an eternal manifestation. Did matter make mind, or did mind make matter? All-knowing mind, to be all-knowing mind, knows how to manifest itself as matter, and still remain mind ; but matter as matter does not know how to become mind, and still remain matter, for it does not know anything. In the manifestation of mind as matter, it need not drop its intelligence, but only add to itself form and continue to be mind; but in the transformation of matter into mind; it drops its essence of form—length, breadth and thickness—and so ceases to be matter. But unless both matter and mind exist eternally, one must make the other. In that case, mind must be the Factor and matter the fact; for, if we suppose that mind, knowing everything, knew how to materialize itself and become visible in form, or to create matter when there was nothing; and that matter, knowing nothing, knew not how to mentalize itself, or to create mind out of itself, we must conclude that mind, which knew everything, made matter; and that matter which did not know how to make anything, did not make mind.

But no one, apart from revelation, knows anything of the origin of either matter or mind. Both have been of old. "As we prolong the vision backward across the boundary of experimental evidence," knowledge is lost in speculation, and speculation is lost in the impenetrable darkness of the eternal mystery. Science may ascribe properties to matter, but science cannot know how, or whence, or what matter is. That inquiry belongs to philosophy and religion. Religion leaves to science the vain effort to solve the insoluble question as to what matter is, and what nature is; but religion worships, by the intuitions of faith, and the conclusions of logic, the supernatural Power as God above and outside of nature. We use the word God as the verbal symbol of superhuman Power, supernatural Mind, supernatural Will.

"All visible things," says Carlyle, "are emblems; what thou see'st is not there on their own account. Matter exists only spiritually, and to represent some idea, and *body* it forth."

So far as we know there is no matter apart from intelligence. Both mind and matter exist. Which is fact and which is Factor? If human mind is a fact, it must have a superhuman Factor. If intelligent nature be denied, unintelligent nature cannot be affirmed; for unintelligent nature cannot take intelligent knowledge of its own unintelligence—it cannot know that it does not know — mindless nature cannot know that it is mindless. And not only must there be intelligence, but there must be consciousness of that intelligence; for unconscious nature cannot be conscious that it is unconscious.

"These speculations," says Wallace, "are usually held to be far beyond the bounds of science; but they appear to me to be more legitimate deductions from the facts of science, than those which consist in reducing the whole universe, not merely to matter, but to matter conceived and defined so as to be philosophically inconceivable. It is surely a great step in advance, to get rid of the notion that *matter* is a thing of itself, which can exist *per se*, and must have been eternal, since it is supposed to be indestructible and uncreated — that force, or the forces of nature, are another thing, given or added to matter, or else its necessary properties—and that mind is another thing, either a product of this matter and its supposed inherent forces, or distinct from and co-existent with it;—and to be able to substitute for this complicated theory, which leads to endless dilemmas and contradictions, the far simpler and more consistent belief, that matter, as an entity distinct from force, does not exist; and that Force is a product of Mind. Philosophy had long demonstrated our incapacity to prove the existence of matter, as usually conceived; while it admitted the demonstration to each of us of our own self-conscious, ideal existence. Science has now worked its way up to the same result, and this agreement between them should give us some confidence in their combined teaching.

"The view we have now arrived at seems to me more grand and sublime, as well as far simpler, than any other. It exhibits the universe, as a universe of intelligence and will-power; and by enabling us to rid ourselves of the impossibility of thinking of mind, but as connected with our old notions of matter, opens up infinite possibilities of existence, connected with infinitely varied manifestations of force, totally distinct from, yet as real as, what we term matter.

The grand law of continuity which we see pervading our universe, would lead us to infer infinite gradations of existence, and to people all space with intelligence and will-power; and, if so, we have no difficulty in believing, that for so noble a purpose as the progressive development of higher and higher intelligences, those primal and general will-forces, which have sufficed for the production of the lower animals, should have been guided into new channels and made to converge in definite directions." (Wallace on Natural Selections, p. 369–70.)

We speak of matter and we speak of Being. Are

they the same or not the same? Has matter intelligence, will, power, and personality? It is the opinion of some, that matter is all, and God or being is not; that God is omnipresent personality. If matter is all God, all God is not matter. The whole subject is incomprehensible. One has no more valid reason for saying that the universe is material, than another has for saying that it is spiritual. The scriptures teach that God created all things by the word of his power. If matter be eternal, it is eternal either in itself or in some eternal existence not known as matter. If eternal in itself, it is what we call God; if eternal in some existence not known as matter, it is not eternal as matter. If eternal in God, then creation is not the coming of something out of nothing, but it is the transformation of being into form; or, as Sir William Hamilton puts it, "all that there is now of existence in the universe, we conceive as having virtually existed prior to creation, in the creator."

In that sense, matter would be the manifestation or mode of Absolute Being; it would be materialized will-power; the visible fact of an invisible Factor; the intangible made tangible; the abstract made concrete—the subjective made objective; spirit manifested as substance. If matter be not eternal, it has been created by an eternal creator, either when there was nothing or out of himself, as the spider converts somewhat of himself into web. But as we cannot conceive of nothing, matter must be a form or manifestation of being; and its eternity, if eternal at all, is the eternity of being materialized in time. Matter, as a manifestation of eternal being, is not eternal.

Matter is the autograph of God. As time is but a segment of eternity; as the age of an undivided whole is the age of each undivided part, so creation has its place in the history of the eternal. Creation was but an echo of existence—existence includes all changes. To God, creation as a purpose, has no chronology.

But matter is not eternal, if it is under the control of mind; for the eternal is uncontrolled. If to crook one's finger shows that some matter is under the control of human will, *a fortiori*, why is not all matter under the control of superhuman will?

If matter, and matter only, be eternal, how explain the mystery of development? Matter is as powerless to change itself, as it is to create itself. If changed, its conditions must be changed ; but who is to change its conditions? It is as impotent or inert to change its conditions, as it is to change itself without change of conditions. The seed in the ground needs outside building from the soil and the sun. Whence the secret of the Protean changes of matter, especially up to life and intelligence?

2. *The first organism, or organic nature.* We have said that the creative method is a way or method of newness ; and, that in inorganic nature it was seen in *the first atom.* We shall now see, that in organic nature, this method of newness was seen in *the first organism..* THE FIRST ORGANISM! whence was it?

The same Power that manifested matter—the first inorganic atom—without life, then manifested matter with life. Mr. Spencer having declined to discuss, in evolution, the origin of the first atom in inorganic nature, is at once confronted with as great a mystery as to the origin of the first organism in organic nature. Mr. Spencer denies both a first atom and a first organism. "The conception of a first organism, in anything like the current sense of the words, is wholly at variance with the conception of evolution." "The absolute commencement of organic life on the globe * * * I distinctly deny" (Ib.).

But, if both matter and life are neither eternal nor created, then that unlimited Power which all admit, must ever be objectifying itself in the symbols called matter, for there is matter, or what Mr. S. calls the symbols or the conceptions of matter. But Mr. S. cannot escape holding either the eternity of matter, of materialism, or the creation of matter by Power; for, when Power was all, there was no matter and no symbol of matter. When Power broke up its infinite and eternal individuality and solitude, and manifested the form and substance of an atom or of the symbol of an atom, then creation began. The first atom or the first symbol of an atom was new and a creation. If Power took form, then form was the form of Power. The presence of form was the presence of Power. But this manifestation of Power in form was something new for Power, and Power out of itself manifested or projected a form of itself—a symbol—called matter.

If there be any validity to these speculations, they prove the universal, continuous creations by Power—that every activity or manifestation of Power is a creation; for Power only is uncreated. Every mani-

festation of Power is something that Power was not
before the manifestation. As that which is uncreated
is that which has always been, so the created is that
which has not always been. Form—symbol-matter
—once was not, for once Power was all. The moment
of creation was the moment that Power manifested
that which Power as Power was not.

In the first organism is the first life in nature.
Whence came that life? Was natural life inherited
from supernatural life, or was it derived from a
supernatural antecedent without life? In inorganic
nature, there is no inheritance—all is unsuspended
creation. But throughout organic nature, like inherits
from like. But species never mix with species. Creative power manifests dissimilarity in its creations.
Power is as unlike its facts as the mould is unlike its
bullets. All chemical changes are creative because
the effects are entirely dissimilar from the causes.
Heat is unlike the electricity that follows it; the
stone dropped into the water is entirely dissimilar
from the wave it raises; light is entirely dissimilar
from the shadow it casts. Creative power as causative power lies between the cause and the effect,
making the cause produce that which the cause in
itself could not be. But the genetic power produces
similarities, and continuously transfers itself from
like to like, as from seed to fruit, and from fruit to
seed. The supernatural power of life is the natural
fact of life—in other words, the creative power of
life in supernature, is the genetic power of life in
nature. We know that life is, but we do not know
what it is. If life lineally descends *in* nature as we

see it does, why should it not lineally descend *from* supernature? We can no more see its end in the future than we can see its beginning in the past. Without life there is no consciousness; and in the proof that human consciousness is from superhuman consciousness, is the higher proof that human life is from superhuman life.

The great, fundamental law of evolution in the correlative integration of matter and the concommitant dissipation of motion, has produced no such result as life; and the almost unanimous voice of scientific learning is, that this correlation between integrating matter and dissipating motion can produce no such result. The Power of life is as much *ab extra* as the Power of motion (104 Psy. 29). The Power of motion may be *in* inert matter, but not *of* it. But, it is at this point of nature that Mr. Spencer takes up evolution. He expressly says, as seen, that he passes over inorganic nature as less important, and takes up the evolution of organic nature as more important. But at this arbitrary skip of science, by which he cuts the phenomena of nature in twain, and accounts for nothing, but describes a few facts of matter, the student of nature must enter an emphatic protest. Evolution must go back, and account for the beginning of the matter of inorganic nature, which is integrated. We think of the first dead form and the first living form, as a commencement of nature, inorganic or organic; but Mr. Spencer tells us that "the affirmation of universal evolution is, in itself, the negation of the absolute commencement of anything." And, yet, 'universal evolution' gives us no account of the first atom or of the first organism. To say that matter, atomized or unatomized, is eternal is what is called materialism; but, the matter-system of Lucretius must be denied, if the Power-system of Spencer be affirmed. If matter could be proved to be eternal, it could not be proved to be infinite, unless space is matter; and so finite matter could not be eternal and infinite in infinite Power. Evolution teaches that matter integrates; but it does not account for the matter or for the Power that integrates it.

All manifesting Power whether creative or genetic, is the same. The same supernatural Power that manifested the inorganic atom and the organic acorn, organizes itself in the acorn to take care of and propagate it. The lifting of the inorganic up into the organic, proves the identity of the Power manifesting both. The organic is the inorganic *plus* life and function. The organizing of the inorganic into the organic, is a creation of the organic upon the antecedent creation of the inorganic.

It is true, that in organic nature--in the transformation of the incoherent into the coherent, and of the indefinite into the definite, matter passes from a diffused to an aggregate state; and the definition of evolution as an integration of matter and concomitant dissipation of motion so far technically applies, if anywhere; but we feel disappointed that evolution ignores the origin of the first atom, or assumes it, and the origin of the first organism, or assumes it, in which theistic philosophy finds its deepest interest. Leave to the world its God, and the minds of men may speculate *ad nauseam*, as to how He has done what He has done. Inorganic nature being given, all else is a study of mere method of Power, personal or impersonal. But here is the battle religion has to fight. Power unlimited in Time and Space is conceded by agnostics; the manifestation of inorganic matter is not denied or discussed, but the question is, is that Power intelligent and personal or unintelligent and impersonal? We claim to here show that it is intelligent and personal. If this claim be valid, we have only to study the methods of an intelligent and personal Power, creative in inorganic nature, and creatively genetic in organic nature. The genetic method is a method of creative Power—or, rather, the genetic method is a part of the creative method.

The first atom, and all the atoms of inorganic nature, and the first organism of all organic nature, are direct creations, because they are new in the universe; while the second organism of organic nature, according to its kind, inherited creation from the first through indirect or genetic creation. They were not created as being new, nor were they eternal as being old; but being *sui generis*, they inherit creative power.

The method in organic nature is genetic, as that in inorganic nature is creative.

Unlimited Power creatively manifested not only inorganic matter or matter without life, but also organic matter or matter with life with power to reproduce or transmit both matter and life. Leaving to the zoölogist and the botanist the technical learning on this point, we simply present the fact of supernatural Power as factor in the phenomena of transmitted life and function. Mr. Spencer speaks of it as a " process of natural genesis " (1 Biol., § 113). The genetic method is a supernaturally natural way of transmission—of reproduction of individuals from individuals. As the first grain of wheat illustrates the creative method, the second grain from the first illustrates the genetic method of universal Power. The genetic method of organic matter is based upon the creative method of inorganic matter. The first thing, whether inorganic or organic, was created ; that is, omnific Power took a form and substance that Power is not. The production of one seed by another seems to deify the reproductive power. In the ancestral worship of the Aryan races, the genetic power was deified. The Power manifested in a tree is the arborescence of supernatural Power, as that of animal life is its incarnation. The Power that is called creative when it originates anything, is called genetic when it propagates what it had originated.

The definition of evolution is not only too narrow as an account of organic or genetic nature, but it is wholly inapplicable to it. What connection can there be between the integration of matter, the correlative dissipation of motion, and the genesis of life and function ? The definition is forced to sustain a theory. The organic is the inorganic, *plus* life and function. The evolution of life has never been shown, and much more, the evolution of function from life has never been shown. The Power that manifested the atom, the molecule and the mass, either from within itself or from without itself, then correlated matter and motion, now by wedging matter apart and now by compressing matter together,—that same Power now adds life to its manifestation of inorganic nature, and lifts it into an entirely new order of nature. Even if it could be shown (as it has not), that the coming and the going of motion and the concentration and diffusion of matter, through the transformation of the homogeneous into the heterogeneous, and the change of incoherency to coherency, and the indefinite into the definite, had been the method of Power in the manifestation first of life and then of function; still, the personal, intelligent Power that manifested itself down this line of phenomena was not disproved by such manifestations. After all, behind nature stands the Power that manifested both inorganic and organic nature.

Science admits a Power unlimited in time and space, but assumes its impersonality. Science treats evolution as a process of impersonal law, and emphatically ignores it as a method of personal Will. Religion treats evolution as a method of personal Will, and emphatically ignores it as a process of merely impersonal law. Materialistic science teaches that impersonal law is primarily all; while religion teaches that, primarily, personal Will is all.

Method, as a way of Power, is either free as supernatural Power, in creation and providence without the method of means; or, as supernatural Power, it is fixed in evolution and correlation, as a method of means. That is to say, supernatural Power both creates without law, other than its own intelligent Will; or, it evolves, with law, as an expression of that Will.

Atheistical science affirms the law, but denies the intelligent Will. Religion affirms the Will, and also law as its intelligent expression. Will prescribes its own methods. The dissimilarity of products in creative manifestations and the similarity of products in genetic manifestations are because supreme Will so wills it. In ourselves we see that will is the executive faculty supreme in each individual; and in all phenomena and life out of ourselves, we cannot suppose that the power of will is less. Each tiny seed, in its genetic life, embodies the creative Power of God Its life is persistent, though possibly dormant through centuries. It never forgets its species. No time can make the seed of wheat produce the tare, or the acorn produce anything but an oak. Nor does the seed ever forget that it must produce a stalk before it can produce another seed. Between the producing acorn and the acorn produced there must be the arborescent life of the grand oak. Unbroken life alone can multiply fish, or bird, or beast, or man.

> As stars that shine by single sun,
> So life in each is life from one.

No wonder that devout imaginations have seen in living nature the grand metamorphosis of God. All living trees, shrubs, birds and insects seem to have an intelligence, a life and a power not their own. The very ground on which our feet stand seems to be holy ground. Creative power is underived; genetic power is derived from the underived creative power. Creation is the fountain, and generation is the issuing stream. Generation is only delegated creation; in other words, creative power confers genetic power. Whatever started nature is creative, whatever carries it on is genetic. This evolutionary Power, immanent in the universe, must be both extrinsic and creative to lift the homogeneous into the heterogeneous ; and intrinsic and genetic, to continue like on into like. But if it is unintelligent, how does it decide, when it grasps a lump of matter, whether it shall evolve into a rock or into a rose? Or is this differentiation altogether a matter of accident ?

LECTURE IV.

METHOD OF EVOLUTION.

The old question, How are we to account for all things? is answered in these days by the old theory of development, under the new name of Evolution. We must decide whether the universe is here as the creation of a Creator, or as the uncreated phenomena of evolution. If we say that the universe is evolved without a Creator, the question arises, Who evolves evolution? If evolution is the derivation of one thing from another, then cabbages are derived from cabbages, and birds from birds, and man from man. But as there must have been a first cabbage, a first bird, a first man, we see that there was original creation as well as derivative evolution. Evolution will do after things get a start; but how did they get a start?

The theory of evolution has been before the world for more than a quarter of a century, and it is difficult to see in it any practical value whatever. No man can manage a bank, sell merchandise, conduct a war, or do anything else by evolution or by knowing what it is. Evolution is a speculation about a method; not a rule of practice: It is for speculative philosophers; not for business men.

There has been an immense deal of talk about evolution; but the vast majority of people are without the slightest knowledge of what it is all about; and all who think they know what evolution is, go on with the duties and interests of life all the same. Its only importance is, as it is arbitrarily made to conflict with the doctrine of the government of a personal God. Every now and then, in the lapse of centuries, rises some new theory, vainly attempting to account, without a God, for all things. At one time it is Fate or necessity; at another it is accident or chance; and now it is evolution. Those who deny the religious basis of things, think that evolution accounts for all things, and nothing more need be said. But what is evolution? Evolution is the homogeneous becoming the heterogeneous. But what is that? It is simply sameness becoming difference. Homogeneity and sameness is unity; heterogeneity is division and difference. An oak is homogeneous in its acorn, but heterogeneous in its roots, trunk, branches, twigs, leaves and fruit. This is evolution; the homogeneous becomes the heterogeneous; the indefinite becomes the definite; the incoherent becomes the coherent; the aggregate becomes the segregate. The evolution of nature has just changed the vesture of our hemisphere. In the process of foliation it is seen from hour to hour. On the naked stem comes a bud, then a bud gradually bursts into a number of different leaves. There is a beautiful and mysterious progress, and beautiful and mysterious difference. This is evolution. It is a *method* of power. But what is that power? Here the conflict between evolution and religion distinctly comes in, if it comes at all. By what power does the homogeneous bud expand into the heterogeneous leaves? The evolution itself is seen and undisputed. All that science has done is to give a new name to an old method of Power; but it neither names nor explains the power. Is the Power, the power of a Person, or the power of Things? Power in action is evolution—in other words, underived power acts in a self-prescribed method, which science calls evolution. That is all there is of it. We are no more advanced in the knowledge of the Power at the origin of things than we were before. Admitting evolution, we know the method, but not the origin of things. As to this origin, we are exactly where we were before, and where we always shall be.

But, we repeat, evolution is only a new name for an old idea. What is now called evolution was, a few years ago, called development. But there are those who think that because the name is new the thing is new. The only difference in the use, though there is none in the meaning, of the two words is, development was admitted to be the method of personal power, while evolution persistently seeks to force itself upon intelligent acceptance as the method of impersonal power. One is theism, the other is atheism. All admit that evolution is only a method or a process; but whether it is one or the other, the whole controversy lies in the old question, whether the power behind evolution is that of a God or of no God, whether it is personal or impersonal.

Now, the first knowledge we get of power is in

our persons, and that of other persons. All fears, whether of children or of men, is of the power of beings, not of things. Things and forces and elements were feared only as they represented personal power. If the power is not personal, then there is no religious morality, no right and no wrong; and persons are only a higher order of things without moral duties ·or moral responsibilities. An impersonal thing or things can give no moral commands to personal beings. A tree or a stone cannot impose duties on a Newton or on an Isaiah. The underived is God; if human beings are underived, then they are gods; if they are derived, they must take the law of their conduct and place from the underived; but the Underived, as a lawgiver, must be personal, not impersonal, for we are persons. All our ideas woven into the fibre of knowledge ascribe personality to a lawgiver. An impersonal lawgiver is utterly unthinkable; so that we must either give up the idea and name of Law, or admit the existence of a personal Lawgiver. To admit this is to admit God; to admit God, makes it unimportant to the ends of religion, whether evolution is a method, or not a method of God.

In ourselves, power is found to be Will; and, if will is power in us, why is it not power in all above us? What should make a difference? Right here is the rub. If infidelity could disconnect power from personal will, it could discard the idea of a personal God, and the victory for materialism would be won. But this it has not done; .and as long as power is in will, and will is in personality, so long su-

perhuman power will be superhuman will, and superhuman will is all that we mean by God. With God
at the head, of the universe, He may have evolution
as a method or not as He pleases. If the method of
evolution covers all that is known of the universe,
then it is both creative and genetic; it is creative in
evolving unlike from unlike as vegetables from minerals. It is genetic in evolving like from like, as
oaks from oaks or wheat from wheat. If this house
is an evolution, it is a creative evolution; for it is not
the generation of any other house, nor can it generate another house. Again, if the vegetables are
evolutions, they are genetic evolutions; because they
descend from other like vegetables.   •

But one thing is certain, that whether the method
be creative or genetic or both, it is only a method.
Science may deal with the method, while religion
personalizes and worships the power. If evolution is
only the method of a personal will, then religion
does not deny it; but if evolution is claimed to be
an inevitable out-rolling of things, then religion does
deny it. There is nothing inevitable to God.

"The other week," says the London *Guardian*,
"there was a meeting held in honor of the tercen-
tenary of the foundation of the University. There
was brought together a galaxy of talent such as has
not been witnessed anywhere in modern times. To
the Scottish capital, and to do honor to one of the
grandest seats of learning in the world, science, art,
literature, statesmanship had sent their leading rep-
resentatives. ·Much interest was centered in the
students' meeting. Here the excitement was brought

up almost to a white heat by the addresses of Minister Lowell, of Count Sacifi, of Helmholtz, of Laveleye, of Pasteur and of Virchow. It was something to see these great masters. It was more to hear them speak. Virchow was the chief attraction. Helmholtz uttered a word of warning against what he called False Rationalism in science; Laveleye reminded the students that their first duty was to seek the kingdom of God, but Virchow surprised, astonished and produced a perfect furor of excitement when he proclaimed with emphasis that evolution had no scientific basis. The Darwinian theory, he said, might be true; but what he demanded was proof, not hypothesis. Such testimony from the greatest anatomist, the greatest master of natural science now living, it was felt was a real triumph for religion. The general conviction produced by Virchow's utterance is, that the tide has turned against infidelity."

What is a scientific basis? Material science investigates material phenomena. Its eye is ever upon inert, lifeless forms. When the phenomena of life appears, then begins an inquiry which utterly baffles science. No scale of science has ever weighed life; no microscope of science has ever seen life; no crucible of science has ever fused life; no alembic of science has ever distilled life. No scientist has ever explained life. The reason that the distinguished Virchow announced that evolution had no scientific basis, lies in the truth, that evolution is a method of facts, but not the power of the facts themselves. Science deals with facts, and facts only. What power *does*, belongs to science; what power *is*, belongs to philosophy and theology. Anything beyond facts is metaphysical, and not scientific. Science may study facts, but not the factors. The essence of Power is beyond the scope of science, but not beyond the studies of philosophy. Rules are for science; principles are for philosophy. Thus Virchow was critically correct—evolution is the subject of philosophical speculations, not of scientific facts. Science may tell us what power does, but not what power is. If evolution is claimed to be a power as well as a method, even then there can be no science as to what power is, there can be no scientific basis for evolution. If evolution has a scientific basis, then it must be admitted to be only a method, and not a power, and as a mere method of power, it cannot conflict with what philosophy and religion reserve as Power.

What religion wants is to get at foundation truths. If science has them not, no material barrier can stop the soul from looking behind the barrier. Let evolutionists explain the power of which evolution is only a method, or be silent when religion attempts, however tardily and gropingly, to get behind the evolution.

No one need deny that evolution, both creative and genetic, is one of God's methods in the universe ; but if there be no God, there is no evolution. There is but one explanation of the universe, consistent with all the facts, conditions, and on-look of things, and that is, that Will—personal Will—Supreme Will —accounts for all. That Will may evolve, involve, revolve, or dissolve, as it may please, and as infinite wisdom may see to be best. Without that Will, we

cannot account for our own Will, or for the complex
ity of phenomena in things without will.   If there be
no such will supreme over all, then blind, unintelligent fate, necessity, chance, or something else impersonal and dreadful grasps the universe in a remorseless and eternal power.   If evolution expresses will,
religion is silent; but if evolution claims to be a
blind, unintelligent power, then religion, by its very
nature, will ever oppose it under whatever new
names it may be known in the future, as it has ever
opposed it under its old name of materialism in the
past.   Evolution is either a process or a method.

1. *Evolution as a process.*   The proposed theory of
evolution as the *process* of an unintelligent, impersonal
Power has not been proved : evolution as a *method* of
an intelligent, personal, Being, need not be denied.
Evolution admits a Power unlimited in time and
space ; and claims that its manifestation is a process,
without beginning or ending, unintelligent and impersonal.   Power is manifested in things, and in their
relations.   Supernatural *Power* is manifested in things,
in what is called natural *Force*.   The manifestation
of Power in things both organic and inorganic, is
called evolution.   When Power is manifested in the
relation or *correlations* of things, we must remember
that the Power that manages the correlation is absolute, and is never itself correlated.   One manifestation is correlated with another manifestation—for instance, Power manifested as the force of heat, is correlated with an equivalence of Power manifested as
the force of electricity.   The Power that as Force
integrates matter is correlatively dissipated as Power

in motion, and is increased or diminished as Force, but is unlimited as Power. From the standpoint of evolution, as formulated by Mr. Spencer, is evolution a process? But we ask, a process of what? Mr. S. says, " we shall everywhere mean by evolution, the process which is always an integration of matter and dissipation of matter" (F. P., § 97). Remember that evolution is always a process of the integration of *matter*. But whence the matter? Mr. Spencer says that

(*a*) Matter is not created. " The creation of matter is inconceivable " (1 Biol., § 112). He denies creation when, in seeking to avoid the charge that he is bound to assume the first organism, says, " the affirmation of universal evolution is, in itself, a negation of the absolute commencement of anything. The absolute commencement of organic life on the globe, *
* * I distinctly deny" (1 Biol., 482, and § 112). But, if it be denied that the first organism is assumed, can it be denied that the first atom is assumed? To admit the assumption of the first atom would be the very materialism which Mr. Spencer formally denies. Whether manifestations of eternal Power be processes or methods, they are both alike within the ways of Power, and are incomprehensible to us. Materialism assumes the existence of matter; but, as we have seen, Mr. Spencer emphatically denies working out a materialistic system. The inference is, that, in his theory of evolution, as in theistic cosmogony,

(*b*)—Matter is not eternal. All admit a Power unlimited in time and space, and, unless matter be infinite, it must be limited in unlimited Power. For such Power to be such Power, it must be supreme. As there cannot be two firsts—two infinite entities (F. P., § 24)—so there cannot be two Supremes. The Supreme is one. Power could have no co-ordinate in matter; for, in that co-ordination, Power would would lose its supremacy, and cease to be Power unlimited in time and space. Therefore, if matter be neither created nor eternal, it follows that—

(*c*) Matter is not at all but is ever becoming—that is, there is no matter, but there always is to be matter. Heraclitus held to a restless, changing flux of things, which never *are*, but are ever *becoming*. " No one," he says, " has ever been twice on the same stream ; for different waters are continually flowing down : it dissipates its waters and gathers them again —it approaches and recedes—it overflows and it falls." His aphorism was : " all is motion ; there is no rest or quietude " (Lewes' Hist. Phi., p. 69). Wherein does this differ from evolution ? The instability of the homogeneous is its pivotal doctrine. The parallel is wonderfully complete. The cosmic theory of evolution is that matter never was created —is not eternal, and is always a becoming. The manifestations of supernature are known as organic and inorganic. These manifestations, of course, have commencements; for, as they are the manifestations of eternal Power, they cannot be as eternal as their manifesting Power. To say that there never has been an absolute commencement of organic life is to make organic life eternal, which is absurd ; or, it is to make evolution to be an eddying stream, ever flowing out of itself in the past into itself in the

future. This *ever becoming* is an eternal process. If
it has results, they are unanticipated results; for
process that anticipates nothing is not a method that
anticipates everything. The process of the emanation of supernatural Power of itself from itself, and
the re-absorption of itself into itself, is Buddhism in
science. But Buddhism is more religious in the conception of this emanating Power as an impersonal
Being, than science is in presenting this manifesting
Power as an impersonal force. The Buddhistic word
"emanation" suggests a going forth of Being itself
from itself; while the word "manifestation" of evolution suggests the metamorphosis of itself as itself, or
within itself—that is, Buddhism is the emanation of
impersonal Being, and evolution is the process of
impersonal Force.

As Mr. Spencer denies that there is any force
within matter, his system cannot be one of dynamics;
and as he also denies that there can be any force
without or external to matter, it cannot be a system
of mechanics; the whole self-evolving process of organic nature must therefore be one of genetic parturition; or, as he expresses it, "the co-operation of
the variously conditioned modes of universal immanent force, internal and external." That is to say,
the universal "immanent force," as an *external* force,
is genetic, or begins to produce something; and, as
an *internal* force, it is parturient. In this system, to
beget and to produce is the same act. What else
can Mr. Spencer mean? Or, is there no begetting, and
is there no parturition? What do these evolutionists
mean to say, and what would they have us believe?

12

Do they give us any more light than we had before as to the origin of the universe?

Evolution is either free or necessary. Supreme Power behind evolution must be free to be Supreme Power. If, therefore, evolution seems necessary to human intelligence, it cannot be necessary to super-human Power. But,

(*d*) Evolution, as defined, is not a necessity. Nothing is necessary that could possibly be other-wise ; but what could not be otherwise to Supreme Will? Mr. Spencer says (Pop. Sci. M., Nov. 1880, p. 105): " The process of evolution is not necessary, but depends on conditions." But on what do the conditions depend? If the conditions are necessary, then, of course, evolution that depends on necessary conditions, is necessary. On what but Supreme Will can conditions depend, if they are not necessary? If conditions depend on Supreme Will, they are not necessary ; for nothing can be necessary to Supreme Will. That which is called necessity belongs exclu-sively to the sphere of nature. Supernature of its own Will may manifest itself in a process, or stereo-type itself in a method ; but we must ever remember that Will-Power—Supreme Will-Power—is not bound by its own methods. Power immutable to us is not immutable to itself. But whether evolution is a method or a process, it is not necessary ; for Power and intelligence could form or not form the method it did form. But if the phenomenon called evolution is a process of impersonal, unintelligent Power, then evolution is necessary ; for unintelligent Power knew not how to make it otherwise. Human intelligence makes a distinction between process and method that superhuman Power does not make. Human names are only symbols of superhuman Power. Mr. Spencer both admits and denies the necessity of evolution. He says : "The doctrine of evolution currently regarded as referring only to the development of species, is erroneously supposed to imply some intrinsic proclivity in every species towards a higher form ; and, similarly, a majority of readers make the erroneous assumption that the transformation which constitutes evolution, in its wider sense, implies an intrinsic tendency to go through those changes which the formula of evolution expresses. But all who have fully grasped the argument of this work (Principles of Sociology), will see that the process of evolution is not necessary, but depends on conditions : (Pop. Sci. M., Nov., 1880, p. 165). Mr. Spencer would seem to hold in the certainty of progress that there is the certainty of the conditions of progress. He says : (So. Sta., chap. II, § 4), " The inference that as advancement has been hitherto the rule, it will be the rule henceforth, may be added a plausible speculation. But when it is shown that this advancement is due to the working of a universal law ; and, that in virtue of that law it must continue until the state we call perfection is reached, then the advent of such a state is removed out of the region of probability into that of certainty. If any one demurs to this let him point out the error." * * * " Progress, therefore, is not an accident but a necessity." The theory of evolution is, that everything is in a state of instability, and that all phenomena are results of that instability, not the creations of originating power, But whence are all things and whence is the instability of all things? If Will is behind all things, and behind the instabil ity of all things, then nothing is necessary in the universe ; for nothing can be necessary to Will and Will be Will. Mr. Spencer says : " All finite forms of homogeneous --all forms of it which we can know or conceive, must inevitably lapse into heterogeneity." (F. P. § 155). " To the conclusion that the changes with which evolution *commences* are thus necessitated remains to be added the conclusion that these changes must *continue.* The absolutely homogeneous must loose its equilibrium ; and the relatively heterogen- eous must lapse into the relatively heterogeneous. * * * And thus, the continued changes, which characterize evolution, in so far as they are consti- tuted by the lapse of the homogeneous into the hete- rogeneous and of the heterogeneous into the more heterogeneous are necessary consequences of the per- sistence of force." (F. P., § 155). It is not clear in the face of these and other doctrinal formulas of Mr. Spencer that we understand him when he says : " The process of evolution is not necessary, but de- pends on conditions." Are the conditions necessary ? To get anything like an adequate notion of evolution, we must study the power that exists before evolution begins, the process, the conditions, the product, and the method of nature. From every consideration, we see that all must be free in the free Will of Power (the personal Power we call God), or all is necessary in the necessary process of impersonal evolution. The fact is, that behind an evolution inevitable as to us, there is the Will of Power, free as to all. To those who deny this Will, what happens, happens. Things could not be otherwise than they are. As we have said, evolution as a method implies intelligence. Evolution as a manifestation of any kind implies Power, and Power is Will. If human Power is human Will, why is not superhuman Power Superhuman Will? We therefore conclude that evolution is a method of Superhuman Will. For that reason,

(*c*) Evolution, as defined, is not eternal. Mr. Spencer teaches that it is eternal. He says "the affirmative of eternal evolution is, in itself, the negation of the absolute commencement of anything." (1 Bio., 482).

If there is universal evolution and there is no absolute commencement of anything, then the matter to be integrated in evolution is eternal, and the process of evolution is eternal—that is, there must be an eternal evolution, by eternal Power, of eternal matter. According to this theory of evolution, eternal Power eternally manifested itself in some eternal thing. The next was eternally to transform that eternal thing into some other eternal thing. Agnostic evolution, in denying the absolute commencement of anything, assumes the eternal existence of matter. According to this evolution, all things were eternal that eternal Power manifested in an eternal instability. The eternal power that eternally made eternal motion, then eternally dissipated eternal motion, and eternally held itself eternally still, and made all things eternally stable. The eternally diffused matter that eternal Power manifested eternally apart, or in an eternal disintegration, eternal Power afterwards eternally integrated or brought eternally together. What eternal Power eternally manifested as eternally indefinite, eternal Power eternally transformed into the eternally definite; and what eternal Power eternally manifested as eternally incoherent, eternal power eternally transformed into the eternally coherent. All eternal sameness was eternally transformed into eternal difference. This brings us to the absurdity of an acephalous universe.

(*f*) If Evolution is not eternal, it is not a process. According to agnostic evolution, eternal Power is synonymous with eternal Process. But evolution is not eternal if there are changes in it; for the eternal is the unchanged. All changes are new, like the revolving views of the Kaleidescope; and all that is new is a commencement, and all that is a commencement is a creation. Creation implies Power; and creating power implies intelligence, as its manifestations are intelligent. Mr. Spencer's reasoning would seem to be that Power was and is all, and all was and is Power. There being no "absolute commencement of anything," eternal Power never did anything that was not eternal. Eternal Power evolved those eternal modes of eternal Power which he calls matter and motion. But can modes be eternal? Can phenomena be eternal? Are changes fragments of the eternal? In a word, evolution is a method of going on after a start; but how about the start? In making evolution universal and eternal, all things are made to go on without having started; but this leads to the absurdity, that as nothing can go on that has not started, and as, according to Mr. S., nothing ever started, nothing has ever gone on.

(*g*) If evolution is not a process, it is nothing. Mr. Spencer himself, says, "Construed in terms of evolution, every kind of being is conceived as a product of modifications wrought by insensible grada tions on a pre-existing kind of being; and this holds as fully of the supposed commencement of organic life, as of all subsequent developments of organic life." (1 Bio. p. 482). Yet he admits that the evolution alluded to in the language just quoted, is not proved by direct evidence. He says: "Though the facts at present assignable in *direct* proof that by progressive modifications, races of organisms that are apparently distinct may result from antecedent races, are not sufficient; yet, there are numerous facts of the order required." (1 Bio., p. 351, § 119).

2. *Is Evolution a method?* Are the manifestations of this admitted Power an eternal process or a prescribed method? The answer to these questions sustains or invalidates agnostic evolution. Evolution, *as defined is a method;* but evolution defined as a method is not a method of evolution, but a method of correlation. Admitted Power, unlimited in Time and Space, is either intelligent or unintelligent. The manifestations of unintelligent Power would be utterly unintelligible; the manifestation of intelligent Power is a method. But whether the Power is intelgent or unintelligent, Mr. Spencer calls its manifestation a process. What is the difference between a method and a process, and wherein is the importance of the distinction? If there be design in the manifestation of Power, it is unimportant whether the manifestation be called a process or a method.

Method in a process makes the process a method; but process in a method does not make the method a process. The process might realize the method; as the process of the growth of a tree realizes the design in the seed.

But Modern Thought, as it is called, uniformly omits all allusion to design, as it would imply a Designer; and there seems to be a growing evasion of the word law, as that implies a Lawgiver. The attitude of Modern Thought is to ignore words of personality, of Will and of Intelligence. It therefore uses the impersonal word " process " in preference, if not to the exclusion of the personal word " method." To a theist method implies nothing less than personal intelligence — no intelligence, no method. To an atheist process implies nothing more than impersonal Power—no power, no process. In method there is plan; in process there is action. That is, method emphasizes personal intelligence rather than imper sonal Power; process emphasizes impersonal Power rather than personal intelligence. Evolution as a process may be impersonal, if such evolution can be at all; evolution as a method *must* be personal. There might be a theistic process, but there could be no atheistic method. The distinction, therefore, between method and process, in evolution, is the distinction between theism and atheism. If evolution were a process, and not a method, it would imply the eternal circle of an endless beginning. As the created is the new, so far as evolution is a process unfolding the new, and never repeating the old, like a method, it is a continuous and unbroked creation. A genetically repeated production is a method. A process never repeats, but always flows on like a river without a fountain. A method is when Power has a way of creating types and generating individuals. All new things are according to a method of newness; all propagated things are according to a method of generation; and all exchange of equivalents is according to a method of correlation. That which is called evolution, but which is the same as correlation, is a method, because it always does the same kind of thing in the same way. It is a process so far as nothing is repeated.

Power observes a *method* when it *always* transforms the homogeneous into the heterogeneous; when it *always* defines the indefinite, or always coheres the incoherent; or when it *always* integrates diffused matter as motion dissipates. This is method and not process; and being a method, it implies personal intelligence, power, and a time when method was not. Evolution, as defined, is an eternal correlation or exchange of matter and motion; evolution, as described, is the process of an eternal coming and going, the flux and reflux of Heraclitus, of matter and its modes. Evolution, as defined, is the barter of matter and force in nature, giving so much of one for so much of the other; evolution, as described, is the allotropism—the chemistry—the metamorphosis of nature.

Prof. Tyndall confesses that "the whole process of evolution is the manifestation of a power absolutely inscrutable, to the intellect of man." But nature makes as high a revelation of intelligence, as she does of Power; but why admit the Power and deny the intelligence behind the Power? Can we think of either without thinking of both? In looking at Grecian Temples, and Christian Cathedrals, do we think only of the strength of the materials in their construction? or, are we not rather impressed with their feeling of aspiration, and the wonderful intelligence of their plan and decorations? In the minute and graceful, do we not think more of the intelligence than we do of the Power they exhibit? and so of the wondrous system of worlds around us. Is the Cosmos a process of impersonal Power, or the method of Personal Will? Why should the Power personalized in human nature be impersonalized in superhuman nature? If all things are manifestations of a power that transcends our knowledge, it is as illogical to deny the personality of that Power as to affirm its impersonality. But how shall we account for *our* conscious personality? If there never has been any absolute commencement of organic life on the globe, as Mr. Spencer emphatically affirms (1 Biol., p. 482), then, human life must have been eternal in the eternity of superhuman life. To say that dead matter is a mode of life is mere assertion, unscientific in its dogmatic tone. If living organisms are eternal continuities of life, let it be shown. The bearing of what is strangely called evolution is to impersonalize Power, and to deny personal creation. It uses the word manifestation in place of the word creation; but the word manifestation will answer for religion as well as for science.

Evolution, as taught by Mr. Spencer, originates

nothing; for, in his theory of evolution, nothing is original, or, to use his phrase, "there never was an absolute commencement of anything." All things are said to be in an eternal activity of flux and reflux. According to this theory, evolution is an eternal process of unoriginated development of one thing out of another, either by eternal generation, or by eternal metamorphosis. There being no matter, as is claimed, either created or eternal, but only our conception, as the symbols of matter, evolution is only the eternal process of the symbols of an Unknowable Reality, called matter. Can it be said to be unknown, when unlimited Power, of which it is a manifestation, is admitted to be eternal?

Materialistic evolutionists deny a prescribed method and affirm an eternal process. A method which implies design may include a designed process, but an undesigned process can never include a designed method. Design lifts a process into a method. Taking evolution as Mr. Spencer defines it (F. P., § 145), it is a method of correlation. Taking evolution as he describes it (*Ib.* § 97), and evolution is a process. He says, "we shall everywhere mean by Evolution the *process* which is always an integration of matter and dissipation of motion, but which, as we shall now see, is in most cases much more than this." As a method, what is called evolution is correlation; an intelligent process is a method. As an unintelligent process, evolution is impossible; for an unintelligent, impersonal process must be an eternal process; and an eternal process of an unintelligent, impersonal Power, is unintelligible. All manifestation of intelligent

Power is either a method or a miracle. If all that is unintelligent be a process, it cannot be a method; if all that is intelligent be a method, it cannot be a process. Method implies intelligence and intelligence implies a method.

3. *Evolution cannot be a process* rather than a method; and this distinction is most important if there is to be any moral conduct. Moral conduct implies the intelligence and will that is implied in method. If intelligent method in evolution be denied, so intelligent conduct must be denied in morality; for a morality without intelligence is without authority, and morality without authority is no morality. The learned writer of the Introduction to the Data of Ethics, says, there are two systems of morality—that which claims supernatural authority, and that which is grounded in nature; one of these must be accepted or all morality is denied." (Intro. D. E. IX). But if nature be an unintelligent, impersonal process, no *system* of moral conduct can be grounded on it. An unintelligent, unauthorized process cannot evolve intelligent, authorized conduct. But intelligence and will implied in a method of evolution is the intelligence and will implied in an authority of conduct. Therefore, if morality be an evolution, as Mr. S. claims, then evolution must be an intelligent method; but if evolution be an unintelligent process, then morality is an impossibility.

Mr. Spencer admits, as we have seen on p. 16, that " all accountable and natural facts are proved to be, in their ultimate genesis, unaccountable and supernatural " (F. P., § 30); and from this we might reasonably expect Mr. Spencer to teach a supernatural morality. He says "amid the mysteries which become the more mysterious the more they are thought about, there will remain the one absolute certainty, that he is ever in the presence of an Infinite and Eternal Energy, from which all things proceed." Pop. Sci. M., Jan., 1884.) Though he thus admits the supernatural—the Infinite and Eternal Energy from which all things proceed — he not only does not expect morality to proceed from this Energy, but says, "The establishment of rules of right conduct on a scientific basis is a pressing need. Now that moral injunctions are losing the authority given by their supposed sacred origin, the secularization of morals is imperative." (Pref. Data of Ethics, vi). The "sacred origin of moral injunctions" is not *supposed* but necessarily *admitted* in the admission of supernature. And again: if from the Infinite and Eternal Energy *all* things proceed, why are moral injunctions excepted, why should the secularization of morals be imperative? If from this Infinite Energy all things proceed, *how can* morals be secularized? That which is essentially sacred cannot become secular.

We expect to show the impossibility of Mr. Spencer's system of morality "grounded in nature," where he exclusively places it; and also to show that morality *must* be from the supernature, which he admits, exactly under the authority where he denies it to be. To admit supernature, admits its moral as well as its material authority. It would be more consistent either to deny the supernatural, or to admit its moral authority. If the basis of morals must be scientific, of course morals must be natural and not supernatural; because there can be no science of the supernatural. Suppose, that, by induction, we try to put morals upon a scientific basis: what must we first do? Mr. Spencer says, "Our preparatory step must be to study the evolution of conduct." (D. E., § 2); that "moral phenomena" (as all else) "are the phenomena of evolution." (D. E., § 23). Is this evolution theistic or atheistic — free or necessary — prescribed or unprescribed? Unless there are two or more kinds of evolution, the laws of the evolution of morals must be the same as the laws of the evolution of matter. Not stopping here to define any terms — nature or supernature—morality or evolution— the logical argument is, that whatever is not prescribed is either accidental or necessary. According to materialistic evolutionists, evolution is not prescribed, and is, therefore, either accidental or necessary. It must be necessary; for, as to morals, Mr. Spencer says (D. E., § 21): "The view for which I contend is, that Morality, properly so-called — the science of right conduct—has for its object to determine *how* and *why* certain modes of conduct are detrimental, and certain other modes beneficial. These good and bad results cannot be accidental; but must be necessary consequences of the constitution of things." A necessary constitution of things makes consequences necessary. Between the constitution of things and necessary consequences, where does necessity begin? What is necessity? Theists contend, that with a divine Will in the universe nothing is necessary.

But to theists it is more easy to tell what necessity is not than what it is. Necessity is not the irrevocable behind us, but it is the inevitable before us. In necessity there is no intelligence, for there is no plan; there is no will, because there is no choice; there is no hope, because there is no escape; there is no responsibility, because there is no freedom. If, then, evolution is not prescribed because prescription implies authority, which materialistic evolutionists deny; and if evolution, especially of morality, is not an accident, as we learn from Mr. Spencer, it is evident from the reasoning of these materialistic evolutionists and from their stand-point, that,

First.—All evolution is necessary evolution. If it is not necessary is it free? If it is free, is it evolution? By evolution, is generally meant phenomena without a God. If all things come from God, it does not matter whether we call the way they come, evolution, or creation, or anything else. Right here, as to whether evolution is free or necessary, is the whole question of natural or supernatural morality. As we know no freedom apart from Will, if there be no Will in evolution, there can be no freedom. If evolution be neither free nor accidental, it must be necessary. Evolution does not claim to proceed from Will, or to address itself to will. It is not free to command, and no one is free to obey. Therefore, it must be admitted or denied, that all impersonal evolution is necessary evolution. If it be admitted, as it must be by all materialistic evolutionists, then, it follows, as all evolution is necessary, and all natural morality is an evolution, that all natural morality must be necessary; and necessary morality is no morality. If it be denied, and it be claimed, that there is a natural morality, which is an evoluntion, but not a necessary evolution, then such evolution must be merely a method of a free Power; and if free, as we are conscious of freedom only in a free Will, we come, in our denial of a necessary evolution, to an all-evolving Will, whose uniformity is not a necessity of evolution.

Mr. Spencer speaks of a "Power manifested throughout evolution work." Does this power work with method or without method? According to Prof. Hæckel, and some other materialistic evolutionists, this Power works without method. He says in his Munich Address, that "those rudimentary organs —eyes that see not—wings that fly not, muscles that do not contract, clearly show, that conformity to an end, in the structure of organic forms, is neither general nor complete; they do not emanate from a plan of creation drawn up beforehand, but were of necessity produced by the accidental clash of mechanical causes." (Mr. Spencer denies "*accidental* consequences.") Can things be necessarily produced that were not necessarily caused? If Prof. Hæckel is right, then nature, (including things "of necessity produced") under necessity and without Will, puts under necessity and without Will, all in nature. If nature is thus necessary, and evolution is a way of nature, then all evolution is necessary. Things evolve because they must; they cannot be otherwise than they are. Whatever is, is inevitable. No intelligent Will started the universe, and there is no intelligent

Will to stop it. The abstract *must* become concrete —the absolute *must* become the conditioned. Mr. Spencer states the doctrine of necessity quite as sharply as Prof. H. He says, " moral principles must conform to physical necessities." (D. E., § 22).

Morality is either evolved or prescribed. If evolved, it is said to be "grounded in nature," and is called Natural Morality. If morality is prescribed, it is said, as blind, unintelligent nature prescribes nothing, "to claim supernatural authority," and is called Supernatural Morality. If nature is necessary, then the supernature admitted by Mr. Spencer, so far as it is not self-limited in nature, must be free. Therefore Morality is either evolved as necessary in nature, or prescribed as free in supernature. In evolution, as nothing cannot evolve something, something must, from itself, evolve something like itself as the necessary from the necessary ; for, if unlike itself, it is something evolved from nothing ; which is impossible. All evolution is under Will, or not under Will ; if not under Will, it is necessary ; if under Will, evolution is only the method of free Will.

But, according to the theory of natural evolution, the homogeneous *must* be unstable ; the instability of the homogeneous *must* differentiate into the heterogeneous ; the dissipation of motion *must* integrate matter ; effects *must* follow causes ; and causes *must* multiply effects. Now, where is there enough freedom of action in all this, for that free action called moral action ? But let us say in passing, that what is *must* to human limitations is not *must* to unlimited superhuman Power.

Second.—All so-called Natural Morality is an evolution. What is morality? Morality is right conduct. What makes conduct right? Mr. Spencer says it is the "adjustment of the acts to ends." (D. E., § 2.) But how is the adjustment to be made, and who is to make it? How are we to answer this question? Adjustment implies personal intelligence and power.

The definition of conduct which emerges is either —acts adjusted to ends, or else—the adjustment of acts to ends; according as we contemplate the formed body of acts, or think of the form alone. And conduct in its full acceptation must be taken as comprehending all adjustments of acts to ends, from the simplest to the most complex, whatever their special natures and whether considered separately or in their totality.

"Our preparatory step must be to study the evolution of conduct." (D. E., § 2.) Moral conduct is either prescribed unevolved, or evolved unprescribed or evolved as prescribed. If prescribed unevolved, or evolved as prescribed, it is prescribed by superhuman personal Will to human personal Will. If evolved unprescribed, it implies impersonality, and excludes Will. Prof. Hæckel and other materialists teach, that nature evolves unprescribed, or in Prof. H.'s phrase, "with no plan drawn up beforehand." Mr. Spencer says, as we have seen, that "Moral phenomena are phenomena of evolution."

But the whole terminology of the evolution theory indicates its origin in materialistic philosophy. "The instability of the homogeneous"—"the integration

of matter is the dissipation of motion " and so on,
show that matter only is in the mind of the evolu-
tionist. When it was extended over the whole field
of the universe, either evolutionary terminology
must have a secondary and figurative meaning as
applied to the sphere of mind, or mind itself must
be materialized ; that this was Mr. Spencer's conclusion we shall see further on. But whether moral
conduct is under nature or supernature or both, in
Mr. Spencer's opinion, it is an evolution. But if
conduct is an evolution and evolution is necessary,
then conduct is necessary, and therefore not under
moral authority or moral responsibility. But, it is
not clear how conduct, which is an act of Will, can
be strictly under the laws of evolution where there
is no Will. And to apply evolution to moral conduct
seems to be forcing the theory ; but for the present
let us consider it as a source of moral conduct, as is
claimed for it.

Third.—Therefore, all so-called Natural Morality
is a necessary evolution. In the end it will be evident that, as to this philosophy, the conduct called
Natural Morality is not only an evolution, as specially
taught by Mr. Spencer, but that it is a necessary evolution, as taught by both Mr. Spencer and Prof.
Hæckel. This conclusion is reached by the argument already given ; and will now be confirmed by
that which is added. Evolution is either natural or
supernatural. If natural, then, as nature, according
to Prof. Hæckel, has no method or plan, natural evolution has no method or plan. If natural evolution has no method or plan, then moral conduct

grounded in nature can have no method or plan. If moral conduct, grounded in nature, has no method or plan, then Mr. Spencer's definition of ethical conduct, as "acts adjusted to ends," is impossible. For, "adjustment of acts to ends," implies a method or plan in nature, which Prof. Hæckel denies. Now either Prof. Hæckel errs in denying method or plan to creation, or Mr. Spencer errs in defining conduct as "acts adjusted to ends." If there is no method or plan of adjustment in an all-including creation, there can be no method or plan of adjustment in a specially included conduct. But, if there is Will—intelligence—adjustment of acts to ends, in the lower sphere of conduct, why is there not Will—intelligence—adjustment of acts to ends in the higher sphere of nature? If there is no plan—no adjustment of acts to ends in universal nature, as Prof. H. teaches, how can there be any adjustment of acts to ends in particular nature of conduct, as Mr. Spencer teaches? To Prof. H. the absence of "plan in creation" is the correlative presence of Necessity. He sees necessity where he sees no plan. In this doctrine of a necessary nature, all materialistic evolutionists agree. Dr. Maudsley (Body and Will, p. 124) says, "It is a law of Nature, and therefore a necessity, that the sun rises day after day." He does not account for the law of nature, and so he does not define necessity.

Mr. Spencer says (D. E., § 22), "Throughout the whole of human conduct, necessary relations of causes and effects prevail." Again : "The connexion between cause and effect is one that *cannot be established*, or *altered*, by *any authority external to the phe-*

nomena themselves." (*Ib.*) It is sufficient that the authority be internal to the phenomena : but whence the phenomena ? Mr. Spencer says (D. E., § 22), " Moral principles must conform to physical necessities." For moral principles to conform to physical necessities, they must be, not only numerically distinct, but they must be essentially different. But Mr. Spencer makes them psychologically the same. If matter evolves mind, or, if physical necessities evolve moral principles, as we understand Mr. Spencer to teach, they are conformed in the very process of evolution. Neither human will nor human intelligence have any conforming to do. Moral principles are so-called as a designation of a special phase or manifestation of physical necessities. Essentially they are the same. Principle is not necessity, nor is necessity principle. If principle is derived from underived necessity, then it is not principle, but only a manifestation or mode of necessity. If principle is underived then underived moral principle cannot conform to underived physical necessity. The eternal cannot conform to the eternal. There is no conformity between equals or co-ordinates. But Mr. Spencer, in making "moral phenomena the phenomena of evolution," and in making evolution an underived, unintelligent, unconscious, impersonal, necessary process, includes moral principles in physical necessities ; and to speak of moral principles as conforming to physical necessity, of which it is already only a mode, is a distinction without a difference. If moral principle and physical necessity are the same, there is identity ; but there can be no conformity of the same to the same. If there must be a conformity between the two that there is not in the nature of things, they must be different in kind, and, if different, there is no *nexus* of necessity between them. The underived is necessary to the derived, as the foundation is necessary to the superstructure; for without the underived the derived could not be.

If there can be no evolution with Will and without necessity, so there can be no morality with necessity and without Will. If necessity is the basis of evolution, so liberty is the basis of morality. If nature be the basis of a necessary evolution, so supernature must be the basis of a free morality. To define nature is to prove supernature; for nature is the known and visible part of supernature, the unknown and visible whole.

Evolution as a method, under intelligent Will-Power, is free; but evolution under Power without method of intelligent Will-Power is necessary. Moral or free conduct must be under a method of power; if not under a method of Power, human conduct is not moral. The simple question is, Is there Will in the universe? Will that is Will, and not a mere necessary energy of impulse?

Here the alternative is fully presented of plan or necessity. According to Prof. Hæckel there is no intelligent, prescribed, created plan or method of evolution, but a direct, sharp, unequivocal doctrine of a necessity in all things. If evolution as a method of Power, is denied, this system of necessary materialism is consistent in matter, whatever may be said of it as to mind. Extracts from the "Data of Ethics"

show how much the idea of necessity runs through
Mr. Spencer's presentation of the theory of evolution and of evolutionary morality. That theory is
understood to hold, that an unintelligent, unconscious
and impersonal, natural Power evolves the universe
of mind and matter; not because it intends it, wills
it, or desires it, but because it *must*. The Power
to evolve Nature is held to be this powerless Power
of necessity—powerless because it has no power to
do otherwise than as it does; and that any system of
Natural Morality must have in it this element of
Necessity.

According to the theory of atheistic evolution,
Nature works only by necessary evolution, without
Will; Necessity ignores Will, and Will ignores
Necessity. "The Power manifested throughout Evolution" is Will in itself, and knows no Will out
of itself. If necessary Nature evolves Will as an
impulse of desire, it cannot evolve the decision of
that Will without destroying the Will itself. Will,
to be Will, must be free. Recognizing Will, moral
conduct is commanded as free, and is not evolved as
necessary. So far as Will is ignored, moral conduct
is evolved as necessary and is not commanded as
free; and just as conduct is not free, so it is not moral.

Morality grounded in nature is called, as we have
said, natural morality, and is an evolution either
natural or supernatural. All evolution with plan *in*
nature is supernatural *to* nature. All evolution without plan is natural, and therefore necessary. All
evolution without plan is necessary rather than contingent, for contingent evolution is no evolution.

"The homogeneous must lapse into the heterogeneous." (F. P., § 155.)

Man, in "Morality grounded in nature," called Natural Morality, by observing what Nature does under certain circumstances, infers what, in nature, is best for him to do under other and similar circumstances. In morality "claiming supernatural authority," man not only observes what nature does, and reflects upon what nature, as a reflection of supernature, makes it wise for him to do, but, looking beyond, around and above Nature, he calls directly to the omnipresent Parent, Lord, what wilt *thou* have me to do? In the latter case a moral law is prescribed by authority; in the former, man infers, not a law, but a certain necessity of conduct! But natural necessity is not natural morality. Morality is obedience to moral law; but evolution is not obedience— it is only the process of a method. What is called Natural Morality is the conformity of the conduct of rational beings to "the constitution of things." It is intelligent, conscious, personal man, watching unintelligent, unconscious, impersonal phenomena, rather than the Power behind the Phenomena.

In evolution force is force. It makes no essential distinction between mind-force and matter-force. It distinguishes mind-force from matter-force only in its degree and attributes. In poetic language, these matter-forces may be said to have moral and immoral behaviour—they have their likes and dislikes—their sovereignty and subordination. It is said that chlorate of potash when heated alone will explode like gunpowder; and yet, when heated in the presence of

a black oxide of manganese, it gasifies in quietness
and safety. The chlorate of potash behaves in the
presence of the manganese as if it knew the presence
of a master. Still, it is only unintelligent force
watching and subjugating unintelligent force. But
will it be contended that mind-force watches the phenomena of matter-force only to avoid, or make them
available? Is mind simply the manganese watching
the heated potash? Is it simply one intelligent force
watching and manipulating all unintelligent forces?
Are the watched and the watcher both only different
modes of matter? Is human personality only a
name for a material evolution to be obliterated in a
material dissolution?

Mr. Spencer himself says, in the Preface to his
" Data of Ethics," " What differences exist between
Natural Morality and supernatural Morality, it has
become the policy to exaggerate into fundamental
antagonisms."

The fundamental antagonism is not between two
moralities; but between the two sources of authority
— nature and supernature — of the one morality.
Authority must be of one above, over one below :
and unless there be supernature, there can be no
authority over nature ; for nature cannot be superior
to itself. If natural morality is the natural manifestation of supernatural authority, these fundamental
antagonisms become fundamental agreements. We
have not two moralities, or two systems of morality,
or two authorities of morality. The authority is one
and the morality is one. The methods of proof are
two—the Natural and the Supernatural—or the proof

in evolution and the proof in inspired revelation. The proof of moral rules and ends in nature, by evolution, is called Natural Morality. This method of morality is agnostic or silent about the power by which evolution is evolution.

Morality is called Natural Morality when, ignoring supernatural authority, it claims to be grounded in nature only. But, does the grounding in nature only, give morality a natural *authority*; or does it dispense with the idea of authority altogether, and make it a mere evolution, as inevitable or necessary as all other evolution is claimed to be? It is calling that natural morality which we expect to show is, in fact, supernatural morality. It denies the invisible part of the visible. It denies the Factor in the fact, the lawgiver in the Law.

"We have become quite familiar" says Mr. Spencer, "with the idea of an evolution of structures, throughout the ascending types of animals. To a considerable degree we have become familiar with the thought that an evolution of functions has gone on *pari passu* with the evolution of structures. Now advancing a step, we have to frame a conception of the evolution of conduct, as correlated with this evolution of structures and functions." (D. E., § 3.) "Conduct is acts adjusted to ends." (D. E., § 2.) "Acts are called good or bad, according as they are well or ill adjusted to ends." (*Ib.*) "Evolution becomes the highest possible when the conduct simultaneously achieves the greatest totality of life in self, in offspring, and in fellow men; so here we see that the conduct called good rises to the conduct

conceived as best, when it fulfils all three classes of
ends at the same time." (*Ib.*, § 8.) This is natural
morality. It is human acts adjusted to human ends.
But acts, ends, and adjustments are evolutions; and,
if evolutions, they are necessary.

Some contend that evolution is the free *creative*
method of an *impersonal* Creator. This would imply
an impersonal intelligence, and an impersonal Will,
and an impersonal " Power manifested through evolution work." From the consciousness of our own
personal Will and intelligence we can form no idea
of impersonal Will and intelligence; and so, in all ages,
human personality has thought of a superhuman personality, to account for its own personality.

Evolutionary necessity being admitted or proved,
warrants the direct conclusion that evolutionary
conduct called Natural Morality, being evolved like
gravitation, electricity, and everything else in " the
Constitution of things,,' should be called mere natural
phenomena, not natural morality. Where there is
no Will, there is no morality—no one to command
and no one to obey—and no responsibility, either
personal or civil.

If, according to Prof. Hæckel, that which is with
out method or plan is necessary, then all natural
evolution, being the evolution of a necessary nature
without method or plan, as distinguished from supernatural evolution with a method or plan is necessary evolution. The alternative is Will or Necessity — nature under supernatural Will, or nature
under natural necessity. If nature is necessary, and
if nature is all, then natural morality is necessary in

the agent, necessary in causes, and necessary in effects. If anything is necessary in the universe, everything is necessary—that is, all is necessary or nothing is necessary. The most pressing question in the evolution of morality is, Is man so far a free or moral agent as to enable him to adjust the acts of his conduct to his own and the happiness of others, as an end? Has he a Will so free that it is in his power to obey or to disobey moral authority? Adjustment is an act of Will, extrinsic or intrinsic. The still earlier question in this agnostic evolutionary philosophy is, Is there any authority, strictly so-called, in the universe? or are the acts of man's conduct necessary evolutions, making his Will identical with necessary desires or motives? How are we to understand Mr. Spencer when he says that "every one is at *liberty to do* what he *desires to do* (supposing that there are no external hindrances) all admit; though people of confused ideas commonly supposed this to be the thing denied?" (1 Psy., § 219.)

The Will which he thus admits to be free, his system proves to be necessary. The moral liberty here admitted, seems to be inconsistent with the evolutionary necessity afterwards affirmed by Mr. Spencer, when he says: "But, that every one is at liberty to desire or not to desire, which is the real proposition in the dogma of free Will, is negatived as much by the analysis of consciousness as by the contents of the preceeding chapters." (*Ib.*) Memory, Reason and Feeling simultaneously arise as the automatic actions become complex, infrequent and hesitating; and Will, arising at the same time, is necessitated by these conditions." (*Ib.*, § 217.) He says, " until there is motive (mark the word) there is no Will. That is to say, Will is no more an existence separate from the predominating feeling than a King is an existence separate from the man occupying the throne." (*Ib.*, § 220.)

" Moral principles" and " physical necessities" belong to contradictory systems of truth. Principles are the beginnings of things, and synonymous with cause. A moral principle cannot be a physical necessity, nor can a physical necessity be a moral principle. The terms represent ideas radically different. If a moral principle be a necessary evolution of matter, then, though it may be called a necessary evolution, it cannot be called a conformity. The potter may form the clay, but the clay does not conform to the potter.

If we are to speak of the evolution of morality as Natural Morality, then, what is its authority? Can Nature authorize itself? This depends upon the question; Is there Supernature? If there is supernature, then supernature is the authority for Natural Morality, or it has none. But as morality without authority is no morality, so, as nothing can be authority to itself, Nature is not authority as such to nature, for natural morality to be morality, it must have supernatural authority; and as the authority of nature is supernature, so, for Natural Morality there must be Supernature. If conduct called natural morality be only an evolution, but a necessary evolution, it is evident, as there can be no authority over necessity, that,

First.—All necessary evolution is without (i) moral authority. What is authority? If we understand Mr. Spencer, he ignores all authority. He says (D. E., § 22), "The connexion between cause and effect is one that cannot be established, or altered, by any authority external to the phenomena themselves." But can there be any authority internal to the phenomena?

Authority as authority is underived personal power, prescribing personal conduct. It is not between personal equals, or between impersonal things. 'It is exclusively personal. There is no authority in impersonal power over persons; or in personal power over impersonal things, or in the power of impersonal things over impersonal things. Authority is prescribed Will. Unprescribed Will is power, but not authority. Though the power to originate is the power to control, yet, authority is original power over the conduct of free persons, as distinguished from the original power over the phenomena of necessary things. Underived personal Will is authority over the personal Will derived from the underived.

Agnosticism teaches a necessary, material system, and denies a free, moral system. Mr. Spencer says, "We have seen that during the progress of animate existence, the later-evolved, more compound and more representative feelings, serving to adjust the conduct to more distant and general needs, have all along had an authority as guides superior to that of the earlier and simpler feeling—excluding cases in which these last are intense. This superior authority, unrecognizable by lower types of creatures which

cannot generalize, and little recognizable by prima-
tive men, who have but feeble powers of generalization, has become distinctly recognized as civilization
and accompanying mental development have gone
on. Accumulated experiences have produced the
consciousness that guidance by feelings which refer
to remote and general results, is usually more conducive to welfare than guidance by feelings to be
immediately gratified. For what is the common
character of the feelings that prompt honesty, truth-
fulness, diligence, providence, etc., which men habit-
ually find to be better prompters than the appetites
and simple impulses? They are all complex, re-rep-
resentative feelings, occupied with the future rather
than the present. The idea of authoritativeness has
therefore come to be connected with feelings having
these traits; the implication being that the lower and
simpler feelings are without authority. And this
idea of authoritativeness is one element in the abstract
consciousness of duty." (D. E., § 46.) The power
that produces a tree does not, as authority, command
the tree to come or to live. In other words, neither
production nor sustenance is authority, because production and sustenance, in materialism, are not prescribed. Superhuman power, as Creator, produces
things; and superhuman power, as Authority, commands or prescribes its personal creatures to produce
actions of their own.

Authority is said to be power over conduct. But,
is there any such power? If not, let us change all
our moral ideas and words. If there is any control
over conduct, let us know what it is. Evolution is

ceaseless production, and nothing but production. It produces everything, but commands nothing, unless production is command. But, if there is anything that may be called Authority in the universe, let us define and obey it; if it is supernatural, let us know and reverence it. By admitting authority, we admit responsibility, and by denying either we deny both; and so, all morality, whether natural or supernatural. Unphilosophical conclusions, negativing authority and responsibility, leave conduct without a guide. What our souls are to our bodies, supernature is to nature; therefore, to take supernature out of nature, is to leave society and individual virtue to ask guidance of a silent, awful, deaf corpse. We contend for nature—for supernature in nature—and for personality to that supernature. As authority is personal, if impersonal nature has a morality, it has a morality without authority. But basing morality on authority, as there can be but one undisputed authority in the universe, so there can be but one undisputed morality in the universe. As said before, natural consequences of conduct are the exponents of supernatural authority. Natural consequences are from supernatural power. Morality is, therefore, natural morality on the side of natural consequences, and supernatural morality on the side of supernatural authority. Authority precedes and consequences follow conduct.

There is nothing in an impersonal effect that we are accustomed to think of as personal authority. Authority speaks before conduct; effect speaks after. Authority prescribes what ought to be done; effects subscribe what has been done. Authority in sovereign sympathy commands; effect in silent apathy records. Authority gives a law; effect is the occasion of an inference. Authority says, if you are wise you will not strike the rock with your hand; effect, holding up its bleeding hand, says, I was not wise, and I struck.

As in materialistic necessity there is no such thing as moral conduct, the words "morality," "authority," " responsibility," in the future of evolutionary terminology would cease to be used; for Will, as we know it, being no longer admitted in human psychology, there would be no ideas for these words to represent.

But Natural Morality, if any, as it includes necessity, excludes from conduct not only all authority over freedom, but all moral freedom itself. All necessary morality is without authority. Necessity excludes authority. That which must be, needs no authority. An unintelligent, impersonal constitution of things may compel but can have no authority over an intelligent, personal being. This whole discussion brings us into the presence of the old question of liberty under supernatural authority or no liberty under natural necessity. Morality is human conduct free under authority; if it is inevitable under necessity it is not morality. Authority requires, but does not evolve; Necessity evolves but does not require. Human conduct required or prescribed by authority, is morality; if conduct is not required or prescribed by authority, whatever else it may be, it is not morality. If conduct, evolved under Necessity, be

14

morality, then what is conduct required under authority? Is that morality too? or is there no authority? If conduct free under authority and evolved under necessity, both be morality, there must be some harmonizing power *ab extra*, to make them consistent; making that necessary which it authoritatively commands, and authoritatively commanding what it makes necessary.

There is no authority, as such, in consequences. Consequences may expose to us the absence of wisdom in our past acts, and warn us not to repeat (as if the acts could be repeated) the acts which caused the consequences; but they prescribe or predict nothing as to the other and different acts we may commit in the future. But if conduct be an evolution, it can never be repeated, for evolution never repeats anything. From sameness it ever works towards difference—from the homogeneous to the heterogeneous. As evolution never repeats the past, it can never warn of the future. It cannot tell us the new things it is ever to do. Its necessity to differentiate its work—its committal to perpetual heterogeneity, makes it valueless to experience. It is useless for the experience of consequences to warn us not to repeat acts that we call bad; because evolution assures us that in its necessity to go on, neither conduct nor consequences can be repeated. The office of evolution is to manifest results, not to prescribe moral law.

Are we to understand, when morality, claiming supernatural authority, is contrasted with morality grounded in nature, that morality under authority is supernatural, and morality not under authority, is natural? Again we ask, what is authority? Authority is the supremacy of personal Will over personal Will, and is more than the mere presence of Power, and more than the manifestation of Power through impersonal phenomena; though it may certify itself through these manifestations. Authority is the sovereignty of personal Power, commanding obedience of all persons subject to its control.

According to Mr. Spencer, the only authority is the lesson of facts, or the inferences of experience. But this is not authority as we have been accustomed to think it. Authority is a personal government. We attribute an impersonal authority to the impersonal sovereignty of the state; but the authority is only so in a figurative sense, as it represents the aggregate of personality in the state.

But it may be asked: What is the need of supernatural authority, or authority of any kind? Why may not conduct be reasonable conduct, under neither authority nor responsibility? If the individual reason is competent to decide upon a moral authority, why is it not competent to decide upon moral questions? Why is not the reasonableness of an act a sufficient authority for the act? To what else, they say, but to reason can a man turn in the moral emergencies of conduct—there are no Urim and Thummim to consult? If, according to St. Paul, "the Gentiles which have not the law, do by Nature the things contained in the law," why may not all, like these Gentiles, take the nature of things, discoverable by reason, as all needful authority? Authority, it is said, cannot make that right which, in its nature, is wrong; nor that wrong which, in its nature, is right.

It may be asked, why not reject the idea of authority altogether; or, if there must be authority, why is not rightness its own authority? But, even if a right act needs no other authority than its own righteousness, whence that righteousness? Personal rights are inherent in personal relations. But whence the relations? They are neither eternal nor self-existent, nor are the inherent rights essential to them either eternal or self-existent. Eternal justice or right is a high-sounding phrase; but, in the nature of things, there can be no justice without relations, and evolutionary relations are not eternal. If relations are derived, so are the inherent rights essential to them. Relations and rights come together one with the other. Rights are either absolute or relative. If absolute, they are commanded because they are right; if relative, then they are right because they are commanded. Only underived existence is absolute; only derived existence is relative. The absolute has no rights, for no one can possibly do it any wrong. Rights come and end with relations.

Personal rights in what is called the nature of things are relative, not absolute, because no solitary person has rights; and they are personal, because such things as trees and stones have no rights either as to each other, or as to persons. If brutes have rights, man does not respect them as rights, even their right to live. Personal rights which are essential to personal relations, are the very purpose—aim—ethics—necessity—congruity—exponent of the relations, and exhibit their own laws of essential harmonies. One cannot be related to himself ; but, the coming of two or more people together, constitutes the relation of many in one. New mutual rights inherent in and essential to the new relations co-exist. Moral conduct, therefore, is obedience to authority—the authority of the underived over the derived. Thus, whether authority be that of impersonal nature, as some insist, or that of a personal God, that is right which is essential to the relation or which this authority commands, and that is wrong which it forbids or which is inconsistent with the relation itself.

We never know where a blind man may step—he does not know himself. As like understands like, mind can communicate with mind. It is only the mind in matter that our minds can understand. Human intelligence can somewhat understand the plans of superhuman intelligence. Human conduct can intelligently accommodate itself to Nature only as it understands what nature means. But for nature to mean anything, it must be intelligent; and this, materialistic logic cannot admit.

If an impersonal constitution of things, or what is called Nature, rewards or punishes conduct, it does so intelligently or unintelligently. If Nature be intelligent, it is personal (if external nature is like the nature within us), and if personal, it is God. If external nature is unintelligent, then there is no intelligent reward or punishment for human conduct. An unintelligent sequence to our conduct is material, not moral. When we do what we call a good act, does Nature blindly grasp the act, and do something, not knowing what it does? Does Nature reward our actions, not knowing that it rewards? Does it punish not knowing that it punishes? By theory, impersonal Nature has no intelligence, and does not know what it is doing, whether it is helping or hurting personal nature. Admitting that Nature knows what it is about, and that it always works the same knowing way, human action might intelligently work to it. But what is the use of human intelligence if there be no superhuman intelligence? How can intelligent, personal Nature understand the meaning of impersonal Nature when it has no intelligence to mean anything? If Nature knows nothing, it cannot know when we do a good action, nor when we do a bad action. If Nature knows nothing, it strikes blindly, both friends and foes. As you find intelligence in superhuman Nature, you find God— the human personality finds and understands something of the superhuman personality. Personality can communicate with personality—this must be admitted, or nothing is admitted ; for rational personality cannot communicate with irrational impersonality. We cannot make our minds known to a tree or to a stone, or to " the constitution of things." These have no ear to hear, nor mind to know. The " necessary consequences" of conduct are the only announcements made by " the constitution of things," and this is after, and not before conduct. But as no experiences are ever alike, the constitution of things stands ready to strike after, but never to warn conduct before, of its consequences.

Authority is a personal attribute. I repeat, there is power but no authority in gravitation, chemic affinity, electricity—in a word, in any impersonal force or principle. Authority is the command of a superior to an inferior. Supernature is the authority of nature, if nature has any authority; for nature cannot be over itself and so an authority unto itself. Impersonal nature commands nothing. Impersonal power is to material nature what personal authority is to personal conduct. Necessity is not authority. Advice is not authority. The origin of authority is will; it is always personal; it may be uniform, but it is not necessary.

So far as evolution takes the supernatural out of nature, conduct in what is called Natural Morality, is under no authority;—nor, indeed, in the theory of evolution, is it possible for it to be. The idea of authority disappears altogether from evolutionary speculations. Necessity takes the place of commands; impersonal law ignores a personal lawgiver; unplanned events come along unbidden; a world goes on that never started; man is a machine evolved from that which was not a machine; the universe comes from nothing and from nobody but itself; and, in the instability of the homogeneous, itself that is, is not the itself that was, and is to be. Succession is not identity.

It is said (Intro. D. E., xxiii.) that " When a man eats because he is hungry, he feels the power, but not the *authority* of appetite. When, on the other hand, he refrains from vicious indulgence because its later effects will be bad, or when he takes a walk before breakfast because he believes it will conduce to his health, though its good effect will not be immediately apparent, he recognizes and feels the *authority* of sanitary rules. In these cases the degree of dissociation between the rule or principle recognized by the mind and the actual facts on which it rests is but slight; yet the rise of *authority* is plainly visible. A rule of conduct once established, the mind, working quite independently of the will of the individual, resents any attempt to impugn its authority. Naturally enough, seeing that to impugn its authority means an unsettlement of all that the rule had settled."

In this reasoning, the more that " the rule or principle is dissociated from the actual facts on which it is said to rest," the more authority arises—full dissociation is full authority. And, *e converso*, there is no authority whatever in the complete identity of the rule or principle with the actual facts with which it is associated. In other words, there is no authority where there is identity of producer and produced—of *Natura Naturans* and *Natura Naturata*, and there is authority just as they are distinct. Authority is defined by describing this distinction. In evolution and evolutionary morality, force and its manifestations are one, under two modes.

All this is only the so-called authority of the wisdom of experience ; but experience is not authority. With the materialist, experience is a historian, not a prophet ; it is information, not judgment ; it may persuade, not command ; at most it is a friend, but never a sovereign. Experience is always *after* conduct, never before it ; it is always different and never the same ; it is always individual and never common ; it is always personal and never impersonal ; it is always in mind and

never in matter; it records the actions of the Will,
and a multiplicity of ·sequences; its knowledge of the
past gives neither a hope nor a despair of the future.
With the idealist, experience is but the human knowledge of superhuman authority. A condition is not
authority. We repeat, necessity is not authority; nor
is uniformity necessity. The inevitable is not authority. Evidence is not authority. The writer of the
Introduction finds *authority* for sanitary rules in the
fact that a walk before breakfast conduces to health.
This is but the persuasion of experience, but it is not
authority. Authority commands, not persuades. It
gives a rule, not a reason. Authority may give a rule
through reason, but not give reason as the rule. A
child in some acts, obeys as required by parental authority; in other things, it pleases itself; yet in others it is passive under circumstances. Passive experience is involuntary, and therefore necessary; obedience to authority is voluntary, and therefore moral;
all other conduct is wilfully indifferent to authority,
and selfish, and may or may not be innocent; but *mo
rality is* obedient *conduct required by authority.* Without authority, you may have selfishness, passive en-
durance, but not morality. In this way we see that to
have morality, we must have conduct under authority.

The issue presented is between a religious morality
under supernatural *authority* and a scientific morality
under *no authority.* But the issue is unreal. Science
only investigates where religion worships. What is
objective in nature is subjective in supernature. Natural facts are manifestations of supernatural power
and authority. Science studies the objective, and ig-

nores the subjective, while religion uses the objective to prove the subjective. The morality is one. Science seeks to know it through nature only, without any authority; while Religion proves its authority through both Nature and Supernature.

But the real *authority* of nature, is the Supernatural Will behind nature. The fire would be powerless to burn the child, unless power was given to it; but the fire was not authority. The originator of the fire is the authority of the fire. Nature proclaims only the Supernatural Will. What is called Natural Morality is but the objective manifestation of, and has its authority in, subjective Supernatural Morality. Authority is always above the plane of its action.

If morality is founded on nature, on what is nature founded? Mr. Spencer says (F. P., p. 16), "information, however extensive it may become, can never satisfy inquiry. Positive knowledge does not, and never can, fill the whole region of possible thought. At the utmost reach of discovery there arises, and must ever arise, the question—What lies beyond? As it is impossible to think of a limit to space so as to exclude the idea of space lying outside that limit; so we cannot conceive of any explanation profound enough to exclude the question—What is the explanation of the explanation? If Supernature is denied, is Nature authority unto itself? If so, one part of nature would command another part; as would be the case if matter commanded conduct, and both matter and conduct were called Nature. But, after all, would not the part commanding be supernatural to the part commanded?

Is morality founded on nature, or on a supernatural authority which controls nature? Why restrict the rules of conduct to the lesson of the facts of nature, and deny their authority in the Will of a supernatural Factor illustrated in the facts of nature? To that Will the human inquiry is driven at last.

If morality has no supernatural authority, has it any natural foundation? or is its natural foundation a kind of natural authority? Or has morality no authority? It would seem that morality must be under authority, if anything must. But, if authority is no longer to have place among moral ideas, what is to be substituted for it? Necessity? From our own human will, we infer a superhuman Will, uniform but never necessarily determined, in the constitution of things. All necessary evolution of conduct thus seen to be necessary, is also without,

(ii) Moral responsibility for conduct, for causes, or for effects. Necessary conduct in moral evolution being a necessity of evolution, of course, as a necessity, must exclude moral responsibility. If " moral principles *must* conform to physical necessities," the real and ultimate sphere of human conduct is physical and not moral. But responsibility belongs to the moral and not the physical.

What is responsibilty? It is the answer made by derived will to the prescribed requirements of underived Will. It is the reciprocal of authority. As the authority so is the responsibility. As authority is the power of personal will over personal will; so responsibility is the return which personal will makes to personal will. As action and reaction are equal and opposite, so are authority and its corresponding responsibility—responsibility is the echo of authority. Moral responsibility begins and ends with the freedom of the Will. Deny that, and you deny the moral system of the universe. One atom is not responsible to another atom ; gravitation is not responsible to electricity ; nor is the outcome of physical necessities responsible to moral principles—in fact, in materialism, there are no moral principles. So far as moral principles must conform to physical necessities, they are not responsible to physical necessities for not conforming. This reverses all former moral ideas. The responsibility of mind to matter—of the moral to the physical—is inverting the pyramid. We are *responsible* to authority. We must *yield* to necessity. If we retain the use and the meaning of the words authority and responsibility, we must continue to admit supernatural personality. To give up supernatural personality, we have left, only natural impersonality ; dethroning moral authority and abrogating moral responsibility.

Nature is under control from without, or from within. If it is under control from without, it is, of course, under supernatural authority. If supernature be denied and nature is under control from within, and nature is all, then all is natural ; and conduct commonly called good, and conduct commonly called bad, are, to nature, equally natural, and are, therefore, to nature, equally right and equally wrong. Nature cannot hold man responsible for what nature makes him do.

We have said that all conduct is free or all conduct is necessary ; so far as conduct is necessary, it is a blind, inexorable energy of matter, as much as is that of gravitation, electricity or chemic affinity: and, as an energy of matter, it admits of power but no authority, unless it be a supernatural authority. So far as conduct is free, it is moral, under supernatural authority, and cannot be necessary.

Can morality be called morality in which supernatural authority is denied, and in which even natural authority, or authority of any kind, is not admitted? Is the idea of moral authority no longer to be involved in the idea of morality, and with the loss of the idea of authority are we also to lose the idea of moral responsibility? If the ideas of authority and responsibility are both to be dissevered from our ideas of morality, what is left, but the inexorable, blind, impersonal, unintelligent power of necessity?

Is the universe under Necessity or under Authority? Blind, unintelligent, impersonal Necessity accounts for nothing, not even for itself; intelligent, omnipresent, personal Authority accounts for everything, except Itself. Necessity is a matter-system, and materializes all heretofore mentalized; Authority is a mind-system, and mentalizes all heretofore materialized. Morality is human conduct with a moral purpose. Under which system is morality possible? If under the matter-system, it is called Natural Morality; if under the mind-system, it is called Supernatural Morality.

Necessity is impersonal, and executes without commanding, as in gravitation; authority is personal, and commands without executing, as in the command to do unto others as we would have others do unto us. All physical phenomena, in physical relations, are, primarily, under physical necessity; all moral conduct, in moral relations, is, primarily, under moral authority. That is, where the power and the act are identical, there is no authority and no responsibility; and just as they are dissociated, there is authority and no necessity.

But necessary conduct is not moral conduct. Compulsion creates no duties. If morality is founded in nature, all conduct must be natural as well as the consequences of conduct. But, if Nature is always right, and conduct be all natural, so all conduct would be right, and there should be no detrimental consequences.

So far as the basis of things is material, it is necessary—in a word, so far as moral principles conform to physical necessities, they cease to be moral principles, and necessary conduct is not responsible. We are not to be blamed for doing what we were compelled to do. There is no guilt in necessity. Nature cannot condemn us for being natural. If we are the higher parts of nature, we are not responsible to the lower parts. Equals are never responsible to equals. We must exonerate Nature from all responsibility, unless we enthrone a Supernature to whom it could be responsible.

If man is not responsible for necessary, evolutionary conduct, no more is he responsible for necessary causes in moral evolution, which necessitated the conduct, as a necessary effect. If the conduct of man is an effect of some necessary cause acting upon him, that necessary cause was a necessary effect of

some necessary cause before it, and so on back *ad
infinitum.*

If there is no moral responsibility for necessary
evolutionary conduct, nor for necessary evolutionary
causes, there is no responsibility for necessary effects
in moral evolution. What are effects? Mr. Spencer
says, "Universally the effect is more complex than
the cause." (F. P., § 156.) How can there be any
more responsibility for the effect of conduct, when,
as we have just learned from Mr. Spencer, "the
composition of causes is so intricate, and from moment
to moment so variable, that effects are not calculable?" (1 Psy., § 219.)

How, then, with complex and variable causes, and
with effects so complex and variable that they are
not calculable, can we so determine the "necessary
relations between causes and effects" as to obtain a
rule of moral conduct, and fix moral responsibility?
We cannot understand cause, but can we any more
understand effect? What is cause — the seed, the
soil, or the sun—to the wheat? What is the effect of
the cause—the wheat, the nourishment to the eater,
the deeds he does, or the thoughts he thinks? Effect
follows, but does not come out of, what we call cause.
Night is not the effect of the preceding day. In the
correlation of force there is all of cause and effect
that there is anywhere ; but in the sympathy of direct
correlation, though the presence of one thing is the
presence of some other things, one does not create
the other into its presence. Good labor is the occasion of good wages; the presence of religion is the
occasion of morality, and so on. In the antipathy of

inverse correlation, the absence of one thing is the occasion not the cause for the presence of some other thing; as, when religion is absent, immorality is present. Cause is power, and power acts where it is, but never where it is not. Cause is in the present, not in the past or the future. The absence of heat is the occasion of the presence of electricity. The going of one is the coming of the other. The movement is one of displacement and substitution.

No satisfactory induction of the rules of morality can be made from any necessary relation of cause and effect; because all causes are indefinite and make more indefinite effects; and because conduct is an act of a derived human Will, and as conduct, is not a cause; and what follows is the discipline imposed by the underived, superhuman Will, and as discipline, is not an effect. These two orders of will, the human in conduct and the superhuman in discipline, we must admit, unless we assume that the human will is supreme in the universe and in both conduct and consequences. When Nature manifests no other Will, the superhuman Will is fixed in the constituted order of cause and effect.

Having shown, as we think, that all evolution is necessary, and that all necessary evolution is without moral authority over either the conscience of conduct, the instability of conduct, or the heterogeneity of conduct; and that it is also without moral responsibility for evolutionary conduct, evolutionary causes, or evolutionary effects, it remains only to state, under the present proposition, that

All conduct called Natural Morality is a necessary

evolution; and, therefore, as such, is without either moral authority or moral responsibility. Indeed, this seems to be the opinion of Mr. Spencer himself, when he says: "Thinking of the extrinsic effects of a forbidden act, excites a dread which continues present while the intrinsic effects of the act are thought of; and being thus linked with these intrinsic effects causes a vague sense of moral compulsion. Emerging as the moral motive does but slowly from amidst the political, religious, and social motives, it long participates in that consciousness of subordination to some external agency which is joined with them; and only as it becomes distinct and predominant does it lose this associated consciousness—only then does the feeling of obligation fade.

" This remark implies the tacit conclusion, which will be to most very startling, that the sense of duty or moral obligation is transitory, and will diminish as fast as moralization increases. Startling though it is, this conclusion may be satisfactorily defended. Even now progress towards the implied ultimate state is traceable. The observation is not infrequent that persistence in performing a duty ends in making it a pleasure; and this amounts to the admission that while at first the motive contains an element of coercion at last this element of coercion dies out, and the act is performed without any consciousness of being obliged to perform it. The contrast between the youth on whom diligence is enjoined, and the man of business so absorbed in affairs that he cannot be induced to relax, shows us how the doing of the work, originally under the

15

consciousness that it *ought* to be done, may eventually cease to have any such accompanying consciousness. Sometimes, indeed, the relation comes to be reversed ; and the man of business persists in work from pure love of it when told that he ought not. Nor is it thus with self-regarding feelings only. That the maintaining and protecting of wife by husband often result solely from feelings directly gratified by these actions, without any thought of *must;* and that the fostering of children by parents is in many cases made an absorbing occupation without any coercive feeling of *ought;* are obvious truths which show us that even now, with some of the fundamental other-regarding duties, the sense of obligation has retreated into the background of the mind. And it is in some degree so with other-regarding duties of a higher kind. Conscientiousness has in many outgrown that stage in which the sense of a compelling power is joined with rectitude of action. The truly honest man, here and there to be found, is not only without thought of legal, religious, or social compulsion, when he discharges an equitable claim on him ; but he is without thought of self-compulsion. He does the right thing with a simple feeling of satisfaction in doing it ; and is, indeed, impatient if anything prevents him from having the satisfaction of doing it." (D. E., § 46.)

Mr. Spencer looks forward to the time in the future of the race when, by its accumulated experiences, man will, as naturally as the sun-flower turns to the sun, adjust his conduct to right ends. He will do this not under what we now call authority, or the command of any supernatural Will, but as a physical function. The words moral conduct, moral authority and moral responsibility will become obsolete, in the perfect adjustment of acts to ends.

All Morality without moral authority or moral responsibility, is no Morality ; all so-called Natural Morality is without moral authority or moral resposibility ; therefore, all so-called Natural Morality is, in fact, no morality.

According to the theory of materialistic evolution all nature is evolved unprescribed, and is necessary ; all natural morality is, of course, under nature ; all conduct under nature is necessary ; all necessary conduct is not free ; all conduct that is not free, is not responsible ; and all conduct that is not responsible, is not moral conduct.

But where is this necessity of natural evolution to begin, and where is it to end ? Mr. Spencer speaks of " necessary consequences ;" but how much necessity is in the chain of antecedent causes ? If cause is an evolution, it is necessary as all else in evolution, for all evolution is necessary ; but, if cause is not necessary as an evolution, then evolution does not account for all in the universe. The whole chain of causes and effects preceding conduct as an evolution, is under necessity, or nothing is under necessity and nothing is an evolution. How about free Will ? An evolved Will is a necessary Will, or rather no Will. From views of evolutionary nature—necessary nature—it is clear that, as there is no Will in evolution, things must be as they are, and because Natural Morality is an evolution, it is, therefore, necessary. If so, whatever else evolved conduct may be called, it is a misnomer to call it Morality.   Morality is free, and therefore, moral conduct.   If not free, it is as automatic as the attraction of the sun, but it is not moral.

4. *Evolution must be a supernatural method*, rather than a natural process, in any scheme of possible mor ality.   At the outset, Morality was said to be either evolved or prescribed, or evolved as prescribed.   If morality is a natural evolution, and natural evolution is shown to be a necessary evolution, then natural morality is a necessary morality, or rather, no moral ity.   But if there is a morality at all, it must be free and not necessary conduct; if it be free and not nec essary conduct, it cannot be a necessary evolution ; if it be not a necessary evolution it cannot be a natural evolution, for natural, impersonal evolution is neces sary; if it be not a natural evolution, it must be a supernatural evolution, if it be an evolution at all.

First.—All prescribed morality is free, not neces sary ; and Morality is prescribed when it is neither accidental nor necessary.   It is prescribed if, before acting, we are told how we ought to act.   This we may be told directly, as an inspired written revela tion ; or we may be told this indirectly, by reflecting upon the consequences of past acts.   But whether we be told directly or indirectly, how we ought to act, before acting, we have our action none the less pre scribed ; the rule of action must be prescribed to be the law of action.

Let us look into the laws of matter, the knowledge of the mind, the constitution of nature, and the civil and social relations of mankind, and see if facts war rant the induction, that, as there are no facts without a factor, there is a Factor in nature which nature is not. The belief in the supernatural has universally affected human conduct. Was the belief a delusion ? The world has wrought under the theistic conviction, as if it were true, and under this conviction, whether well founded or not, has been all true progress.

What is called Natural Morality being necessary, is not prescribed ; for, in a system of necessary nature, there is no one free to prescribe. Morality which is prescribed is free, not necessary ; for nature cannot prescribe or require free conduct of one of her own children not free to obey.

We repeat, all prescribed Morality is free, as opposed to necessary morality ; because only a free power could prescribe, and only a free agent could obey. An unintelligent and impersonal nature cannot prescribe to an unintelligent and impersonal stone, that it must gravitate ; when, by a necessary nature, it cannot help gravitating. For morality to be morality, there must be moral freedom, and moral freedom implies that each person is a law unto himself, or that the laws are prescribed to him, which he is free to obey or disobey. If there is any morality which is not natural morality and therefore not necessary, it must be supernatural morality, which is therefore free.

It may be said that the conduct called natural morality is prescribed to the future by the consequences of past conduct—that the present sufferings of a burnt child prescribe to him a command to keep out of the fire in the future—in a word, that all painful experiences may be said to require men to do or not to do certain things. Persons may prescribe conduct to persons; but impersonal nature can prescribe nothing. Mind prescribes to mind, not matter to mind or mind to matter. Morality is obedience of mind to mind, not the conformity of mind to matter. Obedience is intelligent conformity of conduct to authoritative command. Blind, unconscious action is not moral obedience. If moral conduct is the moral adjustment of moral acts to moral ends, who is the Adjuster? Adjustment implies anticipation; anticipation implies intelligence; and, if like is from like, intelligence in us implies its derivation from a higher intelligence. To anticipate the end from the beginning is to know the end from the beginning. Only omniscient Supernature can know all nescient nature.

There can be no morality in necessary nature; therefore, if moral conduct is either prescribed or supernatural, it must be both. So far as conduct is moral, it is prescribed; and so far as prescribed, it must be supernatural; as natural evolution prescribes nothing. Evolution anticipates its work, or it does not. If it does not anticipate its work, then its work is only blind phenomena, implying neither obedient morality nor disobedient immorality. If it does anticipate its work, then evolution is supernatural and is only the method of the Anticipating Power; and what that Power prescribes is right, and what it proscribes is wrong.

To agnostic Evolutionists, Nature is all, and all is necessary; and, therefore, according to Prof. Hæckel and others, all is unplanned and unprescribed. Necessary, and, therefore, not moral conduct, being unprescribed, of course, free, and therefore, moral conduct, is prescribed. As said before, all morality is evolved or prescribed. All evolved morality ignores all Will, and is necessary. All prescribed morality is free, and implies Will. Free conduct is free under law, not above it; and all law is prescribed. But what is Law? Beginning the study of nature with ourselves, we find that Law is Will; Will is one, as the sun; law many, as the rays; as every ray is all sun, so every law is all Will. Will is eternal Power outside of nature taking form as nature; nature is visible Will. Those who deny that law is will, claim that law is a fact—not a cause—that it is a fact that like conditions produce like results. This fact, they say, is law. It has been said that the idea of law is pushing Will from the throne of the universe.

But is the government of law more comprehensible than the government of Will? The power that is uniform as law can be uniform as Will. Besides, uniformity is only an averaging of diversities. Uniformity is as impossible as stability; and, in the eternal instability of the homogeneous, there can be, according to evolution, no stability, and therefore no uniformity. Both uniformity and heterogeneity cannot be—if one is the other is not. But as to Law and Will, distinction of names is not a difference of power. Will is power. Supernatural Will is before, and in, all natural entities. Without will there can be no law. Law implies the uniformity of Will.

Nor can there be law without a lawgiver. With no supernatural intelligence behind unintelligent nature, there is no certain basis for science; for there can be no knowledge of future, unintended movements. All uniformity of law implies plan. Persistent repetition implies purpose and intention. Unless nature is intelligent in the uniformity of to day, we have no intelligent certainty of what is claimed to be an unintelligent uniformity to-morrow. Is the uniformity of nature intentional or unintentional? If intentional it is a personal intention and therefore free; if it is unintentional, the uniformity is impersonal, and is therefore either necessary or accidental. But as uniformity to be uniformity can be neither accidental nor necessary, it must be intentional and therefore personal. What is called impersonal law is only the uniformity of diversities in personal Will.

As relations and their incidental rights are not eternal, but derived, they must be derived from the Underived, which is eternal; and that Underived is authority to all temporal things derived from it. If the Underived Power is thus older than the derived right commanded, then right is because it is commanded, and is not commanded because it is right. If right is commanded because it is right, then right is underived, and existed as right before it was commanded; but right is not older than the relation to which it pertains, and in which relation it was derived and originated. If rights are derived, they are derived directly by command or indirectly in relations. A derived relation expresses the Will of underived Power. Without that Will the relations cannot be; and with that Will all relations begin, with all incident and inherent rights. But the command or constitution of the relation is conceived before the relation and its inherent rights exist. Without the command neither relation nor incident right exists.

Second.—All supernatural morality is prescribed, because so-called natural morality is not prescribed but evolved; and evolved morality, being natural, is therefore necessary. If all that is necessary is all that is natural, then, all that is free is all that is supernatural. Morality being impossible as a natural necessity, we shall see that it is possible only under a Supernatural Power. The Power that made the human mind can prescribe to the human mind. Has it done it? Is there a supernatural Power, and has it prescribed any law to Mental Phenomena?

Mr. Spencer says (F. P., § 105) as we have seen, that "The progress of intelligence has throughout been dual. Though it has not seemed so to those who made it, every step in advance has been a step towards both the natural and the supernatural. All accountable or natural facts are proved to be, in their ultimate genesis, unaccountable and supernatural." If the ultimate genesis of all accountable and natural facts is proved to be unaccountable and supernatural, why is not the ultimate genesis of the authority for moral conduct supernatural? Does supernature restrict its moral manifestations to the natural constitution of things? Supernature may talk by works as well as by words. A tree speaks for supernature as well as the words of a Prophet.

The supernatural is admitted by Mr, Spencer as "absolutely certain." He says (*Pop. Sci. Monthly*, Jan., 1884), as we have seen and now repeat, "Amid the mysteries which become more mysterious the more they are thought about, there will remain the one absolute certainty that he (man) is ever in presence of an Infinite and Eternal Energy from which all things proceed." Is this energy merely natural, and do "all things proceed" by evolution impersonal or personal, or by creation of a personal power? These questions are answered by Mr. Spencer, when he says, " all accountable and natural facts are *proved* to be, in their ultimate *genesis*, unaccountable and *supernatural*." But, if "all things proceed" by an "ultimate *genesis*," what becomes of a continuous *evolution?* or is evolution, in its beginning, a "genesis"? The teaching of religion is, that "all things" are created, and then proceed by the power genetically derived.

We are compelled to admit a basis of things, and that basis, according to Mr. Spencer, is supernatural; so, to exclude supernature from nature would involve the necessity to deny the basis of nature and so nature itself, which nature our senses affirm. Nature is the monogram of Supernature. Where anything is found, we find something supernatural, or the bodying forth of the supernatural. Religion simply adores as a Personal Presence, whatever is admitted to be at the background of things, whether called cause—law—force—or Being.

According to Mr. Spencer, "the natural and supernatural" are "dual," and different not in degree but in kind; therefore, if there be in nature that necessity which is taught by both Mr. Spencer and Prof. Hæckel, then *all* necessity must be in nature, and none whatever in supernature; for that which nature is, supernature is not. If nature is under necessity and supernature is not, then Supernature is the only Power free to prescribe morality.

The Supernatural Power and Person being proved, as we claim, we see that all moral conduct must be under its authority and responsible to its sovereignty. We are now prepared to show that so far as morality is an evolution, it must be a supernatural morality, though a supernatural method of evolution; if we may call it evolution. It is evident, as the opposite of necessary conduct, that moral conduct is conduct prescribed or required by some competent authority. Nature, according to Prof. Hæckel, prescribes nothing. Further: It has been said that we must have a morality claiming supernatural authority or one grounded in nature; but nothing is grounded in nature that has not supernatural authority. Natural morality is the exponent of supernatural authority, not of natural necessity. Nature is but the manuscript of supernature. Nature is the phenomenal side of nomenal supernature. Therefore so far as nature teaches a morality, it teaches under supernatural authority. Nature is an open letter, addressed to all who can read it. Nature is but inspired things, telling in their way what cannot be so well told in any other. But how does the Supernatural *prescribe* morality? How can the Infinite communicate with the Finite? We see the fact to be that like communicates with like. By a sort of fixed inspiration called instinct, the human mother communicates with her offspring. The bird-mother, the brute-mother, and the human mother have no difficulty in making themselves sufficiently understood to their young. There is no difficulty in the Infinite making itself understood and prescribing to the Finite; Impersonal Facts prescribe as they are exponents of a personal Factor. A personal Factor may express his commands through his works as well as through his words. Works then become object-language. A Supernatural Person can talk through natural things, if he chooses to do so; the simple question is: Has he done so? So far as nature is the foundation of morality, it prescribes it,

(i) In Works. We learn from St. Paul (Rom. i., 19), "That which may be known of God is manifest in them; for God hath shown it unto them. For the invisible things of him from the creation of the world are clearly seen, being understood by the things that are made, even his eternal power and Godhead, so that they are without excuse." Beside God's revealing manuscript in Nature, there was a code of moral law given to the conscience of each man. God, at one time "suffered all nations to walk in their own ways; nevertheless he left not himself without witness, in that he did good and gave us rain from heaven and fruitful seasons." (Acts xiv., 17.) St. Paul says, "When the Gentiles, which have not the law, do by nature the things contained in the law, these, having not the law, are a law unto themselves; which show the works of the law, written in their hearts; their conscience also bearing witness, and their thoughts the meanwhile accusing or else excusing one another." (Rom. ii., 12). "The heavens declare the glory of God, and the firmament showeth his handiwork. One day telleth another and one night certifieth another. There is neither speech nor language; but their voices are heard among them. Their sound is gone out into all lands, and their words unto the ends of the world." (Ps. 19, 1-4.)

(ii) In Words. The Bible is written in the language of man, interpreting what God says in His works, and in the events of the world. There are worlds; what do they say? There are events; what do they mean? The prophet, lawgiver, or philosopher, or priest, is the one who reads the doings of God, with infallible correctness. God uses no words of any language. But what He does is what He says. Creation is the language of God. Moses was moved by God (who certainly knew how to move the mind of a creature of His hand) to tell, in his own Hebrew words and style, what God did say, from what He had done, and was doing. St. Paul interpreted God, using the Greek tongue. Newton told what God had done and was doing in gravitation, using the English tongue. So that God is truly and fully interpreted, it matters not what tongue is used. God uses none that man uses. God's teaching is object-teaching. A star, a leaf, a death, means the same to a Gentile as to a Hebrew; though each gives to each thing a different name. The Prophet is so near to God as to understand Him—the godly understand God. We cannot read writing beyond the focus of our vision. Distance from Him, as from all else, blurs the writing we seek to read. Nature is the materialized language of Supernature—the divine pantomime of Time. Some facts speak louder than some words. Science reads in nature the divine hieroglyphics of the message of all that nature is not.

As there is will in the universe, Supernature must prescribe its own mind and Will to Nature; for nature, being necessary, has no will of its own. The larger imparts to the smaller. The whole includes the parts, as Supernature includes nature. Nature ever increases or decreases. To decrease persistently is to cease to be. To increase, is from within itself or without. To increase from within itself is to be superior to itself, and to produce something from nothing. All increase of nature from without, is from supernature. The natural is ever the unbroken evolution of the supernatural.

Modern Scientists in attributing uniformity called law to the operations of Power, deny its personal Will, and call it nature; and all religions, in attributing a personal Will to Power, deny its uniformity, and call it supernature or God.

It is claimed that "all laws shall be conformed to natural morality;" but, if our argument has been valid, there is no natural morality. What is the Power behind Natural Morality, by which it is Natural Morality? The authority, if any, for all morality, is in some supernatural Will, whether supernaturally revealed in Scripture or naturally revealed to mere reason in the deductions of experience, or by the inductions as to what is right and wrong in "the necessary consequences" of actions. Morality is not merely natural morality because nature manifests the consequences of immorality. Natural testimony is not natural power. The witness is not the Court. In supernatural Power, natural morality and supernatural morality are the same. Nature is only a manifestation of supernature. Is there an evolving power *above* evolution manifested *through* evolution? That is the simple question. In other words, is natural morality prescribed by supernatural power?

Mr. Spencer says: "It must be either admitted or denied that the acts called good and the acts called bad, naturally conduce, the one to human well-being and the other to human ill-being. Is it admitted?" ("Data of Ethics," § 18.) If so, what then? Acts that naturally conduce to any results, must have power naturally so to conduce ; that power is either derived or underived ; if underived, it is Supernatural Power (God), acting directly as nature, as the ancient polytheists and nature-worshipers thought ; if derived, it must be derived from the Underived, or is Supernatural Power (God) acting indirectly as nature, as some theistic scientists now think.

Therefore if, as we claim to have proved, the Factor in law is supernatural Will ; if the energies of the mind are supernatural in its present and future attainments, moving from nescience towards omniscience ; if the science of nature reveals a power in nature for which nature cannot account ; if the theistic idea works out in civil society as the surest civilizer, we claim,

Third. Therefore, as all supernatural Morality is free, there can be no natural or necessary morality. There is nothing necessary in the universe, if there is any free will in it.

If evolution covers mind as well as matter, it must be because matter becomes mind, or because mind is as necessary as matter. But the moral system is something that the material system is not. The material system of evolution is government without a Governor—it is intelligent work without intelligence in the worker. But such conclusions are not consistent with known facts and phenomena. Will in its work cannot be accounted for as mentalized matter. For this Will, Supernatural Power, Mr. Spencer says: " Right, as we can think it, necessitates the thought of not right, or wrong, for its correlation ; and hence, to ascribe rightness to the acts of the Power manifested through phenomena, is to assume the possibility that wrong acts may be committed by this Power. But how came this to exist, apart from this Power, conditions of such kind that subordination of its acts to them makes them right, and insubordination wrong ? How can Unconditioned Being be subject to conditions beyond itself ?" (" Data of Ethics," Ch. xv., § 99.)

Unconditioned Being is not subject to conditions beyond itself. We cannot ascribe rightness to the acts of the Power manifested through phenomena, and therefore by no possibility can wrong acts be committed by this Power. Whatever this power, manifested through phenomena, may do, is *sovereign*, and so is neither right nor wrong. Right is obedience to sovereign authority ; and wrong is disobedience to sovereign authority, but sovereign authority can neither obey nor disobey itself. But why admit the Power and deny the intelligence manifested through phenomena ? And, if we admit the intelligence, why deny the Will; and if we admit the Will, why deny the personality, and if we admit the personality, why deny God ?

Is a supernatural method suitable to Will, quite different from its method in matter that has no will of its own? The moral system is based on commands prescribed by superhuman Will to a human Will. In the material system, there are no prescriptions or commands, but work is done without commands. There are no commands, because there is no ear to hear commands, and no Will to obey or disobey commands. If the materialistic system, which is the system of evolution, be the true and only one of the universe, then the material nature did a useless work in evolving human Will.

But in accepting either natural or supernatural morality, both are accepted; for nature and supernature are as inseparable as sunshine and shadow. The rose without the sun in its color, and in its perfume, is no longer the rose. Without supernature, nature is no longer nature.

There is no assortment of moralities. If, according to Prof. Hæckel and Mr. Spencer, nature is necessary and has no plan, then, as plan *in* nature, must be supernatural *to* nature, all evolution—all evolution of moral conduct—with method or plan, or, in the language of Mr. Spencer, with "adjustment of acts to ends"—with purpose, with Will—must be supernatural. Do we observe any *plan* in nature? If evolutionary conduct be not natural and therefore necessary, it must be supernatural and therefore free.

Morality is possible only through freedom under a supernatural Will, revealed in written form, or developed in the consequences of conduct, or in both. If it be admitted, that, it is only under supernatural

16

authority, that acts commonly called good, and acts commonly called bad, naturally tend, the one to human well-being and the other to human ill-being, there will be no disagreement. It is not that morality is an evolution, but only as that evolution is denied to be a supernatural method, that the disagreement arises. Natural evolution is a mere process, without authority or responsibility, and cannot possibly evolve a morality. To supernatural evolution only, as a method of Will, is a morality possible. As Nature according to Prof. Hæckel, being necessary and without method or plan, prescribes nothing, so all prescribed conduct must be supernatural.

We have said, that there is no Natural Morality; for, if Nature is all, then all is natural, whether it be conduct commonly called good or conduct commonly called bad; and Nature does not hold man responsible to nature for conduct which Nature prompts. But if Nature is not all, then all that nature is not, is Supernature, and is authority to Nature for all the conduct required of man, and is also the Power for all the phenomena of Nature. Supernature to be Supernature must be *authority* to require of Nature, what Supernature may determine. Nature is the FACT, Supernature is the FACTOR.

If what is called Natural Morality, is not required or prescribed by supernatural authority, and if natural morality must have an authority, and nature can be no authority unto itself, then there can be no natural morality. That which is called Natural Morality, has, in fact, a supernatural authority, if any, and is ultimately, a Supernatural Morality. Supernatural morality is none the less supernatural because it has natural methods and verifications. Natural Morality must have either no authority, or a natural authority, or a supernatural authority. To say that natural morality has no authority, is to say, that it is necessary, and is therefore no morality. To say that natural morality has a natural authority, is to say, that conduct is an authority unto itself, which is impossible. To say that Natural Morality has a supernatural authority, is to say that with a supernatural authority, it is supernatural, and not natural morality.

Natural Morality as a natural evolution, is a necessity, and there is no authority in necessity and therefore no morality. We first meet authority, when we first meet personality, in all human associations. Impersonal authority is a conventional arrangement, and not an essential reality. Though, in philosophical discussion, traditional opinion of minds ever so eminent is not argument; yet it is significant, of the idea of the fundamental constitution of things, that nearly all who have professed a belief in what, in any sense, might be called Natural Morality, have also been believers in a Supernatural Authority, behind it. A supernatural Person has, almost universally, been admitted to exercise ultimate personal authority over impersonal nature.

Mr. Spencer stops at nature, where science stops. He does not deny supernature, but affirms it; but he announces no specific trace of it in Nature. He admits a phenomenal connexion between what he admits of supernature and what he knows of nature. The both are, and he admits that all accountable and natural facts are proved to be in their ultimate genesis, unaccountable and supernatural, and there he firmly stops. To draw the inferences from what he admits of supernature, furnishes the proof of the religious supernatural person—GOD.

Natural and Supernatural morality are two names for the same moral economy of one power. That morality which is verified in natural conseqences, is authorized in supernatural law or Will. This one Power of the universe, stereotypes the rules of what some call natural morality in "the constitution of things," as well as specially reveals them in human utterances. The evolutionary school of thought recognizes only the physical basis and an impersonal power; but how it can affirm the power and deny the intelligence, or how human personality can deny superhuman personality, is inexplicable. If like is from like, then the fact of personality in man implies a personal Factor of that personality. With religion, a personal power and intelligence gives the law of conduct, and adapts upon its violation, such consequences as it may determine, and, though the systems of manifestations may be two, there is but one morality. Now, whether this one morality should be called natural or supernatural, depends upon the answer to the questions: Do we admit the supernatural any where, and what is its relation to nature, and what control has it over conduct? Has morality any authority of law or not? If not, how is it morality? If it has any authority of law, is that law natural or supernatural? Authority is the control of an inferior by a superior. Nature, therefore, must be under the

control of supernature or be under no control; for
it cannot be superior to itself and so control itself, or
be inferior to itself and put itself under the control
of itself, or make its own laws inexorably unalterable
over itself; for if it made its own laws, it can repeal
or suspend its own laws. If nature is thus its own
lawgiver, it is superior to itself, which is impossible.

Every human act is either necessary or not necessary. If necessary, it is no more morally responsible
than the necessary phenomena of gravitation or of
electricity. If not necessary, the act is moral. For
every moral act there is a moral law and a moral consequence. The moral law *pre*scribes what the moral
consequence of conduct will be, and the moral consequence *sub*scribes or testifies what the moral law is.
Law implies consequence, and consequence implies
law—one looks to the other.

Now, if moral consequences are from moral law,
from what is moral law? As the universe is *under*
law, so law is *over* the universe. In other words,
from Supernature must come the laws of Nature.
Therefore, the natural consequences of a moral act,
prove the supernatural authority of the moral law.
All will agree to a natural morality which manifests
a supernatural authority.

We call morality supernatural when we fix our
attention upon, and magnify the supernatural law,
and lose sight of the natural consequences of conduct: and we call morality natural morality, when
we fix our attention upon, and magnify the natural
consequences of conduct, and lose sight of the supernatural law. For instance, the natural consequences

of drunkenness is disease—it naturally tends to the ill-being of the drunkard. From these consequences, the law is deduced that drunkenness is wrong. One says that this law is a natural law because testified to by what is called nature. Another says, that all natural laws are but an expression of supernatural authority. In fact, all nature is the objective side of supernature. Certainly, if the consequences of of conduct are natural, the law by which consequences are consequences, must be supernatural: for the law must be above the consequences of its violation. That is authority to another which has power over that other; and, thus, in the power of supernature over nature, it is authority to nature. The supernatural, in the sense of eternal intelligence, justice and power, *does not command things because they are right, but things are right because commanded by the supernatural.* We are accustomed to speak of things as *eternally* right or wrong in the nature of things. But the supernatural only is eternal; and nothing was either right or wrong before supernaturally constituted. Rights and wrongs belong to relations; but relations are neither eternal nor unchangeable. Therefore, the Absolute Being we call God, having no relations, cannot, except in an accommodation of terms, be said to be either right or wrong. To be one implies the possibility, at some time, of being the other; but, as the Absolute by no possibility could be wrong, so by no possibility could the Absolute be right: In a word, the Absolute, excluding all relations, is entirely apart from all rights and wrongs of relations, and there are rights and wrongs no where else than in relations. Obedience and disobedience, reverence and irreverence, holiness and unholiness, are quite different states. We must look for knowledge of right and wrong to supernatural authority, however attested.

There can be no relation between the concrete and the abstract—between the noumenon and the phenomena—between Power and the shapes it manifests. Relations are either personal or impersonal. Impersonal relations reveal only impersonal forces. There can be no moral relations of right and wrong between the acorn and the oak—between the falling stone and the man it kills—between any merely physical cause and its merely physical effect.

Personal relations of men to man primarily reveal what are the laws of the relations, and what are called their rights and wrongs. These personal relations are either mutual or reciprocal. Rights and wrongs come and go with these personal relations. The laws of the relation are fixed in the relation. The relation reveals that as right which never was a right or a wrong before. As the relation so are the correlative rights and wrongs. The question is, was it right or wrong to establish the relation? Did Power establish relations because they were right, or were relations right because they were established by Power? It was neither right nor wrong for Power to establish what it did establish. Shall the clay say to the potter, why has thou made me?

God never made a right or a wrong except as He made it in a relation. He made man a creature of relations, and gave power to man to act; and man's acts are right as they consist with the relation, and wrong as they do not. Under delegated power an agent may misuse his power; but the guilt is in the misuse of the power, not in its bestowment. Physical ills may or may not be connected with moral guilt. Moral action is only human and individual. Moral guilt is human conduct violative of human relations to man and to God, and duty to himself. What are called rights and wrongs are names we give to human actions in human relations. All that is from God in these actions is the power to act, and the persuasion to act for the ends of the relation. We cannot call the stroke of the lightning right, nor can we call it wrong. Nor can we call the destructions of the whirlwind right, nor can we call them wrong. Nor can we call the bite of beast or reptile wrong, nor disease nor pain, nor death, wrong. There is no right and no wrong to the action of impersonal forces or to the inevitable; but there is right or wrong as we act according to the prescribed laws of our relations. Rights and wrongs go no further. God appoints the relations, and we do right or wrong in them. Wrong is something purely of human will. Superhuman Will has nothing to do with the origin of wrong. It is the act of created Will first, last and all the time. If men could be regenerated into gods, there would be no wrongs, and rights would be known as conditions, not as rights.

President Noah Porter says (Moral Science § 46): " Moral distinctions are not originated by the arbitrary *fiat* or *will of the Creator.*" Why not? Are these moral distinctions older than the Creator? Moral distinctions originate in moral relations, but who established the relations? Moral distinctions are not eternal—not older than the relations to which they pertain. They are not of the nature or being of God, for they pertain alone to relations, and God is Absolute., not relative. Municipal law for municipal ends, distinguishes between *mala in se* and *mala prohibita*. But all wrongs are *mala prohibita*, express or implied ; and may be *mala in se*, because they are *mala prohibita*. All human actions essential to human relations are imposed by the very relations themselves ; and the constitution of the relation in itself prohibits its disregard. New relations are new laws. Law is in the relation. The evolution of human experience is codifying the *lex non scripta* of human relations. From all this we conclude that rights and wrongs are exclusively in human relations ; and rights are right because they are established, and not established because they are rights. The establishment of rights and wrongs in human relations was a manifestation of absolute sovereignty. The absolute owes no rights and can do no wrong, for the Absolute is antecedent to all spheres of the relative. Divinely appointed self-preservation and self-perfection and progress, are the end of all rights, and in themselves the implied Prohibition of all as wrong that prevents these ends.

Conventional morality or the avoidance of conventional *mala prohibita*, is the obedience of individuals to society. What we here call conventional morality may be essentially immoral, in arbitrarily forbidding two relative rights as if they were wrong, or in commanding wrongs as if they were social rights. *Mala prohibita* are not always *mala in se*. *Mala in se* are violations of the ends of divinely appointed relations; while *mala prohibita* are violations of the ends of socially appointed relatives. Their guilt is measured by the authority disobeyed. We must remember that might does not make right. Only supernatural authority, whether express or implied, direct or indirect, can constitute the act in a relation as right, and consequently forbid an act as a wrong. God's will only is right.

Finally, all free Morality is responsible; all supernaturally prescribed Morality is free, therefore all supernaturally prescribed Morality is responsible. All responsible conduct is prescribed Morality; all supernaturally prescribed conduct is responsible conduct; therefore, all supernaturally prescribed conduct is Morality.

Again ; take a thousand years, say from the beginning of the secularization of law in the Twelve Tables, B. C. 500, down to the close of the Schools under Justinian, A. D. 530, and the Fall of the Empire, and we see that the human will as evolved and adjudicated as natural morality and as a center of political life, had been moving to its maximum ; and also, sad to say, to its long sleep in the mental prostration of the Dark Ages. After the Superhuman Will opened the doors of light, civilization awoke to a new dawn and a new life. Final progress is in the persistent supremacy of Superhuman Will.

The following tables and figure show the evolution and correlation of ancient religions, ancient philosophy, and ancient Roman Civil law, for over 1,000 years; by these we may see at a glance, the great factors working to the great results exhibited.

LAW.

PRIVATE RIGHT. REPUBLIC.
Laws, as the will and reason of Man.

1. Senatus Consulta....B. C. 735-222 A. D.
2. Leges of the Centuriata......B. C. 500
3. Plebescites of the Tributa......446-286
4. Twelve Tables......445
5. Connubium......444
6. Edict of Pretor (*Urbanus*)......364
7. Pretor gave inheritance to blood-kin.

OFFICIAL RIGHT (STATUS). Plebians as:

1. Military Tribune......445
2. Consul......366
3. Dictator......356
4. Censor......351
5. Pretor......337
6. Pontiffs and Augurs......300
7. Pretors Peregrinus......247
8. Universal Reason as Law.
   Jurisconsults.
   (a) The Scævola......Circ......185
   (b) Servius Sulpicius......124-87
   (c) Cicero......106-43

EMPIRE.

Of 88 Emperors.

1. Imperial Constitutions.
   (a) Edicta,
   (b) Rescripta.
   (c) Decreta.
   (d) Mandata.
2. Institutes of Gaius.
3. The Perpetual Edict.
4. Jurisconsults.
   (a) Papinian and his pupils......193-211
   (b) Ulpian......228
   (c) Paulus......222
   (d) Modestinus......Circ......225
5. Codes.
   (a) Gregorian......306
   (b) Hermogenean......365
   (c) Theodosian......438
   (d) Justinian......528
       Code.
       Digest.
       Institutes.

1000 Years of Law.

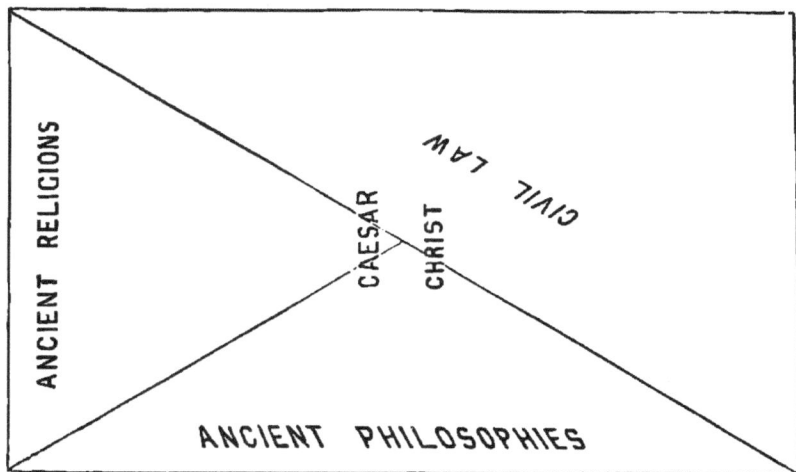

ANCIENT RELIGIONS — ANCIENT PHILOSOPHIES — CAESAR — CHRIST — CIVIL LAW

1000 Years of Philosophy.

PHILOSOPHY.   B. C.

Thales......Living Water......639
Pythagoras......Unity......584
Xenophanes......Pantheism......550
Anaximander......Motion......547
Anaximenes......Air......527
Parmenides......Pure Being......529
Heraclitus......Fire......500
Anaxagoras......Theism......500
Zeno of Ela......Refutation......500
Democritus......Atoms......490
Protagoras......The Sophist......490
Empedocles......Four Elements......444
Socrates......Common Sense..b. 469
Plato......Ideal Truth......429
Diogenes......The Cynic......400
Aristotle......Deduction......383
Antisthenes......Pleasure an Evil......371
Aristippus......Pleasure a Good......366
Zeno the Stoic......Fortitude......351
Epicurus......Ease......341
Arcesilus......New Academy...b. 315
Pyrrho......Skepticism......d. 270
Carneades......New Academy...b. 213
Chrysippus......A Stoic......208
Philosophers banished from Rome.155
Panætius...Eclectic Stoicism.180-111
Posidonius......Rhetoric......135-50

NATURE.   MAN.

ANNO DOMINI.

Seneca............Morality. B.C. 7-65 A.D.
Philosophers banished by Vespasian..70-79
Epictetus............Morality............94
Philosophers banished by Domitian......94
M Aurelius......Morality...... . 21-180
Boethius.. 470-525
School of Philosophy at Athens closed
   by order of Justinian......526
Dark Ages.

This table exhibits the utter insufficiency of what is called natural morality, evolved in the uninspired moral wisdom of the Philosophers and the Jurisconsults, as against the supernatural morality of Moses and the Messiah. Never before or since has the morality of human wisdom without religion been so signally tried, and never has it so signally failed. Not that the Justinian Codes were without value. As adjucated civil morality, they have been unsurpassed; and their value, warmed and enlightened by a great religion, has been great; but nothing merely human is sufficient. "Our sufficiency is of God."

> From shining star to lowly grassy sod,
> Is naught but forms unfolded by a God.
> Like deepest shadows cast by brightest day,
> All evolution is His veiléd way.
> For Supernature, fixed in nature's laws,—
> That brings effects from out itself, the cause,—
> Evolves small things from great, not great from small;
> For God it is who worketh all in all.

LECTURE V.

METHOD OF CORRELATION.

Everything is related, but everything is not correlated. Without mutuality or reciprocity there is a mere relation in time and space between a stone and a chair or between a mountain and a star; but there is correlation when, by a fixed law, things follow as consequences in cause and effect, or co-exist in pairs, as husband and wife, or as uniform sequence in light and darkness. In other words, correlation is either a *method*, a *state*, or a *movement*.

1. *Correlation as a method.* The most terrible certainty in all the economy of nature is the law of equivalence. Correlation is its method, which we are now to consider. The light of science that reveals the behaviour of forces in matter also unveils and emphasizes the awful law of moral exchanges. For so much wrong, we get an equivalent of suffering. But if we measure the moral magnitude of the cause by the multiplicity of its effects, and their undying continuance, we shall see that though a cause is only one thing, it is vast. In physics. we can see so much of one force given for another; but in moral move-

ments the equivalence of a wrong is never full. Men reap one hundred grains for the one they sow. That which we measure to others, they measure to us again; good measure, pressed down, and running over, is surely returned to us.

The nature of things, as seen in correlation, admits of no escape. Nature may heel the wound you make, but she will mark its place with a scar. If you injure moral character, like footprints in the snow, it can never be smooth again. The one sin of woman has its equivalence in an outcast's life. The law of heredity perpetrates ancestral disease to remote generations. Men erect for themselves moral tombs or moral thrones, and each act is a block in the structure built without hands. Consequences are remorseless demons; and, as has been so beautifully said, are as much beyond our control as are a handful of feathers which you scatter to the winds.

2. *Correlation as a state.* Things are related as unconnected parts of a connected whole, such as is the relation of sea, house, tree; or they are correlated, as we have said, into co-existing and inseparable pairs. Heraclitus taught that nothing exists without its contrary, and that to speak of one is to suggest its opposite. Pythagoras and Aristotle mention ten of these pairs:

Finite and Infinite,	Rest and Motion,
Odd and Even,	Straight and Crooked,
Unity and Plurality,	Light and Darkness,
Male and Female,	Good and Bad,
Right and Left,	Square and Oblong.

These co-existing pairs are sometimes of persons, as husband and wife, parent and child, guardian and ward, master and servant, vendor and vendee, buyer and seller, and mortgagor and mortgagee; sometimes in pairs of co-existing forms, as concavity and convexity; or of quantity, as much and little, *plus* and *minus;* or of attributes, as straight and crooked; or of direction, as up and down. Thus we see that, in correlative *states*, pairs of dissimilar things' must co-exist, and that the mention of one of the pair suggests the existence of the other. The husband ceases to be husband when the wife dies. Without a child there can be no parent, without a servant no master. Take away one of two parallel lines, and the other is no longer a parallel, as a line cannot be parallel to itself. As the describing of a curved line makes one side concave and the other convex, so the obliteration of that curved line obliterates both the concavity and the convexity. Forces are in accord or in discord with each other. Accordant forces are in direct correlation; discordant forces are in inverse correlation.

3. *Correlation as a movement* is where one thing is as its correlative is, like labor and wages; or one thing is as another is not, like right and wrong. Correlation is either direct or inverse.

(*a*) Direct correlation is seen when any two quantities. qualities, or forces mutually increase or decrease together in the same ratio. Thus wages vary directly as work; that is, the greater the work the greater the wages, and the less work, the less wages." This is illustrated by the two opposite and equal triangles, formed by the perpendicular line A C, in the square A B C D, in the figure below.[a]

(i) In matter force it is a demonstrated principle that *action and reaction are equal and opposite.* Exactly as your finger presses the table, the table presses your finger. That which you strike, strikes you back. If you disappoint the moral sense of society, the moral sense of society will disappoint you. As

---

(*a*) In this law of direct correlation, the forces are in accord—both are positive or *plus* or both are negative or *minus*—the minimum of one is the minimum of its correlative, and the maximum of one is as the maximum of its correlative ; both increasing or decreasing in the same ratio. Read across the figure from left to right. Notice, that the perpendicular of the square, standing on one of its angles, is the diagonal of the square on one of its sides, as in Fig. 2.

DIRECT CORRELATION.

Fig. 1.

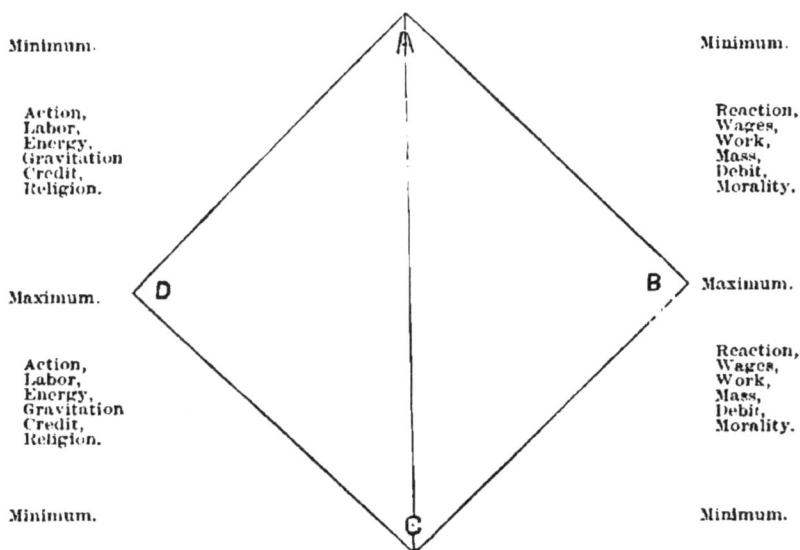

Minimum.

Action,
Labor,
Energy,
Gravitation
Credit,
Religion.

Minimum.

Reaction,
Wages,
Work,
Mass,
Debit,
Morality.

Maximum.

D

B

Maximum.

Action,
Labor,
Energy,
Gravitation
Credit,
Religion.

Reaction,
Wages,
Work,
Mass,
Debit,
Morality.

Minimum.

C

Minimum.

your hand warms the marble, so the marble cools your hand. The gun with which you kill the bird before it, recoils and bruises you behind it. We cannot electrize a substance without magnetizing it, nor magnetize a substance without electrizing it. Before the laws of matter everything is equal. Nature enforces obedience. Every atom protects itself, instantly arresting, judging, and punishing each of fender against its rights. Man cannot lie to Nature, nor extort upon her, nor rob her. Her motto is, *semper fidelis, semper paratus.*

(ii) In moral forces this direct correlation is no less evident. These antitheses and syntheses of forces are seen in the movement of demand and supply ; in credit and debt ; and in cause and effect. Some things are inverse as to one movement and direct as to another. For instance, religion is inverse as to immorality, and direct as to morality. Labor is inversely as to poverty, but directly as to wages. Velocity is directly as to force, and inversely as to time. Law is inversely as to morality, but directly as to crime. Civilization, generally, is directly as to worship and knowledge and inversely as to ignoance and irreligion. Passion correlates itself in a corresponding expression. Anger is violent, grief weeps, pleasure smiles, and hope rejoices. Persecution and oppression beget resistance, and injury correlates itself in revenge. The more alcohol the more is the intoxication. Food correlates itself in strength. The rose pays its debts to the sun, in its perfume and color. Vice has its exact equivalent in loss of character, and known fraud, in loss of credit and business.

17

(*b*)   Inverse correlation[a] is where dissimilar qualities or forces are so related that when one is increased
by any law of change, the other shall equivalently
decrease by the same law.   The purpose of this lecture is to show, through the laws of inverse correlation or conversion, how one force seems to become
or be converted *into* another.   The process is rather
displacement and substitution than conversion.   It is
transposition as distinguished from transmutation, but
it is substitution rather than either.   It is one thing
for another.   But as in direct correlation neither of
the co-existing pairs we have mentioned can be *absent*
at the same time, so now, in inverse correlative movement, both reciprocal energies cannot be *present* at
the same moment.

This illustrates how the many effects of the one

(*a*)   INVERSE CORRELATION.

Fig. 2.

Read across the figure.

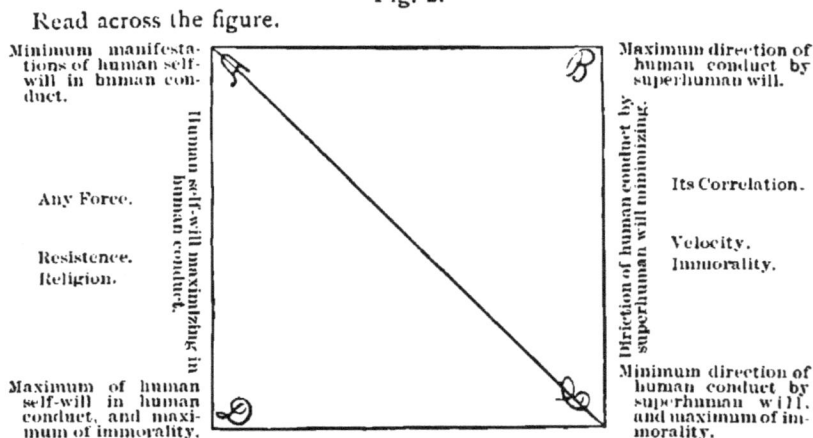

When the square of Fig. 1, marked A B C D, is placed upon its side
C D, the line that was a *perpendicular* from A to C in Fig. 1, is a *diagonal*
from A to C as in Fig. 2.

Power, that seem to us to conflict, do not conflict to Power itself. Power is one; its manifestations are many. That which to us is plurality in nature is, some how, unity in supernature. The same thing is different in different views. Correlations that are direct or inverse to us are not so to correlating Power. Relativity is a law of doubles: two cross lines make four angles. It does not require one act to make one side of a curved line convex and another act to make the other side concave; the opposite sides are made by one act. For instance, matter integrates as motion dissipates: that is, the integration of matter is *plus* as the dissipation of motion is plus; but it is just as true to say, that the integration of matter is *plus*, just as the absorption of motion is *minus*.

Herbert Spencer says that "one force, in giving origin to the next, is itself expanded or ceases to exist *as such.*" When the lower chamber of the hour-

---

Shakespeare expresses this correlation, in the play of "Coriolanus," when Aufidius says:
> "One fire drives out one fire; one nail, one nail;
> Rights by rights foiled, strengths by strengths do fail."

Benvolio tells Romeo:
> "One fire burns out another's burning;
> One pain is lessened by another's anguish;
> Turn giddy, and be holp by backward turning;
> One desperate grief cures with another's languish.
> Take thou some new infection to thine eye,
> And the rank poison of the old will die."

Lear tells Kent:
> "Where the greater malady is fixed,
> The lesser is scarce felt."

And so Virgil, when he says, "*Uno avulso non deficit alter:* Where one thing is absent, another takes its place."

glass is full the upper is empty. We must be careful
to remember that the force which expires may be a
cause or only an antecedent to the one that survives or takes its place. We cannot say that that
causes electricity, but only that so much of one goes
as so much of the other comes. When a virtuous
man is perverted into a vicious man, his virtues are
not a cause of his vices; or when a vicious man is
converted into virtue, his vices are not a cause of his
virtues. When day precedes the night, the day is
not the cause of the night, nor night an effect of
the day because it follows the day. The horse is
not a cause of the cart because it is before it, nor
the cart an effect of the horse because it follows the
horse. Substitution is not causation. Sequences are
not consequences. But there is a correlative movement in the dropping of the sand in the hour glass,
from the upper chamber to the lower; unless one be
emptied, the other cannot be filled. The chain that
pulls up a full bucket lets down an empty one. The
rod dropped from the hand of Moses became a serpent on earth. Exactly as one, so was the other. The
unknown quantity of the equation is ever transfer-
ring or correlating itself into the known. Ignorance
shrinks as knowledge expands. Both in the material
and moral world, when one thing is more, something
else is exactly that much less. The force is the same,
the manifestation only is different.

(i) In matter force this inverse correlation takes
place when one unconscious force exchanges itself
for another, and acts inversely as the other ceases.
Herbert Spencer says, that " when a given force

ceases to exist under one form, an equal quantity must come into existence under some other form or forms." You cannot both expend and keep a force. The butterfly begins to live as the mother-worm dies. In the revolutions of the wheel, one part cannot come up except as the other parts go down. The grain of wheat is quickened as it dies. Water leveling itself from one vessel to another decreases its quantity in one exactly as it increases it in the other. Increasing light contracts but intensifies the shadows. In other words, the maximum of one manifestation of force coincides with the minimum of its correlative force. If you gain motion you lose heat, and as you gain heat you lose motion. Though nature is always in debt, yet she keeps a careful balance-sheet with exact and scrupulous honesty, returning what she borrows, and paying for what she consumes. In agriculture, you must restore to the soil an equivalent for that which you take from it. If nature uses heat, she pays in electricity or some other force; if she dissipates motion, she compensates by integrating matter. In all action she pays by equal and opposite reaction. Nothing is fruitless. When the unheated rifle-ball strikes the iron plate, the plate stops the ball, flattened and heated. The brake on the wheel takes motion from the wheel, but gives it heat instead. Both the ball and the wheel lose one energy, but gain another that is a fair equivalent. But a force and its equivalent in reciprocal or inverse correlation are both present at the same moment. As an electrical rod cannot have both positive and negative electricity on the same end; and as, generally, two opposite energies cannot both be present at the same time and place, yet, if one be absent the other will be present. Nature is vigilant but economical. When she uses one force, she rests some other. Like a relief of sentinels, when one is off duty, another is on. Correlation shows, as we have seen, how one " matter force," in giving origin to the next, is itself expended or ceases to exist *as such ;* and how much one mode of force is the equivalent of so much of another mode. It has been likened to a mart where we barter or exchange one kind of force for its equivalent in another. It is rather a bank from which we do not draw the identical coin we deposit, but only its equivalent in other coin. But as no credit is given, we must first deposit before we can draw at all. Every force, as it has been said, is preceded by some other force. The law of compensation that adjusts the exchange in this correlation gives one force *after* another. In brief, nature keeps things exactly where she wants them, and in perfect harmony, looking and moving in the direction of ultimate perfectibility.

Correlative movements in matter are necessitated by three universal and omnipotent principles in nature : *First*—All physicists, from Aristotle down, say, that nature abhors a vacuum. Everywhere must be something, solid or fluid, and but one. A moral vacuum is as impossible as any other. If man has not virtues he will have vices. *Second*—Though there can be no vacuum, and nature fills every place with something, she only puts one thing in any one place at the same time. In things that run in successive pairs, such as day and night, virtue and vice, you will have exactly as much of one as you do not have of the other. Just as morality goes immorality comes. They are not companions. Two kings cannot sit on the same part of the throne at the same moment. Nature never attempts the impossible. The laws of impenetrability forbid space to have too much of anything. The driven wedge or nail, or the stone in the water, each displaces its own bulk, and no more. Shadows increase with the departing sun. The roots of the tree displace their own bulk of earth in which they are fastened. Two opposite trains cannot pass each other on the same track. In addition to this abhorrence of a vacuum and this law of impenetrability of matter and of incompatibility of morals, there is, *thirdly*, the fact of universal unrest. Nothing is stationary. Forces are ever in unstable equilibrium, and character is ever oscillating to an average. As, if you mix a pint of the seed of tares with a bushel of wheat, you will average upward in value, so you will average downward if you mix a bushel of tares with a pint of wheat. The moral average of character and conduct will depend on the proportion of its virtues to its vices. In colors, you will have a shade or a tint, as the light or the dark predominates in the hue.

(ii) In moral force there is also an inverse correlation. Systems do not conflict, but agree. As in matter, force is any power that does work, such as gravitation, heat and electricity; so, sacred or moral force is any power or influence that affects conduct or shapes civilization, such as love, adoration, and awe in worship, the sacredness of domestic relations, and the highest mental and moral education of man. Secular force includes the seeking of power for the sake of power, the love of money, war for personal or territorial aggrandizement, and the separation of the state from religion. Things that have their opposite, not *in esse*, but *in posse*, such as morality and immorality, and things that do not co-exist at the same moment in the same subject, can be correlated into that opposite : as heat into electricity, or virtue into vice, and the reverse. If things will change, it is important to know the law of that change as it affects conduct and society.

Looking at the past through the perspective of history, it will be seen that the increment of secular forces is exactly equivalent to the shrinkage in the sacred forces, and the reverse ; and that the correlation of sacred and secular forces is as rigidly demonstrable and measurable as that of any and all other forces. This correlation is seen in the fact that the maximum of sacred forces coincides with the minimum of the secular, and the maximum of the secular force is the minimum of the sacred. In other words, a given quantity of one has been displaced and an exact equivalent of the other has been substituted—the one coming as the other goes. High civilization is in the suppression of disorganizing force, and the substitution of its equivalent in one of harmony ; a result ever coming and ever to come. The tendency in the ebb and flow of events is from extreme sacredness to extreme secularity, and the reverse. Take the case of one addicted to vice, say to drunkenness, and the power of vice will strengthen exactly as the power of the will weakens. Discipline is correlated into indulgence. Lawlessness increases as restraints are removed. Immorality increases as spiritual or religious power decreases.

Do we not in this transmutation or manifestation of physical force—the increment of the one corresponding to the decrement of another, or the increment of one corresponding to the increment of another, and the reverse—grasp a principle which underlies the action and reaction of all changes, whether physical, moral, or political? Fraud, defamation, falsehood, impurity, malicious violence, and theft, have their place in the universal chain of cause and effect, of integration and disintegration, of propagation and growth, of evolution and devolution, of conservation and correlation. Can the perpetrator of wrong escape all consequences of his act? Is wrong the only thing in all the universe released from responsibility, or that does not propagate itself, or from which the doer instantly disconnects himself, and leaves his wrong to its solitary effects? Can a man separate himself from his shadow? Let no one, especially the young, deceive himself as to the inexorable laws of all things. The character of actions becomes the character of the actors. The bed of mineral saturates the stream that passses over it. Wrong-doing poisons all subsequent life. Evils change, but never die. Philosophize about it as we may, we cannot be blind to the universal fact that somehow, in the end, right gets even with each wrong. As said before, the law of equivalence, or compensation, is the most terrible of certainties to all who do wrong. Deferred payments only accumulate the debt. Money loaned must come back with interest. Time becomes an awful and avenging factor. It neither conceals nor forgets; but as seconds added to seconds make up the ages, so does a retribution to come enlarge and intensify itself. Wrong is immortal. Moral equilibriums are inevitable. Let every man who has broken a moral law know that, whether asleep or awake, in whatever continent or zone he may be, the remorseless law of correlation, of equivalence, of compensation, of equilibration, is ever in pursuit, and knows exactly where and when to find him for reparation or for punishment. The police of the universe is ubiquitous, its justice infallible, and its punishments complete and resistless.

LECTURE VI.

METHOD OF CORRELATION OF FORCES.

1. *Correlation between unconscious forces.* This lecture extends and applies the principles of the preceding lecture. What is force? Whatever moves matter is force. I take the bulb of the thermometer in my hand by the act of my will-force, and the mercury rises in the tube by a force that is not the act of my will. I am conscious of the will-force that takes hold of the thermometer, but I am not conscious of the action of the heat-force that moves the mercury up the tube. One force, therefore, is conscious and personal; and the other is unconscious and impersonal. The inverse correlation of the unconscious and impersonal forces that we are now to consider, will suffice to explain the direct correlation of these forces as well.

This supernatural will-power manifests both matter forces, such as heat, electricity and gravitation, and also mind force, such as animal will, conscious and personal in man, and unconscious and impersonal in animals below man. Correlative forces are exchanged —blind matter force with blind matter force, as heat with electricity, and conscious, superhuman mind force, with conscious human mind force, as when man gives up his own will and takes God's will—the human and the superhuman wills concurring.

Grove says that the term correlative means a necessary, mutual or reciprocal dependence of two ideas, inseparable even in mental conception ; thus the idea of height cannot exist without involving the idea of its correlative depth ; the idea of parent cannot exist without involving the idea of offspring. There are, for example, many facts which cannot take place without involving the other ; one arm of a lever cannot be depressed without the other being elevated ; the finger cannot press the table without the table pressing the finger.

Force is force, and if impersonal forces may thus be correlated, exchanged, bartered, so much of one for so much of another, why may not personal force be correlated ? Force is a mode of power, and power is will, and will is a personal attribute of choice coupled with an attempt to realize itself, and why may not the personal will force of one be exchanged or correlated with the personal will force of another? And why may not the superhuman will force of an infinite person be correlated with the human will force of a finite person?

Grove, speaking of the physical forces, viz.: heat, electricity, magnetism, chemical affinity and motion, says that they are all correlative, or have reciprocal dependence ; that neither, taken abstractedly, can be said to be the essential cause of the other, but that either may produce or be convertible into any of the others ; thus heat may mediately or immediately produce electricity, electricity may produce heat ; and so

of the rest. (Grove on Correlation of Forces, p. 19.)
But one force cannot be said to produce or cause
another. The going of one force may be the occasion
but is not the cause of the coming of the other, nor
does a retiring force become another force by the motion or act of retiring. The maximizing of the human
will cannot cause or compel the minimizing of the
superhuman will, and the reverse. We cannot explain
this any more than we can explain why any one force
maximizes as some other force minimizes. Science
tells us that this is a fact, and history and observation
tell us that the other is a fact also. The correlation
of mind-forces is as certain as the correlation of matter-forces—that is, as will is force, and as force correlates, *a fortiori* does will correlate.

Correlation is a method, and as method it implies
will and intelligence. If supernatural intelligence and
will power be denied, so all methods in the universe
must be denied. *Method* of impersonal and unintelligent power is unthinkable.

Correlation is neither a process, a creation nor a
generation. It is a method. It is merely an equiva-
lency of forces or things—so much of one for so much
of something else as its correlative. It neither produces atomic matter, nor organizes atomic matter, nor
vitalizes atomic matter, nor personalizes atomic matter. It deals with matter and force furnished to its
hand, already existing.

The correlation or conservation of force is thought
by some to be the distinguishing discovery of the age;
but that depends upon what force is, and what correlation is. We expect to show that there are no forces

as such to be correlated; and that all that correlation is, is the correlative manifestations of the *one* supernatural will-power. In any one correlative act, the correlative forces as force, are two, but the Power is one. Supernatural will is the one power, and natural force is a special manifestation of this supernatural power.

The scope of what Mr. Spencer calls the process of evolution, is a denial of creation, and is only a method of correlation. As stated by Mr. Spencer, "the affirmation of universal evolution is, in itself, the negation of the absolute commencement of anything." Mr. Spencer says: "Evolution is an integration of matter, and concomitant dissipation of motion." This is simply a method of correlation; and nothing more.[a]

In other words, evolution *defined* as a method is the eternal correlation of eternal matter. Evolution *described* as a process has been considered before. We have seen that after the order of supernature in nature, when things have been produced, as in

(*a*) We may here see:

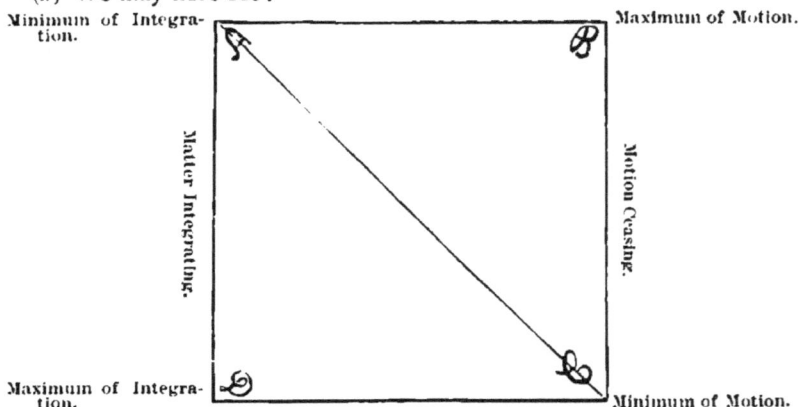

Minimum of Integration.

Maximum of Motion.

Matter Integrating.

Motion Ceasing.

Maximum of Integration.

Minimum of Motion.

the creative method, and after their propagation has been delegated, as in the organic, genetic method, Supernatural Power exchanges its several substances and forces, one with another, in a method of equivalence, called the method of Correlation. This is seen in objects in nature without wills, and in objects in nature with wills. Correlations in objects without wills, Mr. Spencer calls evolution, as when Power or the one Supernatural Will correlates the natural things of matter and motion. He says, "the formula finally is: *Evolution is the integration of matter, and concomitant dissipation of motion; during which the matter passes from an indefinite, incoherent homogeneity, to a definite, coherent heterogeneity; and during which the retained motion undergoes a parallel transformation."* (F. P., § 145.) If this is a definition of evolution, then what is correlation? If this is a definition of correlation, then what is evolution? The first part of the above definition is of a mechanical action, and the second part is the description of a mechanical result. Mr. Spencer's inaccuracies are the more remarkable, as he aspires to formulate a synthetic philosophy. He admits that "Involution would much more truly express the nature of the process" which he calls Evolution. As an authority he should have used the word he ought to have used, and have corrected popular usage, if wrong. But the word involution, admits extrinsic force, would open the door to the theistic idea of personal power; and so he retains the impersonal idea of evolution from intrinsic power. But he is no more fortunate in his definition of evolution; for, as he defines it, evolution is a method of correlation between matter and motion, producing nothing and by nothing produced.

Mr. Spencer says: " The *processes* thus everywhere in antagonism, and everywhere gaining now a temporary and now a more or less permanent triumph over the other, we call Evolution and Dissolution. Evolution under its simplest and most general aspect is the integration of matter and concomitant dissipation of motion; while Dissolution is the absorption of motion and concomitant disintegration of matter." (F. P., § 97.) The phrases, "dissipation of motion" and "absorption of motion," do not convey accurate ideas. Motion as power in action may *cease*, but no power, active or inactive, can be dissipated. Motion may *cease*, but not be absorbed, for that cannot be absorbed which does not exist. Motion absorbs force so far as it absorbs anything, and force causes motion, but there is no motion to be absorbed until force creates it. Force may be reflected, transmitted, or distributed, but not motion. Motion ceases, but is not dissipated; it is caused, but not absorbed.

Mr. Spencer says: " We shall *everywhere* mean by evolution, the *process* which is *always* an integration of matter and dissipation of motion." (F. P., § 97.) The *method* of the correlation of matter and motion is thus called a *process* of evolution. This assumes the existence of matter and motion, but does not account for the origin of either. Again, Mr. S. says: " Evolution is the passage of matter from a diffused to an aggregated state. (F. P., § 139.) So, then, Mr. Spencer's definition and description of evolution, which should be called correlation instead of evolu-

tion, teach a pre-existing Power, pre-existing matter
and a pre-existing, diffused state of matter.

We have already seen that the mere mechanical
method of correlation is, the fixed correspondence
of states and motions, and the equivalence of quantities. But whether things are manifested in a process
of evolution or are equivalently correlated, we must
account for the commencement of the things themselves. Evolution does not do this; for evolution
does not consider or admit the absolute commencement of anything, Correlation does not account for
things; for it is only a method of the equivalence of
things. So, under the treatment of the correlation
of things, we are attracted back to the consideration
of the origin of things themselves. In correlation
there is :

(*a*) Pre-existing Power. The consideration of
this we have somewhat anticipated. How long has
this Power pre-existed? Mr. Spencer speaks of it as
a Power of which the nature remains forever inconceivable, and to which no limit in Time or Space can
be imagined." (F. P., § 194.)

We must not understand that the integration of
matter is one act and the dissipation of motion is
another. The one wedge makes two forms of matter.
They are correlative results of the same act of Power;
just as the quantity of space on one side of the diagonal of a square is positively more as the other side
is negatively less; or just as the space on one side
of a perpendicular line positively increases as the
space on the other side positively increases.

As, according to Parmenides, unity excludes plu-

18

rality, so the unity of power excludes the plurality of forces. Forces are but several radiations of one power—many streams from one fountain. We may call energies of power forces, but the name does not change the essence. For the sake of convenience we may call one manifestation of will-power heat and another electricity ; but after all, force is simply will-power doing different things under different names.

Omnipresent and omniscient will envelopes, pervades and is the force of all phenomena. When personal, supernatural power impersonalizes itself as so-called natural force, so much is this so-called natural force and supernatural power one and the same, that while we worship the personal power, we should not fail to see the action of Supernatural Will in what is called impersonal force.

There is a personal pantheism that is not impersonal atheism, and there is a personality in theism that is pantheistic in presence. Theism and personal pantheism are human expressions for the one, omnipresent person of God. God is the name of the infinite Power ; and nature is the name of its finite manifestation.

We have seen that Will is Power—that Power manifests itself as force—that force is said to be exchanged or correlated with force, as heat with electricity, or energy with velocity ; but, after all, forces are only energies of the one supernatural Will-Power, and are not exchanged or correlated at all. When Will-Power withdraws a given amount of energy of one kind *ipso facto*, it manifests an equivalent amount of some other kind. The correlation is between the different decisions of the Will-Power within the will itself, not between the so-called forces or energies themselves. As Will ceases to do one thing, it begins to do some other corresponding thing. There is no moment of time, no object in space, no sound in the air, no change of relations not subject to the omnipresent, unsuspended, ever effective, sole power of God's will. As all fingers are parts of the hand, all members parts of the body, all colors parts of light, so all forces are special manifestations of one Power. Where gravitation is, there is God's will; and so where heat, electricity, or chemic affinity is, there is His will. If force is will, there can be no correlation of force, for there can be no correlation of God's will. That will may act uniformily, and we may call it law, or it may specially will those phenomena that we call providence and miracles. This supernatural Will-Power manifests both a positive and a negative condition; that is, the negative is the absence of the positive. To will atoms to move, is to will that they shall not be at rest. To will that atoms be at rest, is to will that they shall not move. We see how starlight fades into day-light, and day-light fades into starlight; we see how the leaf gives out the carbon at night and the oxygen in the day; we see when the upper chamber of the hour-glass is empty, the lower is full; we find in ourselves personal mind and impersonal matter. Why should not the supernatural Power-Being exist in any condition of his own choosing? There is now in and around each one of us, personal minds and impersonal matter; and the personal and the impersonal are so blended or inter-mingled in ourselves that we cannot separate their boundaries any more than we can say how far in the outside of a block goes or how far out the inside comes. Personification of nature abounds in the Bible. Is personification of trees, rocks and seas only figures of oriental rhetoric, or is it expressive of a fact of personality in the awful totality and constitution of things? The power and presence of a personal God are around and in impersonal rocks and trees that the heathen personify as God. Indeed, while they see no similitude yet they hear a voice.

The Power to manifest is the Power to create, and the Power to create is the Power to generate, and the Power to generate is the Power to correlate. We infer that this power has an underived Will, because from this all-manifesting Power, we derive our own Will. As this Power manifests matter and motion as its symbols, it integrates its symbol of matter, and dissipates its symbol of motion, in a method of correlation, having less of one as it has much of the other, and the reverse.

The integration of matter and the dissipation of motion is simply the correlation between matter and force ; but, as all force is Will, the correlation is really between matter and Will. But, as matter itself is only a manifestation of Will, the correlation defined as evolution, is essentially between modes of Will—Will in a material manifestation and Will manifested as force in motion. Subjective Will-Power objectifies itself as matter and as motion. What is called correlation of force is simply that one manifestation of God's will becomes less as another manifestation becomes more ; or rather that, in willing one thing he does not will another, its opposite. So, in willing integration of matter he does not will its disintegration. Will, as force, attracts; and Will, as force, repels. Both forces are but phases of one Power, and correlate according to mass and distance. It is called integration when the attractive force is greater than the repellent; it is called disintegration, when the repellent force is greater than the attractive; so that what is called evolution, which really is correlation, may be defined to be the integration through attraction of diffused matter or the disintegration through repulsion of concentrated matter, as the strength of the one force may be. The dissipation of motion is the dissipation of force; and the absorption of motion is the absorption of force; and force is Will. Supernatural Will is natural force.

Power manifests itself in nature as one kind of Force at one time, and as another kind of Force at another. Power integrates its matter as the force of attraction, and it disintegrates its matter under the force of repulsion. One Power manifests itself as many forces; but many forces sympathize as one Power. Thus it is, that the correlation between matter and motion is really the correlation between two different manifestations of the same Power—that is between supernatural Power as motion and supernatural Power in the shape of matter; in other words, Power manifests itself as matter, and then, as force, controls the matter it manifested as Power. One act of God's will as a force is part of God's will manifested as matter; and so one act of God's will does not conflict with another act of God's will as such.

Strictly speaking, one Power is doing it all (see Figs. 142, Lect. V.), just as a diagonal drawn in a square makes two opposite figures, one increasing as the other decreases ; or, using the diagonal as a perpendicular, one figure increases as the other increases. Power cannot conflict with itself ; as by one act of our will we raise one hand and lower the other. One Power, at the same moment, does different if not opposite things ; even as the will of the musician variously moves the several fingers of the same hand, at the same moment. The many facts can have but one factor. We say that matter is a manifestation of God's will ; the diffusion of matter is a manifestation of the same will ; the integration of this matter is by the same Will ; its disintegration is an opposite will of the same Power. Motion does not correlate or exchange with matter ; but the Will-Power that integrates matter at one moment disintegrates the same matter in the next. There are not two forces, but two manifestations of one force Power. Supernatural will at one moment pulls diffused matter together, and in the next it pushes aggregate matter apart. The same Will that at one moment manifests heat, the next moment ceases that act of willing, and wills that there shall be an equivalent amount of electricity. There is one Will, not two forces ; and yet the two manifestations of the one Will are called two forces.

Science can have as much certainty in this view of the mystery of phenomena as it could have in any impersonal law. Will can be uniform as law. Supernatural Will-Power can and has made itself certain in nature ; but supernature is not the slave of its own uniformity. It *can* be multiform and variant. That it *is* uniform is a uniformity that it prescribes to itself. Science can rely upon the uniformity of omniscience, but it can have none upon that of nescience. We may confidently expect that what infinite intelligence saw to be best in the past, it will see to be best for the future, or that compensations in phenomena will make something better. But who can know what a universe without sense or intelligence may do? A universe without an intelligent plan goes not as it pleases but as it happens.

Power, like a wedge, works two ways at once. One act divides an apple into two parts. The antithesis of Power is exhibited when matter integrates as motion dissipates, just as the pendulum swinging between two points lengthens the distance behind it as it shortens the distance before it, or as the curved line convexes one side as it concaves the other. The loss of one is the gain of the other.

At the margin of the sea, the Pillar of God, was light to the Israelites and darkness to the Egyptians. Apparently conflicting phenomena are opposite sides of one Power. Power is the center of all circumferences, and the unity of all pluralities. One Power is at the angle where centripetalism and centrifugalism diverge. The one Power has two supplemental motions of integration and disintegration. The power that at one moment is integrating matter, is disintegrating matter at the next. The correlation is not between matter and motion, but between a diffused condition of matter, and a condensed condition of matter. Uniform power has multiform manifestations. The power that is behind any one manifestation is behind them all.

How the integration of matter and the dissipation of motion, could ever result in life, evolutionists do not explain. It is exactly in this *nexus* between matter and life, that evolution without a living God, breaks down. There must be some uniformity to harmonize all multiformities, whether that uniformity be called impersonal Power or a personal God. With a God, both correlation and evolution, as two actual among other possible methods of God, need not be denied. In the methods we see God. To admit one is to prove the other. Integration and disintegration of matter are opposite manifestations of the same Power. Sometimes that Power acts as a wedge, and sometimes as a compress; in other words, sometimes Power is the power of centripetalism, pulling diffused atoms together; and sometimes it is the Power of centrifugalism, pulling concentrated atoms apart. There are not two powers contending in the mastery; but the Power is the one Power unlimited in Time and Space, harmonizing its movements. It is the supernatural managing the natural, and is, in a sense, itself both.

Supernatural Power has not left itself without witness. There are three points in the process of evolution, when that Supernatural Power is obviously present in direct action. The first point is where motion begins to dissipate and matter to integrate. The second point is when repulsive motion begins to be absorbed, and integrated matter to disintegrate. The third point is where the process of special evolution stops and the process of special dissolution begins. The processes of evolution and dissolution are natural: the power that stops one and begins the other is supernatural. Universal evolution is not followed by universal dissolution. Special dissolutions are parts of universal evolution.

Power of unfixed quantity manifests itself as force of unfixed quantity. Evolution has rhythm, but no exhaustion, because supernatural will has no exhaustion. Omnipotent Will has omnipotent energies. Mr. Spencer says, on the contrary, that "evolution has an impassable limit." (F. P., § 170.) He says that "Motion as well as Matter being *fixed in quantity*, it would seem that the change in the distribution of Matter which motion effects, *coming to a limit* in whichever direction it is carried, the indestructible motion thereupon necessities a reverse distribution. Apparently, the universal co-existent forces of attraction and repulsion, which, as we have seen, necessitate rhythm in all minor changes throughout the Universe, also necessitate rhythm in the totality of its changes -- produce now an immeasurable period during which the attractive forces predominating, cause universal concentration, and then an immeasurable period during which the repulsion forces predominating, cause universal diffusion—alternate eras of Evolution and Dissolution." (F. P., § 183.) [Italics our own.]

But where is the evidence that the quantity of Matter and Motion is fixed? Mr. S. says "the quantity of Force remains always the same." (F. P., § 58.) But that depends on what is force. The action of force may be limited, but its quantity is not fixed. Unlimited Power may have changeable limits of force. In our personal consciousness, and according to the teachings of Herschell, Wallace, and Carpenter, we know of no other source of power or force in ourselves than that of our wills. If Will is Power and Power is force, force can no more be an absolutely fixed quantity; for force and Will are only different names for the same power. Natural force is Supernatural Will-Power. The quantity of motion as Will is unfixed, for Will is a Power, but not a fixed Power or force; and, if we may assign Will as a cause for human motion in human, why may we not expect to find superhuman Will a cause for superhuman motion? If Will is fixed, it is fixed by the Will itself, and the Will may unfix itself.

The distinct formula is, that all things are manifestations of Power. Is motion a manifestation of this Power, or is it this Power itself in action? If motion is unlimited Power itself in action, then, of course, the quantity of motion is not fixed, for unlimited Power is not fixed, and to say that Power unlimited in Time or Space is limited in matter or motion, is a contradiction. Indeed, Power cannot be limited in anything.

Scientists admit that they do not know what matter is. How, then, can they advance the dogma, that the quantity of matter is fixed and that matter can be neither created nor destroyed? If Power materializes, or if Will materializes, or if matter mentalizes, matter cannot be a fixed quantity. Matter is much or little as Power may manifest of itself, or as Will may

choose to make out of itself; whether you call it
Power or Will, that takes form. The essence of matter being unknown, its quantity cannot be said to be
fixed ; and where we do not know we should not say.

If all things are manifestations of Power does this
Power have nothing to do with the rhythmic limit
and alternatives of Evolution and Dissolution? According to the notion that Matter and Motion have a
fixed quantity, evolution and dissolution would seem
to result from an exhaustion of force. But the Power
of the universe has no limits in Time or Space. If,
then, motion has no limits in unlimited Power, motion must be limited if at all, because Power saw fit
to limit it. And here we may ask, if Power limits
motion or matter, does Power act intelligently or unintelligently?

If all things are manifestations of Power, then those
manifestations imply that Power must control its own
manifestations. If matter and motion are manifestations of this Power, either their quantity is fixed or
not fixed by that Power—in short, they do not fix or
limit themselves. Or are we to conclude that matter
and motion are limited, because unlimited Power
must limit them in the nature of things? Unlimited
power is its own limit. When agnostic speculation
singles out the one attribute of Power from the other
attributes of the Supernatural Person we call God,
and pass by the other attributes of intelligence, and
holiness unnoticed, it entangles itself in the perplexity of accounting for all things by mere power, when
the evidence of supernatural intelligence is no less
than is the evidence of supernatural power. But, if

mere power is all, then Power materializes, for there is matter ; Power mentalizes, for there is mind ; Power combines, for there is combination ; Power vitalizes, for there is life ; Power personalizes, for there are persons. We see that power, whether personal or impersonal, intelligent or unintelligent, both begins and continues things —that is, it both originates and transforms. Agnostic science ignores the origin of the universe, for which religion accounts, and occupies itself only with the transformations of the organic matters of the universe, which it calls evolution, and which religion calls methods of Power in correlation.

(*b*) Pre-existent matter. But how has matter pre-existed ? As atoms, molecules or masses? We are told that its first form was an atom. Was that atom evolved out of nothing or created out of nothing? Is the atom eternal ? We beg to repeat that matter could not be said to be until it was known to be ; and when it was known to be there was mind to know it. If matter is not only eternal, but has been eternally known to be, then there has been eternal mind to know. Are there two eternals, or if only one, then, was eternal mind eternal matter, or eternal matter eternal mind ?

Evolution is limited to the mere behaviour or correlation of motion and of the molecules of matter, not of an atom of matter, as an atom. An atom is already integrated, and no dissipation of motion can make it more integrated. Therefore, evolution does not apply to matter as matter, but only to matter in a diffused or in a diffusable condition. But an atom can neither be more integrated or more diffused than it is in itself.

Mr. Spencer protests that he is not working out a materialistic system (1 Biol. 490), but if he were a materialist he would believe in the eternity of matter; and though he does not believe in the eternity of matter, he does not believe in its creation; for that would be the commencement of matter, which he denies. With him all that now is, is all that ever has been; and all that ever will be, is all that now is. Mr. Spencer emphatically denies that he is bound to assume a first organism in organic nature, but he cannot deny that he assumes a first atom in inorganic nature. According to his theory, there could be no such commencement; for he says, we have seen, that "the affirmation of universal evolution is in itself a negation of an absolute commencement of anything." That which has never commenced and is not eternal when all is eternal, is not at all. So, as matter is neither eternal or has a commencement, there is no matter. And yet, he everywhere means by evolution the process which is always an integration of matter. If Mr. Spencer does not mean to assume matter, when he says that it integrates, he must go back and show how matter, before it integrates, came to be matter at all.

If Power materializes, and evolution is the integration of matter, then evolution is the integration of materialized Power—in other words, matter is only a form of Power. Integration of matter is a new name for gravitation, the centripetalism, the unification, the aggregation, the synthesis of matter. It is simply a new description of old ideas. As we have said, evolution is the paradox expressed by Plato in his Parmenides, that "all unity tends to plurality, and all plurality ends in unity." When did this pre-existence of matter commence? Mr. Spencer says, as we have seen, that " the affirmation of universal evolution is in itself a negation of the absolute commencement of anything. He also says: " The absolute commencement of *organic life* on the globe, I distinctly deny." (1 Biol. p. 482.) But, we repeat, he cannot deny the pre-existence of the *matter* which is integrated in evolution—in other words, the integration of matter does not originate the matter integrated. Then when did matter begin, if ever?

We have said that we start with Power, but we do not start with evolution; for, as evolution is the integration of matter, there can be no integration of matter until Power has materialized itself, or until Power has manifested, created, or evolved matter to be integrated. The question right here is, what is the *nexus* between power and matter? Did Power become matter or did Power create matter when there was no matter? Infinite power, in manifesting matter, decides for itself whether it will *be* matter or *create* matter. Matter is manifested in either one way or the other.

We start with omnipresent, formless Power. In some way Power manifests Form. Omnipotence is parturient of all forms and substances, and the creation of something out of nothing is no more incomprehensible than that Power should materialize itself, or that matter should be eternal, or that matter should mentalize itself. And yet some minds, to whom two incomprehensibilities are equally difficult, can bring themselves to accept one incomprehensibility and reject another. And yet to say that matter is a shape of Power does seem more thinkable than to say that matter is eternal where there was only eternal Power. If evolution is the method of the universe, then it covers inorganic atoms, which must be creatively evolved, *ab extra*, or not be evolved at all, as each atom holds only its own Power. One atom may affect but cannot evolve or manifest another atom. Power must manifest the atom before the atom can take its place in the process of correlative evolution. But if the process of evolution is to include the origin of the atom, as well as its integration, then evolution includes more than the integration of matter—and it includes its origin as a creation as well as its genetic organisms. Atoms are before the integrating evolutions of atoms. Evolution is the integration of matter it did not evolve.

Nearly all systems of philosophy are cosmological and not ontological. They are but methods of effects, or *how* the universe was constructed, not Whence or by Whom. To these atheistical systems the universe is automatic, impersonal and unintelligent. From Lucretius down, we have had the Matter-system; from Plato down, we have had the Idea or Mind-system; and now, in evolution, we have the Power-system. Power, as Power, is neither matter, nor mind, nor being; but, as modes, Power might be, as it would seem, either or neither or both. Power is its own measure. Power is its own interpreter. Whether the power of evolution is or is not one of dynamics or internal Power, or of mechanics or external Power, it certainly is a problem of three methods. One method of Power is directly creative, as in the origin of the inorganic atom ; another is the causitive combination of one atom with another, where, of course. there is no life ; and the other method of Power is derivative, as in organic nature, where, of course, there is life. Mr. Spencer chooses to magnify the genetic method of organic nature by discussing and formulating it, and to minify the creative method of inorganic nature by passing it over. Correlation implies not only pre-existent power, pre-existent matter, but it implies

(*c*) Matter pre-existent in a diffused state. That cannot come together in integration which is not apart in disintegration. Plurality may become unity : but unity cannot become unity, because it is already unity.

It follows that matter not in a diffused state is not subject to the process of evolution. One atom is matter, and so far as it is an atom, it is not in a diffused state, nor can it ever be more aggregated in and by itself than it is. Several atoms may be compounded, as those of oxygen and hydrogen in water, but each atom can never be internally diffused or changed. So, if evolution be the integration of matter, the question arises, what matter, and in what quantities? Matter in atoms, in molecules or in mass? Integration of matter neither accounts for the atom —matter—to be integrated, in inorganic nature, nor does it account for the life in organic nature where life is the distinctive force. Notice that the integration is of matter ; not of force, nor of Power, nor of principles ; but if evolution be possible, as defined, there must be matter in a diffused state that can be integrated, while there is atomic matter that is not diffused, and therefore cannot be integrated in evolution. Considering, therefore, the atom as the basal matter in inorganic nature, we must logically conclude that correlative evolution of diffused matter does not apply to the whole of inorganic nature, as it does apply to the undiffused, inorganic atom. So, that, if the theory of atomic matter be affirmed, the theory of universal evolution of all matter, and especially the undiffused matter of an atom, must be denied. Thus we see how pre-existing Power, pre-existing matter, pre-existing in a diffused state, can integrate as motion is dissipated. There are three states of matter—the hypothetical atom, the group of atoms called the crystalloid, and the group of groups called the colloid. An atom may be moved by external force, but it cannot absorb any force or motion that will disintegrate it as an atom. A group of atoms, or a group of groups, may absorb force or motion, and be disintegrated as a group. But once an atom always an atom. An atom is not diffused matter; an atom is not integrated, because it never was disintegrated. It never was diffused, but was always indivisible. What is called correlation has been seen to be correlative movement, under the name of force, of the same Will; but now we come to consider the correlative movement, not of one Will, but of two.

2. *Correlation of conscious forces.* Wills, conscious and personal in man as distinguished from wills unconscious and impersonal in brute animals, correlate

19

exactly as the unconscious, unintelligent forces correlate.

Direct correlation of wills is when two wills agree, and increase or decrease together; as, when it is the will of man not to have its own will, but says "not my will, but thine O Lord, be done."

The promise of the Lord to St. Paul was: "My grace is sufficient for thee: for my strength is made perfect in weakness. Most gladly, therefore, will I glory in my infirmities, that the power of Christ may rest upon me. Therefore, I take pleasure in infirmities, in necessities, in persecutions, in distresses for Christ's sake; for when I am weak, then am I strong." (2 Cor., xii., 9, 10.) God says, "My thoughts are not your thoughts, neither are your ways my ways, said the Lord. For as the heavens are higher than the earth, so are my ways higher than your ways, and my thoughts than your thoughts." (Isa. lv., 8-9.) "And I will come near to judgment; and I will be a swift witness against the sorcerers, and against the adulterers, and against false swearers, and against those that oppress the hireling in his wages, the widow and the fatherless, and that turn aside the stranger from his right, and fear not me, saith the Lord of Hosts. For I am the Lord, I change not: therefore, ye sons of Jacob are not consumed. Even from the days of your fathers, ye have gone away from mine ordinances and have not kept them. Return unto me, and I will return unto you, saith the Lord of Hosts." (Mal. iii., 5-7.)

St. Paul illustrates the direct correlation of the two wills that agree, when he says, "Ye are the temple of the living God; as God hath said, I will dwell in them, and walk in them; and I will be their God and they shall be my people." (2 Cor., vi., 16.) God draws nigh to us as we draw nigh to Him. As we give Him up in our actions, He gives us up to our consequences. As our day with Him, so is our strength; and as our day without Him, so is our weakness. God moves on one uniform line; it saves us as we move with it; and it destroys us as we move against it. The correlation is of man's making. As man's will agrees with God's Will, there is a maximum of good and a minimum of evil; and as man's will disagrees with God's Will, there is a minimum of good and a maximum of evil.

Inverse correlation is when, as one will-power maximizes, the will-power of the other minimizes; and the reverse, as one will-power minimizes, the will-power of the other maximizes. This inverse correlation is a see-saw of will-powers, like the two ends of a beam, one end going up as the other goes down. Universal Will-Power of God may become latent or restrain itself, just as the derived will-power of man becomes active. As the manifestation of one will is, the manifestation of the other is not. The Superhuman is more, as the human is less, and the Superhuman less as the human is more; just as active force or energy changes into the potential, or the potential into the active.

We are not to consider how there came to be two wills; but that there should be two wills, is no greater mystery than that there should be one. We know, as a fact, that each intelligent individual, whether man or beast, has a will. Whence we came is no more incomprehensible than what we are. One will of a high grade implies the possibility, indeed, the probability, of another will of a higher, as we actually see that there are wills of a lower grade. As man is no permanent summit of anything, his will cannot be the summit of anything, his will cannot be the summit of will.

Supernatural will-power then, in some way, manifests from itself will-power in the conscious will of man and will-power in the unconscious will of animals below man. The will-power in these lower animals is a force, not so low in grade as the matter-power in unintelligent things, and not so high as the mind-power in intelligent persons. Unconscious will-power is energetic instinct. The correlation we are now to investigate is the correlation of the limited will-power in man and the unlimited will-power of God. In this, one will-power is not doing two different things, as between two forces called impersonal, but two will-powers, one unlimited and the other limited, are with or against each other upon the same thing. Whether there shall be much of heat as there is less of electricity, or less of heat as there is much of electricity, is all in the choice of one will; but whether there shall be much of the human motives in conduct as there is less of the superhuman, or much of the superhuman motives in conduct as there is less of the human, is a question of two wills. Is not their action correlative to each other?

For the sake of a convenient antithesis, we here make a verbal distinction between the supernatural

and the superhuman. The supernatural is the antithesis to the *whole* of the natural. The superhuman is the
special supernatural antithesis to *human* nature.

(*a*) The superhuman and the individual human
Will. Heretofore we have considered one universal
will as one universal power, manifested in the forces
of material nature. Now we come to consider the
correlative manifestation of two will-powers in the
sphere of human life. The underived will we call
underived power, the derived will we call derived power in intelligent nature, conscious in man
and unconscious in brute animals. Power delegated
in material nature we call force. The underived
superhuman will as power, including and manifesting
all force, correlates with the manifestations of the
derived human will as force. The manifestation of
the superhuman will, whether called power or force,
correlates with the manifestations of the human will,
whether called will or force.

Will is in all animal nature. Has animal nature a
monopoly of will? We claim to have shown that human will implies a superhuman will. Can these two
wills correlate? Certain it is, that there is most of
superhuman will manifested where there is the least
of any other manifested, as in irrational, organic nature. As there is much of the superhuman in the
motives of conduct, there is less of the human ; and
as there is more of the human in the motives of conduct, there is less of the superhuman. The correlation is not the same between two wills that it is between two forces. The superhuman will manifests
the two forces, and then correlates them ; and one will-
power does both the manifestation and the correla-

tion. But in the correlation of two wills, the case is different. The same universal power that specialized its will as force, and that set off the human will to act for itself, permits that human will somewhat to resist it, as the strong is patient with the resistance of the weak. So, within limits, there is the general fact, that the minimum of human will in the motives of conduct, is the maximum of superhuman will in help and approbation.

Personal, conscious, supernatural power manifests unconscious, impersonal forces, and then interchanges or correlates them according to methods and aims of its own. But this supernatural will-power, *ex mero motu*, gave a limited power to a limited creature which, in itself as creator, was unlimited. This conscious, supernatural will correlates its own power as force in all unconscious nature ; for there is no conscious will in unconscious nature with which to correlate ; but it correlates as personal will, not as impersonal force, with the conscious will of human nature. That power which is blind force in a stone, is intelligent will in man. That is, as to the stone, God's will is its will ; as to man, God has given man his own will.

When we speak of the correlation of two *forces* in matter, we are really speaking of one Will acting in two opposite ways. As we have said, in speaking of the correlation of unconscious forces, there is not one Will in the integration of matter and another Will in the dissipation of motion ; but one will in doing one thing, incidentally does another ; just as a person in moving *to* one point is moving *from* another. As the sun goes to the west the shadows go to the east. So in describing a curve line, the same act forms two opposite figures; one concave and the other convex. So, in drawing a diagonal, one line makes a hypothenuse common to two adjacent angles. In the correlation of two Wills, the result is the same. A superhuman Will willing to bless an obedient human will, cannot bless a disobedient human will. Change of action always changes relations. The obedient human will puts itself in accord with the Superhuman Will, as by its disobedience, it puts itself in discord with the Superhuman Will.

Personal force correlates with personal force, as the correlation of the human with the Superhuman Will; and impersonal forces, so called, correlate with impersonal forces and things. There is a correspondence between the Power and its methods: intelligent method implies intelligent Power: personal methods imply personal power. The supernatural and personal Power, we claim to have proved, implies supernatural, personal methods. Instead of the psychological term Will, or the metaphysical term Power, suppose we use the more scientific term FORCE, and say that the Underived Force correlates with the derived force. Like sensitive balances, their equilibrium is easily disturbed; or like the balanced beam, one end goes up as the other goes down. Long lines of history show the alternate prevalence of one or the other of these two will-forces. Their correlation is as certain as the correlation of matter and motion or of any two forces, by whatever name known. Sometimes this Superhuman Will so hedges the human will with difficulties, as to seem to coerce it unconsciously into conformity, leading men and nations by ways they know not. The human will is not consulted as to whether, as an inhabitant of this sphere, it will be at the nadir or at the zenith of the terestrial orbit; but it is consciously free all the time. The fish in the vase are free, but are not consulted when they are moved from one part of a room to another. The correlation of the manifestations of the human will with the manifestations of the Super-human Will, each will being automatic, is the one moral and spiritual problem of human life and destiny. Religious ethics are the basis of civilization. As related, religion is supernatural ethics, and ethics is natural religion. Ethics is the obedience of the human will to the superhuman Will; religion is the worship of the human soul of the Superhuman Being. By the correlation of the individual human Will, and the Superhuman Will, we mean that certain consequences invariably correspond to certain agreement or disagreement of these two Wills. Wills themselves, of course, are not exchangeable but they act interchangeably. The human and the superhuman Wills may be said to be correlated as they affect conduct. The conscious conformity or correlation of the human will to the Superhuman Will, is expressed in the submissive words of the Virgin Mary to the Angel, " be it unto me according to thy word;" as it was afterwards to those of her divine Son in the Garden, " not as I will but as thou wilt." As by generation we are human, so by regeneration we become Superhuman—through ways not our own, we become partakers of the divine nature. In conduct we become supernatural. The human, when it reaches up to the superhuman, is so emptied of its own will, as to be filled with the Superhuman Will. As the one is less, the other is more. " I seek not my own will, but the will of my father which hath sent me." (John v., 30.) " If I do this thing willingly, I have a reward ; but, if against my will, a dispensation of the gospel is committed unto me." (1 Cor., ix., 17.) Will is Power (see first lecture) and Power is force, and force correlates with force ; as force is Power and Power is Will, so Will correlates with Will—that is, Superhuman Will, conscious and personal, correlates with human will, conscious and personal. We have already said that, as force is Will, the correlation of force with force is only the correlative manifestation of the universal Will-Power with its own special manifestations of Will-Power, called gravitation, heat, electricity, chemical affinity, and so on. Indeed, these special manifestations are special modes of itself ; and, yet, the mode is not the Power as such, any more than the wood of a throne or of a ship is the tree whence the wood came.

We expect to show that, as Supernatural, personal Will-Power has manifested what are called impersonal, natural forces, and that these impersonal, natural forces are correlated, so the manifestations of the underived Will of God correlates with the manifestations of the derived will of man. The same law of correlative exchange which God has established between one force of his Will and another force of his Will as force, he has established between his Will as Power and man's will as Force.

Universal Will-Power, like the special forces it manifests, may be active or inactive. That is, when the Superhuman Will-force of an infinite Person is active, the human will-force of a finite person may be inactive or concurrent; and the reverse, when the human will-force of a finite person is active the Superhuman Will-force of an infinite Person may be forbearingly inactive or concurrent. Or, as a direct correlation at times they both may be active or inactive together. We see that a force is active in one object, and inactive in some other object. As Grove said, one object cannot be heated without another being cooled; one body cannot be positively electrified without some other body being negatively electrified. So, the will-power of God is less in our lives, as our own will-power is more, and the reverse. This is evident in all Scripture, and in all experience and observation. These two wills are automatic. In the correlation of the manifestation of the supernatural, personal Will, with the manifestation of the impersonal forces, the one supernatural Will, like the sun, is the Power, and many natural forces, like the rays, are the manifestations. But in the correlation of Superhuman Will with human will, the two wills act *ex mero motu.* The Superhuman Will says to the human will "come unto Me that ye may have life." The human will responds to the Superhuman Will, " I will not." We contend that the human and the Superhuman are correlatives both in terms and in facts; and that if material force can be correlated so can mind-force; and that as force is power, and power is will, the human and the Superhuman Will may be correlated like any other forces of universal Power. Syllogistically, we may say, that all forces may be correlated; all will is force; therefore, all will may be correlated. The human will and the

Superhuman Will either agree or disagree; in other words, are correlative.

(*b*) The superhuman and the collective human will. If all human beings governed their lives by the direction of Superhuman Will, they would progress to a Superhuman experience, which, if less than supernatural, would be more than natural. From the beginning of history, we see that, as the motives of life become less superhuman, they of course become more human. As men relied upon their own wisdom, they sought less the wisdom of God. " By me Kings reign and princes decree justice. By me princes rule, and nobles, even all the judges of the earth. I love them that love me ; and those that seek me early shall find me." (Prov. viii., 15.) Civilization is supernatural so far as Supernatural Will controls human affairs, and is the motive of human conduct. When the Supernatural Will has its way with persons as it has with things, the correlation of the human will with the Superhuman Will is complete, and all is peace, order and progress. But when the human will is filled with its own ways, all is war, disorder and destruction. This method of correlation is illustrated in the history of any long era of civilization.

Civilization is the direct correlation of the two Wills—the human and the superhuman. Events are evolutions out of the domination of one or of the other will, as the case may be. Under the Superhuman Will highest progress is evolved ; under the human will lowest regress is evolved. Religious superstitions are groping in the direction of the Superhuman ; but superstitions are only human misinterpretations of the superhuman. Unintelligent nature never mistakes the supernatural, and never makes false steps to be retraced, as man does. Civilization is a fact and must have a Factor. If civilization is a natural fact then, as the Factor must be above and before its fact, so this, as every natural fact, must have a supernatural Factor. The highest civilization is men and society at their best ; and the human is at its best when it is in accord with the superhuman—that is, when the derived will accepts its law from the underived Will. There can be no discord in true civilization. Human progress is a segment of some better whole—an echo of the harmony of the universe. Civilization is said to be evolved because circumstances render unstable its primitive condition, and instability is the occasion of all evolutionary and progressive changes. All social elements are broken up ; social ideas change. New foreign relations change old domestic conditions. New opportunities change new enterprises. Revolutions readjust classes, interests and power. When, by experience, revelation, or the condition of environment, the human Will correlates with or knows and obeys the Superhuman Will, then is the lifting of the human towards the Superhuman, as trees grow towards the sunlight. Nations have gone up or down with their creeds and their worships. There is creative method of supernatural Will and intelligence in all inorganic, and in the creative and genetic forms of all unconscious organic nature. Here the manifestations of evolutions are many, but the Power is one ; but between the human Will as force and the Superhuman Will as Power, there is a *correlation* of Wills as Power and Force, but *no evolution*, as Mr. Spencer defines it.

Civilization is not an organism, but an organization in unstable equilibrium. It is the action of human will midst superhuman methods. The race is an aggregation, not an organism. Mr. Spencer thinks otherwise. (See F. P. § 111.) What is organism? Any living unit, not an aggregate, is an organism? A grain of wheat is an organism, because it is a living and productive unit; but a bushel of grains of wheat is not an organism, because as a bushel of wheat, it is not a living unit, but only an aggregate relation of living units. Unity only can have organism; plurality may have system, but not organization. There is a celestial *system*, but not a celestial *organism*. There may be a social system, but there cannot possibly be a social organism. Organisms as individuals may descend from individual organisms; and organisms may be related to organism; but the relation of organisms cannot, because of the relation, be itself an organism. Some of the gravest errors in social science result from the confounding relation with organism. Society, as its name imports, is the companionship or unity of harmonious will. The form of companionship is purely constitutional, and companionship itself is natural. In some associations it is enforced, as in monarchies; in others it is called free, as in democracies; in others, it is fraternal, as in perfect Christianity.

Hasty utterances of modern thought restate the medieval error of confounding nominalism with realism—that is, giving to the relations of things the name of things themselves. As society is only a name for a conventional relation, and not of an entity, it cannot be said except by metonomy, of putting one thing for another, to be either organic or inorganic. But science deals with realities, and not with figures of speech ; therefore to the scientist there can be no social organism as such—that is, social science is not the science of social organism, but only the science of the changeable *relations* of social units. Superhuman power controls human affairs, if human affairs are under any extrinsic control at all. · Natural Evolution is a process. Supernatural evolution, if any, is a method of control. The plan of nature is supernatural to nature. Intrinsic power evolves ; extrinsic power controls. Civilization, like everything else, is partly created, and figuratively genetic. The Personal Will of supernatural power omnipresent in the universe, originates the personal units of civilization by indirect, creative act ; and then leaves much to the human will as to the breadth and character of the society that follows. Supernatural Power begins human life, to be worked out and watched by supernatural Power under natural conditions.

The inverse correlations, illustrated by the four adjacent angles of the following Figure No. 3, show the movements of civilization for over three thousand years. It will be observed that the correlation was not between the two religions, Polytheism and Monotheism, which were successive, not contemporary ; but between either of these with the civil basis of morality on the one side, and the speculative one of philosophy on the other. Speaking of this conflict, Bagehot says : " Those kinds of morals and that kind of religion which tend to make the foremost and most effectual character are sure to prevail, all else being the same ; and creeds or systems that con-

duce to a soft, limp mind tend to perish, except some
hard extrinsic force keep alive. Thus Epicureanism
never prospered at Rome (though Cæsar, Lucretius
and Horace were Epicureans), but Stoicism did; the
stiff, serious character of the great prevailing nation
was attracted by what seemed a confirming creed,
and deterred by what looked like a relaxing creed.
The inspiriting doctrines fell upon the ardent character, and so confirmed its energy. Strong beliefs
win strong men, and make them stronger. Such is,
no doubt, one cause why Monotheism tends to prevail over Polytheism; it produces a higher, steadier
character, calmed and concentrated by a great single
object; it is not confused by competing rites, or dis-
tracted by miscellaneous deities. Polytheism is
religion *in commission,* and it is weak accordingly.
But it will be said, the Jews, who were Monotheists,
were conquered by the Romans, who were Polytheists. Yes, it must be answered; because the Romans
had other gifts; they had a capacity for politics, a
habit of discipline, and of these the Jews had not the
least. The religious advantage was an advantage,
but it was counter-weighed." [a]

On the following page will be found a figure illustrating the correlative movements of events for three
thousand years, beginning with polytheism at and
before the time of Moses, fifteen hundred years before
Christ, and coming on down to the fifteenth century
after Christ; with a statement of general principles, and
results at either side; with such deductions under-
neath as are explanatory of the conclusions reached.

(a) Physics and Politics, 767.

Fig. 3.

ANCESTRAL WORSHIP.

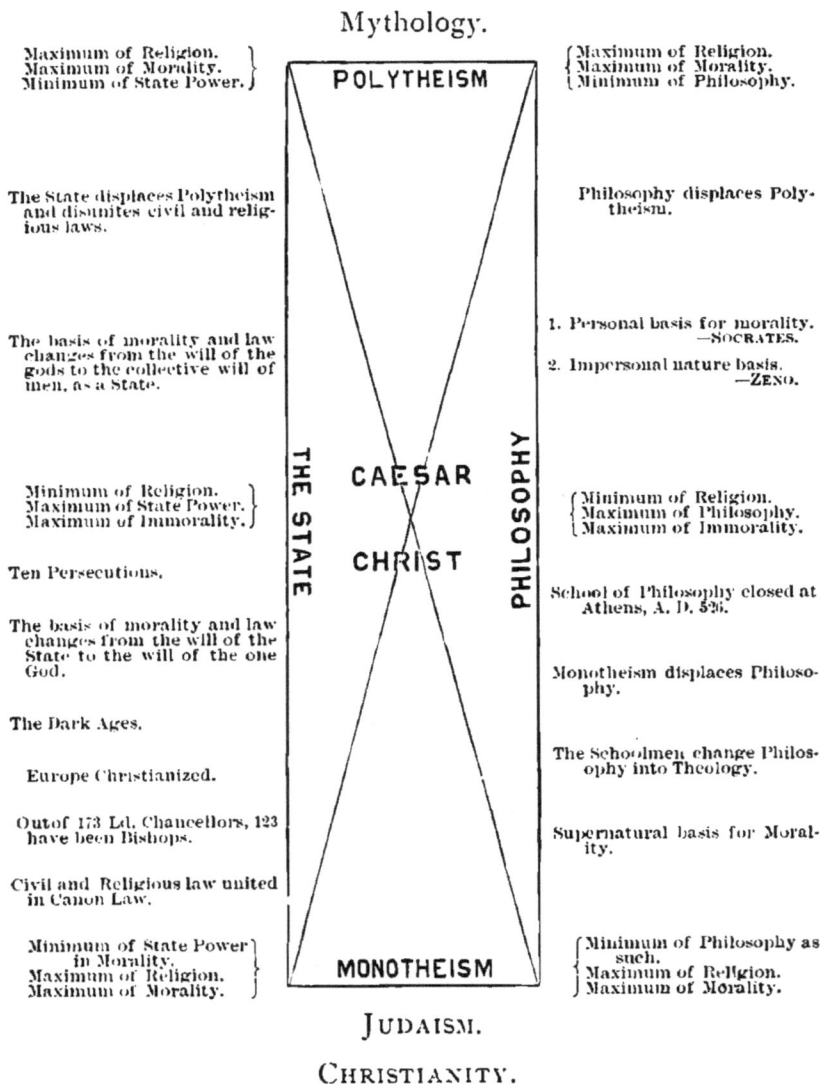

Mythology.

Maximum of Religion.
Maximum of Morality.
Minimum of State Power.
}

POLYTHEISM

{ Maximum of Religion.
Maximum of Morality.
Minimum of Philosophy.

The State displaces Polytheism and disunites civil and religious laws.

Philosophy displaces Polytheism.

The basis of morality and law changes from the will of the gods to the collective will of men, as a State.

1. Personal basis for morality.
—SOCRATES.

2. Impersonal nature basis.
—ZENO.

THE STATE

CAESAR

CHRIST

PHILOSOPHY

Minimum of Religion.
Maximum of State Power.
Maximum of Immorality.
}

{ Minimum of Religion.
Maximum of Philosophy.
Maximum of Immorality.

Ten Persecutions.

School of Philosophy closed at Athens, A. D. 526.

The basis of morality and law changes from the will of the State to the will of the one God.

Monotheism displaces Philosophy.

The Dark Ages.

The Schoolmen change Philosophy into Theology.

Europe Christianized.

Out of 173 Ld. Chancellors, 123 have been Bishops.

Supernatural basis for Morality.

Civil and Religious law united in Canon Law.

Minimum of State Power in Morality.
Maximum of Religion.
Maximum of Morality.
}

MONOTHEISM

{ Minimum of Philosophy as such.
Maximum of Religion.
Maximum of Morality.

JUDAISM.

CHRISTIANITY.

From the foregoing figure, we observe, first, that when Polytheism is at its maximum, the State is at its minimum ; and that as the State maximizes, Polytheism correlatively minimizes, and so does morality. Second, that when Polytheism is at its maximum, Philosophy is at its minimum ; and that as Polytheism minimizes, Philosophy correlatively maximizes, and so does immorality. Third, that, with the State at its maximum and Philosophy at its maximum and Polytheism at its minimum, there is a reverse movement ; and that while the State is at its maximum Monotheism is at its minimum ; the State minimizes while Monotheism maximizes, and so does morality. Fourth, that while Philosophy is at its maximum, Monotheism is at its minimum ; and that as Philosophy minimizes, Monotheism maximizes, and so does morality.

> Omnific forces all things fill;
> All will is force ; all force is will.
> No will or force was first in man ;
> Another was whence his began.

LECTURE VII.

METHOD OF PERSISTENCE.

Mr. Spencer says (F. P. § 59) "the persistence of force is an ultimate truth of which no inductive proof is possible;" yet as (in § 58) he says, " the quantity of force remains always the same," it must of course persist. To be is to continue. It is the order to "gather up the fragments that remain, that nothing be lost. If Power manifests all things, and all things go back into the manifesting Power; then Power persists producing, recalling, and reproducing forms of itself. This is quite near the Buddhistic doctrine of emanation and reabsorption, if it is not the doctrine itself. But we are not manifestations of impersonal, but of personal Power. If human personality disappears, it reappears or expands into superhuman personality; illustrating the doctrine, that "we go on to perfection," even " partaking of the divine nature."

The persistence of force — unsconscious force — is one of the confident assumptions of science. According to the definition of force, the mind or soul is a force, as we shall see. Will the soul-force persist as such?

Another law, universally and invariably true, is, that what is called death of each, is a gain of the succeeding whole. All other things gain by dying : why should not man? The soul is self-created, or it is created by another. If self-created, it is a power to itself forever. If it is created by another, then that other can take care of it in the future, as it has in the past. So, whether we exist of ourselves, or by the will of another, there is within and behind us an immortalizing power, looking, to say the least, in the direction of immortality, and showing its possibility.

But is there a probability of it? When the body dies, we see no soul depart, nor has one ever come back to give evidence of its disembodied existence.

But in this, as in everything else, the past answers for the future. Though no one can have a *present experience*, in the body, of a *future state* out of the body, yet the reasoning from present physical phenomena to future physical phenomena is neither different nor more certain than that from the present existence of the soul to the continued future existence of the soul. The rising of the life-bearing sun to-morrow cannot, in the nature of things, be a matter of observation to-day. In the omnipresence and omnipotence of law, by which both matter and mind continue to progress, we have as much certainty of the continuance of the individual immortality of the soul, as we have of anything in the future.

But, as we have said, we cannot possibly answer experimentally now a question whose solution must be entirely in the future. Do we not live now under a law of persistence, by which it is seen that we must

live hereafter? We exist now, and why should we not
continue to exist? We expect to exist to-morrow,
and why should we not expect to exist one hundred
or a million of years hence? In the life of the race,
we have not only an expectation and a start in existence, prophetic of its continuance, but in our present
lives, as conscious individuals, we have already entered upon immortality. We are in the grasp of the
law of persistence, and those who deny immortality,
must prove conclusively that the law has been repealed, and the grasp released. In short, the doctrine
of immortality cannot be disproved.

According to materialism the individual has no immortality in himself. Out of himself his race or type
only persists.[a] But so far as science can establish a
principle of continuity or persistence of beings in time,
it helps religion to a line of reasoning, which points
to their persistence in eternity. ' *We are* conscious
beings, and *therefore shall be*.' Life once begun must be
supposed to continue, not only in this world, but also
in the next, unless it be proved to have ceased. Some
say that this proof is made when the material body
has no longer life in it. But the separation of the
soul from the body cannot be a cessation of the existence of the soul, for this separation partially takes
place every second, and yet we live. At no two moments do we have the same bodies, though ever the
same souls. As our entire bodies are new every
seven years, as it is said, while our life and consciousness are one and the same, it is evident that we do not

(*a*)   "So careful of the type she seems,
   So careless of the single life."—*Tennyson.*

give up our consciousness when we give up our bodies, in what we call life, and why should we be held
to give it up when we give up our bodies in what we
call death?

We have said that whatever moves matter is force.
We also say that mind moves matter; therefore, mind
is force. Again they say, all force is imperishable;
all mind is force; therefore all mind is imperishable.
This proves that mind, as force, is imperishable.
This much is settled. But, it is asked, as the horse
has mind, why is not the mind-force of the horse im
perishable? This raises the question as to the form
or mode in which force is imperishable. Mind-force
is both conscious and personal in man, and unconscious and impersonal in brute animals.

1. *Conscious, personal mind-force persists.* As said
before, each one is conscious, that his mind is his own,
and continuous. Each one has the same reason to
believe in the individuality and continuous personality of his own mind, that he has to believe in its
existence. And we may as well expect the mind
itself to perish, as to expect its individuality, consciousness, and personal continuance to perish. We
know that we know; in other words, we are conscious, and therefore immortal. The exercises of the
mind arise and vanish, and are each separate and distinct from others in their appearance; but the same
mind is in and through them all, and holds them all
in its one consciousness. The thought which was
yesterday or last year in consciousness, and the conscious thought of to-day are both recognized as being
in the same self-consciousness. The self-conscious-

ness has not changed, while the exercises have been coming and departing. The mind thus remains in its own identity yesterday and onward into the future, perpetuating the same mind. Through all development of its faculties, in all states, the mind itself neither comes nor goes, but retains its self-sameness through all changes. Its phenomenal experience varies *in* time, but itself perdures *through* all time." (Hickok, Science of the mind from Consciousness, Chap. I, p. 3.)

" Consciousness has been very differently apprehended by different writers, and certainly not seldom misapprehended. Some have considered it as scarcely to be distinguished from personal identity; others as a separate faculty for knowing the action of all other mental powers; and others again as the complement and connection of all mental exercises, inasmuch as they are all held in one consciousness. Consciousness is doubtless ever one in the same person, otherwise some actions would be in one consciousness, and some in another, and man's life could never be brought into one experience. But this does by no means confound consciousness in personal identity, for identity continues in and through a great number of states of consciousness." (Ibid. 88.)

Consciousness persists because, first, it is intelligent Power, and Power is immaterial, uncompounded, and, therefore, indissoluble; and second, because it is at the summit of being, and survives as the fittest. Consciousness is either inherent in matter, or it is an independent Power. If it inheres in matter, it inheres in each and every atom, or in a combination of atoms. If it inheres in a combination of atoms, then it must inhere in each atom ; for, as nothing can communicate what it has not, each atom must have inherently in itself the consciousness which it communicates to a combinations of atoms. As consciousness is personality, if each atom is conscious, each man is not one person, but as many persons as there are atoms in his body. But as our bodies are no two seconds the same, if each atom is conscious, and, therefore, a person, we are not only a congress, but an endless procession of persons, which is inconceivable. The nature of every cause must decide its effects ; but, as we cannot conceive of anything being and not being at the same moment, so the nature of unconsciousness cannot include consciousness ; and unconsciousness cannot, therefore, be the cause of consciousness as an effect. If consciousness be indivisible, it cannot be an inherent energy in divisible matter.

Consciousness can become extinct in only one of three ways: first, either by *dissolution*, which is impossible, as consciousness is a single, not a compound substance, and cannot be dissolved ; or, second, by *privation* of a part of its essence ; but as consciousness has no parts, it can be deprived of none ; or, third, by *annihilation;* but this could only be by its own act, which is not supposable, or by the external act of God, whose existence materialists deny.

As a principle of unity, the soul is indiscerptible and indestructible ; as a principle of motion, it is incapable of rest ; as a principle of vital force, it is incapable of annihilation ; as a self-conscious principle, it is incapable of oblivion.[a]

(*a*) Heard's Tripartite Nature of Man, p. 3.

The immortality of the soul is not impossible from any connection with matter, for it is not matter.   As nature, it is said, can make no leaps, unconscious matter could never have become conscious matter. That matter should think is unthinkable.   The body changes constantly, but never the consciousness. Each persists or not by its own laws.   Herbert Spencer says that there is no conceivable kind of consciousness which does not imply continued existence as its datum.[a]   Nature confines some life in unconsciousness below.   Supernature enlarges other life in consciousness above.

If consciousness or the soul itself be an effect, then it persists; for all effects not only succeed, but survive their causes.   The soul or mind is something, or it is nothing.   If it be nothing, then as nothing it cannot be destroyed.   If it cannot be destroyed, then it must be something, for destruction implies something to be destroyed.   But if it be something, it cannot be destroyed; for while nature changes all things that are changeable, she destroys nothing that she values as anything.   The soul to be a soul must retain its individual and conscious personality.   But in any view we may take, immorality is sure.   We see the proof of it in this, among other considerations: Consciousness makes a person and distinguishes man in the scale of being, whether he be an

---

(a)   First Prin., chap. VI., sec. 62.   See in the Popular Science Monthly for July, 1878, a most admirable article, by R. G. Eccles, Esq., on the "Radical Fallacy of Materialism," wherein he says, at the conclusion of a line of most convincing argument : "If we declare matter and energy to be eternal, then we must declare the same of consciousness." p. 360.

original type or a derived individual; whether he be the fountain or the issuing stream. If man derives this being, it must be from some underived conscious cause. If he originates his own consciousness, he creates it as a God, and he can continuously transmit it as a God. In his consciousness, man shows that he is either descended by creation from some conscious God, or that, in consciousness, he is himself a God to his conscious descendants. Therefore, whether he begins in a God as a source of conscious being, or a God begins in him as a source of conscious being, he is immortal, for nothing divine ever dies.

Does nature change by receding or advancing? Does she ever tear down anything except to build up its elements in something better? When she decomposes vegetable life, is it not to build up animal life? If our consciousness be destroyed, must it not be for some condition above consciousness? What do we *know* of the origin of life? of organization? of the connection between matter and mind? What we *do* know is limited, but what we do *not* know is unlimited.[a]

Does matter mentalize itself, or mind materialize itself? Evolutionists have never answered the question whether the egg preceded and was adapted to the chicken, or the chicken to the egg; whether the male was made before and for the female, or the

---

(a) See Dr. Montgomery's "Monera, or the Problem of Life," Pop. Science Monthly, August, 1878; Supplement Pop. S. M., May, 1878, Virchow, 12, 73; also, July number, p. 334; Tyndall, Address, Norwich, 1868.

female before and for the male; whether the honey was made for the bee or the bee for the honey. The Unknown is vast indeed! Do not all things advance? If advance seems to be in accordance with a law of nature in the past, who can prove that it has been repealed as to the future.

But, it is asked, if nature tears down the vegetables on one plane to build up the animals on a higher plane, why should not the brute develop into something above itself? If man can become an angel, why not the brute become a man? If, as according to the analogy of nature, conscious man is to be lifted into some power above consciousness, ought not the unconscious brute to be lifted above itself into consciousness? If, as asked, development is to be expected in men, so it ought to be expected in brutes.

While we can look below us and see that no brute ever does become man, we cannot look above us in the same way to see what a man may expect to become. Immortality is necessarily to be expected from nature in either man or brutes, or both, unless she can be stupid enough to stop in sight of what would glorify her most. If she can produce life for awhile in man and brute, why not forever? Has not nature as much reason to go on as she had to begin? And since beginning, has nature not in fact steadily advanced, and held every gain? As to thinking animals, no intelligence short of consciousness is considered a gain. At least we have no knowledge of it. Whatever mind the brutes may have, so far as we now know, seems limited to their animal wants. It is directive, not reflective. But man has mind for far more. Brute mind is imperishable, only as an impersonal, unconscious mode of force, in the same grade of force it is now ; but lacking consciousness, it is perishable as individual mind. The mind-force of man must persist in its consciousness if it persists at all. It is consciousness which lifts mind from a mode or manifestation of force into force itself. Conscious mind is force.

Nor in distinguishing between impersonal individuality and individual personality, do we make a distinction without a difference? Consciousness is the grand difference between impersonal individuality and individual personality, and is a new order of existence. Nature preserves its best things, and these only. If it preserves not consciousness, what else would it preserve?

When brutes die, the intelligent but unconscious force that was individualized in them for a time, obeys the law of all unconscious, unpersonalized force, and losing whatever individuality it may have exhibited when it has performed any special work, is correlated back into something else, or reabsorbed ; as, after electricity has been captured and made to fire guns, ring bells, explode mines, and carry messages across vast oceans and broad continents, it drops its temporary mode of individuality, and lapsing back like a wave of the sea, becomes again an undistinguishable part of electricity elsewhere, or is correlated into heat. Individuality was no part of its nature, but only an impersonal, unconscious temporary manifestation of it. So the individualized mind of the brute, not having gained consciousness, or enough to lift it into the higher order of personalized force, drops its individuality when its animal work is done, as a tree or an oyster drops its individuality ; and being only unconscious force, is conservated, like any other unconscious force, by correlation or reabsorption. But the personality of man, including the transient individuality common to the brute, and also a consciousness which is peculiar to man, is a vast flight upward ; and manifests, if it does not originate, as before said, a new order of force in which individuality, now lifted into personality, persists. Consciousness, or life, on nature's highest terrace, is a gain to be conservated, if any is to be conservated. To individuality there has been superadded, in conscious intelligence, moral power and spiritual responsibility, all that is meant by personality. Nature advances as much in moving from unconsciousness to consciousness, as she does when the animal kingdom rises above the vegetable kingdom. Is there a greater difference between these kingdoms than there is between conscious man thinking about his thought, and the unconscious brute thinking only about his mate and his food ? If the law of progress be admitted, then immortality begins where consciousness begins, and ends where it ends. Disembodied life is not new in the nature of things, if mind preceded matter. Conscious mind is either a mode of matter, or it is above matter. If above, it can survive in the future, as in the past, the absence of that which is beneath it. If mind be a mode of matter, it must be a supreme mode, conscious, individual, and personal ; and as such, it must exist forever, because no matter perishes. If, in other words, matter becomes a person, then as personalized matter it is imperishable. If matter becomes conscious, then it must exist as conscious matter."

As said before, every person is an individual, but every individual is not a person. We cannot transcend our personality. A person is an individual that is conscious of his individuality—a thinker conscious of his thought—one who knows that he knows. A stone or a piece of metal is an individual mass or lump which may be separated into parts, each of which shall continue to have the same qualities as the whole. That which cannot be parted into several things of the same nature is an individual whole ; as, for instance, a seed, a plant or an animal, when separated into parts, loses its identity or individuality, which is not retained by any of its parts. We refuse *personality* to a stone or a metal, because these things exist for others and not for themselves. We refuse it also to a mere animal, because, though it may have individuality, it is not conscious of its individuality. We ascribe personality to man because that which he is, he is for himself, and has consciousness of it. Consciousness, or the ability to study our own minds, pre-eminently distinguishes man from the brute—the personalized individual from the non-personalized individual. It is the dividing line between imperishable personality and perishable individuality. Until personality is attained, there is no such individuality as needs or does persist. Though consciousness is not in itself a force, yet, when force becomes conscious, consciousness persists with the persistence of the force that manifests it.

It is true that the individual or unconscious animal part dies, but not the conscious or personal part. The unconscious die and not the conscious? We can conceive of no consciousness that does not continue. To resolve personal consciousness back into impersonal unconsciousness is not to correlate or transform, but to destroy it, and nature destroys nothing.

Nature destroys the individuality of the brute at its death; that is she drops it but seems not to consider the obliteration of any individuality short of conscious individuality, rising into personality, as a destruction or loss. We repeat, consciousness is at the summit of all things, and it is consciousness that makes individuality a type, and so a gain. Personality is equal to a type, but if personal consciousness does not persist, then it is a total loss, and nature works in vain, preserving her lower, impersonal types, and annihilating her highest personal, conscious, individual type. Such an exhibition of power, such vacillating weakness of purpose, and such permission of loss, if not wanton destruction, would proclaim nature to be an idiot and a suicide. She may convert impersonal and unconscious force, and exalt conscious force, but not destroy it. The elements of everything that dies can be and are used over again, such as the carbon and other elements in the animal body; but that which cannot be used over again does not die. The consciousness of one cannot be used again in the consciousness of another, and unless each man's consciousness persists under all changes, then consciousness, which is the most exalted of facts, must perish altogether. Does nature in anything else so destroy its best work? It is in consciousness that man is in the likeness of God, or whatever is supreme above him. In the pyramid of stars surmounted by the sun all serve and glorify the one at the top; as in the universe, consciousness looks down upon all unconscious forms below it.

Brutes are not immortal, because, while they have individuality they have not consciousness, or anything that nature cares to preserve, except their material elements. Having no conscious personality, they must forever remain in the class of impersonal things, and be correlated or transmitted from one impersonal thing to another. Below personal individuality, no individuality persists.

2. *Unconscious, impersonal mind-force persists.* If the mind force of the horse is conscious, he cannot assert it. Lower animals, as the horse, the dog, the elephant, the beaver, and such insects as the bee, have intelligence and memory, but we have no knowledge that they are conscious. Those who affirm their consciousness must prove it. We are severally conscious of our own consciousness; but we are neither conscious of the consciousness of another man, nor can we prove the consciousness of another man or of an animal. Nature has not yet been so unmerciful to the horse as to make him conscious of his lot. Instinct is not consciousness. We are conscious that we are men and not lower animals, but we have no evidence that they think anything about it. But

consciousness or no consciousness, settles the question of the brute animal's immortality. The difference between these two kinds of force is this, as said before. The man thinks and he thinks about his thought—he knows that he knows—he is conscious of his consciousness. The horse thinks, but he does not, from all we can judge, think about his thought. He may know, but he does not know that he knows. If he was conscious of his strength, he would kick into eternity the brutal wretches who inhumanly mistreat him; and yet, as the man belongs to a grade of immortal creatures, he is to be imperishable in his personality and the poor horse imperishable in his impersonality. As men are to be men in eternity, the horse may be thankful that he is not to be a horse in eternity. If the elephant was conscious of his strength—if the lion was conscious or knew how to rend his iron barriers, how terrible would be his revenge. If all animals in the lower plane are to serve man on the higher plane, consciousness must be denied them. Man knows, captures and bridles the lightning, because it does not know how to resist. The conscious must ever be master of the unconscious.

Conscious mind-force belongs exclusively to man, making him a *person*; and unconscious mind-force belongs equally to brutes; leaving them in the class of thinking but unconscious impersonal *things*.

We have seen that each man has in himself two orders of force: a conscious, personalizing, regulative mind-force, as seen in his will, elevating him into a person; and an unconscious, impersonal, regulated matter-force, as seen in the heat of his material body, which he has in common with mere things. The brute has the same two orders of force, but its mind-force is as unconscious as its matter-force. Its intelligence is called instinct, and only directive, not reflective, and is limited, unconscious, impersonal, and without moral responsibility.

Impersonal mind-force persists as impersonal. The mind-force of the horse as of the man is imperishable for exactly what it is, and not for what it is not. It is impersonal mind-force here, and will be imperishable as impersonal mind-force hereafter. Man's mind-force is personal mind-force here, and will be imperishable as personal mind-force hereafter. If the mental force of the horse is unconscious and impersonal force here, why should it be a conscious and personal force hereafter? If a horse is not a person here, why should it be immortal as a person hereafter? It may be said that this is hard on the horse ; but you must question evolution about that, if you deny a God ; and if you do not deny a God, then you should not question the God which you admit. Now comes the question, why should the impersonal mind-force of the horse lose its individuality and be reabsorbed only as impersonal force, like gravitation, or electricity, and the personal mind-force of man be preserved as personal, individual force?

The proposition is that all force is imperishable ; but that not all individualized quantities or manifestations of force are imperishable in individual quantities. A bottle of electricity is an individualized quantity of electricity ; the electricity as a force will

21

be preserved, but not the individualized quantity as an individuality. Strictly speaking, individuality cannot be predicated of anything inorganic. It is only by way of accommodation that we can individualize portions of the elements or speak of a bottle of electricity, or a quart of oxygen or of hydrogen, or a pound of gravitation, or a yard of space, or a handful of water. We may enclose space, but we do not individualize it. The individual is the indivisible. The thoughts of all animals are their individual thoughts, but until intelligence is developed into conscious intelligence, nature does not preserve its individualities. This is proved by the law and the facts of the case.

It is a law of nature to hold all gains. The unconscious impersonal intelligence of impersonal animals was a great gain, and Nature holds it exactly as she gains it—an unconscious impersonal, intelligence. But the conscious, personal intelligence of man was a greater gain, and Nature holds that exactly as she gains it—as conscious, personal, individual intelligence. The unconscious intelligence of the horse and the conscious intelligence of man are imperishable, exactly as force. That which is once a force is always a force. That which is once a conscious mind-force is always a conscious mind-force. A person once is always a person. If consciousness has been added to mind-force and mind-force is imperishable, of course its essential consciousness is as imperishable as the force to which it is essential, is imperishable. As the outside is imperishable, so must be the inside; and so, if the mind is imperishable as a force, all must be imperishable that belongs to it as mind. As we have said before, nature holds its gains. When nature rose from homogeneity to heterogeneity—from genera to species—from species to conscious individuals—it held its gains. Force once an individualized person, is individualized forever. We know that we have minds only by our consciousness; but we are as conscious of our individuality as we are of having minds at all. Each is conscious that his mind is his own and not that of another. If our consciousness knows our mind at all it knows it to be essentially individual, and therefore personal. To obliterate the individuality of the mind of man, is to obliterate the mind itself; a human mind without individuality is no human mind. But the mind is a force—an individualized force—and, as a force, cannot be obliterated; therefore the individuality of the human mind cannot be obliterated.

Individuality belongs to it as mind-force. In other words, if the whole force is imperishable all its essential characteristics, such as consciousness, are imperishable. Unconscious mind-force in time will be unconscious mind-force in eternity. Personality retains its individuality; impersonality drops it at death. To impersonality, individuality is accidental. To personality, individuality is essential. It is conscious force that individualizes force, and it is conscious individual force that personalizes force; and personal force once is personal force always.

A jar of electricity, though losing whatever individuality it had as a separate quantity of electricity in the jar, does not lose, on being discharged, its force as electricity, but it does lose its individualization of quantity. It is reabsorbed into the totality of electrical force. All personality is individual, but all individuality is not personal. Impersonal force ever continues to exist in the impersonal totality of force, and personal force exists as personal individual force, or not at all. If it is reabsorbed into the totality of impersonal force, it ceases to be a force at all; for individuality is its essence. A drop of the ocean is individual so long as it is a drop, but it loses its individuality on being returned to the ocean.

When nature advanced from whatever of intelligence may be claimed for the habits of plants, the lower intelligence of lower animals, we see that as nature came on up the ascensions of being, it made different kinds of mind-force, in the habit of plants, the instinct of some animals and the intelligence of others, and the consciousness of others. Consciousness is at the summit of intelligence. This consciousness of man makes him a person, and the want of this consciousness leaves the horse an impersonal creature.

Place before your imagination a battery or a bottle of electricity, a vessel of water, and a living horse. You have a blind force in electricity, a blind force in chemic affinity, a blind force in gravitation, an intelligent force in the mind of the horse, and an intelligent, conscious force in your own mind. If you discharge the electricity through the water, the force of chemic affinity is overcome by the electric force, and the water is decomposed into its original elements of oxygen and hydrogen. If the circuit is complete, the electric force passes on into the horse and overcomes the mind-force of the horse and kills the horse.

Thus your own conscious, mind-force has not only made blind electric force overcome the blind chemic force in water, and the impersonal, organic mind-force in the horse, but your conscious mind-force has per-mitted the blind force of electricity to go free. Can it be that these blind forces, managed by man's con-scious force, shall be imperishable in their imperson-ality, and man's conscious mind-force that manages them, shall not be imperishable in its personality?

But notice, it was your personal mind-force that first captured, confined and then liberated the force of electricity. Personal mind force is master. It makes electricity dissolve compounds, carry mes-sages, turn wheels, lift weights and light up the world. This personal mind-force harnesses gravitation and makes it do the work of countless millions of giants. It compels heat to work the engines of civilization and even to evolve electric force itself—in a word, the personal mind-force of man, not the impersonal mind-force of the horse, masters all other forces.

At this point, let us resume the consideration of the persistence of conscious, personal mind-force as a soul-force.[a]

3. *The persistence of conscious, personal mind-force is immortality.* Personal mind-force persists as personal mind-force. That which supernaturally exists in any form supernaturally persists in some form. Un-conscious things such as vegetables and brute ani-

(a) See pp. 309–319.

mals change their form and disorganize, but do not destroy any of their atomic substance. Conscious persons change their substance, as from the physical to the psychical, but not their form. This change is progressive, not destructive.

The argument is that the mind, whether of man or of beast, is imperishable in the persistence of force. We claim not only that the persistence of force proves the imperishableness of the mind as force, but that the persistence of consciousness shows the mind of men to be individually and personally imperishable, and the mind-force of the horse perishable as an unconscious individuality, but imperishable as an impersonal force. Consciousness immortalizes the individuality of individual intelligence.

All force is not the same force. To our observation there are two orders; first, a mind-force, underived and supreme in the Unoriginated Power—personal, intelligent, conscious, and dominating all below it; and second, matter-force. such as heat and gravitation, impersonal, unconscious, unintelligent and secondary to all force above it. Scientists say now that there is but one force in all the universe, conscious in mind and unconscious in matter. Though they do not prove this unity of force, yet, admitting it to be so as the last conclusion of science and for the sake of the argument, even then the unconscious, such as heat and electricity, must be a mode of the conscious, having its basis, as Herbert Spencer says, in Absolute Being, and not the conscious its basis in the unconscious. Even if all force is but eternal power in action, conscious in mind, unconscious in matter, it must ever go forward, but never backward. So that if matter-force cannot be annihilated, neither, *a fortiori,* can mind-force, of which matter-force is the unconscious, impersonal mode.

How do you prove that *any* force is imperishable? Scientists prove the imperishableness of any and of all force, by the fact as claimed that its quantity is fixed ; that is, that force can be neither increased nor diminished, neither created nor destroyed. Such is the theory by which scientists try to account for phenomena that they can, as yet, account for as well in no other way.

Herbert Spencer says[a] ' the persistence of force is an ultimate truth of which no inductive proof is possible.' Youmans says ' it is not without its difficulties, which time alone must be trusted to remove.'[b] Grove, Faraday, Stewart, LeConte and Bain assume, rather than attempt to prove, the doctrine of the conservation of force. There is such correlation as heat into electricity, and of electricity into heat ; but we do not see gravitation correlated or transferred into any other manifestation of force, or of any other force into gravitation. Besides, if force can be and is exhaustively correlated backwards and forwards, how can the theory of evolution be true, that everything progresses forever? The constancy or inconstancy in the quantity of force depends upon whether its source is personal or impersonal, and this question of source must be first settled. Supreme Will may

---

(a) First Principles, Chap. vi., § 59.

(b) Introduction to Cor. and Con. of Forces, xiv.

will that there shall be what we call force, or supreme Will may be that force itself. If force, personal or impersonal, be the Will of a supreme Being, force cannot be a fixed quantity; for supreme Will cannot be a fixed quantity; and so, if the quantity of force be fixed, force cannot be will itself. Supreme Will can will all things except to will that it will not will. It is true that the Will that could will our personal wills into existence, and yet not be those wills, could will impersonal force into existence, and not be that force. A supreme Will may will that our mind-force be imperishable; but if there be no supreme Will, then our mind-force is necessary, and *must* be imperishable. · That which necessarily began in the past, necessarily continues in the present, and will necessarily [continue forever. Necessary evolution makes a necessary immortality.

The manifestation of impersonal force, that is, force manifested in things rather than in persons— such as the blind force of heat, electricity, or gravitation—is as an ocean of force lifted and broken at times into individual waves that lapse and subside into the infinite fullness. Personal or will force, originating in the mind of an Infinite Person, is deposited and perpetually correlated in the wills of finite, conscious persons. If a Person did not create force, force has certainly created a person; for man is here. If there be no God, and unintelligent and unconscious eternal Force created everything, then it was indeed a miraculous leap for the conscious force manifested in every man's will, to come up out of what is called unconscious force lurking only in matter. If unconscious force originated everything, which one of its forces did the work? Did unconscious gravitation create everything? Did unconscious electricity create everything? Did unconscious chemical affinity create everything? If the quantity of force be fixed, who is to fix it? If the quantity of force is fixed it is *infinite*.

It is more logical, and not so difficult to suppose that creative Power, in originating and fixing the quantity of force, would have provided an infinite quantity, than to suppose that it would have experimented upon the possible insufficiency of a finite quantity. If nature had any plan to which it invariably worked, we might suppose that it would have known exactly how much and what kind of force it would need, and might, with good reason, have fixed its quantity in finite limits; but as Bückner, Vogt, Moleschott, and Hæckell, deny that there is design or plan in nature, it could not, therefore, know how much force it might need in its blind work, and might well be expected to fix enough once for all, and make it infinite. Any way, nature, in the prodigality of its works, seems to be quite confident of having enough stuff and force to keep up, and even extend, its phenomena. If there be no God, the quantity of force must be infinite or self-limited. But if any say that it is not infinite, then they must prove definitely how much less it is; because if it be not infinite it may be zero, and vanish entirely. Force is in the universe. Those who assert a given quantity must define and prove the quantity. The fact is, no one knows much about this thing called force. The definition of force here used is about as good as any, if not the best; but keep in mind that we argue this question from the exclusive standpoint of science.

So far as these authorities can settle it, force has its basis in Absolute Being. If this be so, the quantity of force is not necessarily fixed, but may vary with the decisions of His omnific will, and so transcend the domain and methods of science.

Explain it as we may, it is a fact that *all real advances persist.* Nature never recalls or intermits progression; never mistakes the end or the means; never changes in vain; never sees a reason to undo what she has once done; never goes down, but always upward and forward.

So much for phenomena from impersonal nature! And yet there is no true explanation. The mind, accustomed to abstraction, is the dupe of an illusion when it takes laws for realities. Laws are symbols of order—of Will; they do not account for order.

Mill says that to explain one law of nature by another, is simply to substitute one mystery for another. We can no more assign a *reason* for the more general laws than for the more partial.[a] And yet, all reasoning that proves anything for science, proves more for religion.

For Nature, with her immanent, necessary instinct, does not perpetuate, as real gains, such transformations as heat into electricity, or of electricity into heat; of gases into rocks, or of rocks into gases; of minerals into vegetables, or of vegetables into ani-

---

(a)   Mill's Logic, p. 276.

mals. In these ebbs and flows of matter, these working correlations change everything and gain nothing
that persists.

Nature advances from chaos and gains organization; she advances from vegetable life to animal life.
These types are these gains. If they are not, what
are? If we mount by terraces, is not each terrace a
gain in altitude, quality of atmosphere, and extent of
view? Has not the man on top of the mountain
gained much over the man at its base?

The man at the top has gained, but not the brute
in any grade, for whom sublimity is in vain. It
needs no lofty tower or mountain-peak to enable it to
study the stars in their courses. For it in vain the
soft influence of the Pleiades, or the face of Orion or
Arcturus. It aspires not from nature to supernature.
All it wants is food. For it there need be no loom
or spindles. It has appetites, but no desires. Its
organization is low, and its future is limited. It
never acts upon any ideas, except those which conduce to its two aims, its personal well-being and its
propagation; consequently, we may conclude that its
brain only resolves a certain class of forces, and that
another class appreciated by men are not cognizable
by the brute.[a] Like the collodionized plate, the unconscious self registers only one class of phenomena.
The beast lives for itself, for its animal nature; it has
no other pleasures, for it has no other nature. A
horse is indifferent to the rainbow, because the rainbow in no way affects its well-being.[b] The human

---

(a) Baring Gould's "Origin and Development of Religious Ideas," 51.
(b) Ibid, 5.

mind is open to a chain of pleasurable impressions, in no way conducive to the preservation of man's sensual being, and to the perpetuation of his race. He derives pleasure from harmonies of color, and grace of form, and from melodious succession of notes. His animal life needs neither. He is conscious of desires which the gratification of passion does not satisfy, for they are beside and beyond the animal instincts. Man derives his liveliest gratification and acutest pain from objects to which his animal consciousness is indifferent. The rainbow charms him. Why? Because the sight conduces to the welfare of his spiritual being.[a] The religious instinct, (which is a desire to follow out a law of our being) is the feeling of man after an individual aim other than that of his animal nature.[b] Brute intelligence is not a conscious intelligence, and therefore no gain.

Does the the artist who moulds in clay, consider himself to have gained anything by the image which he breaks? or the painter who thinks in chalk, anything in forms which he rubs out as soon as finished? Can nature be said to have gained anything in individualities which she ever most remorselessly extinguishes? She makes the individual crystal, and dissolves it into gas. She shoots up countless blades of grass, and lifts up the forms of shrubs and trees, and draws them back dead into her mysterious workshop. She quickens the pulse of insects, brutes and birds with individual life, and beats them down again in indistinguishable dust, leaving in the universe

(a)   Baring Gould's "Origin and Development of Religious Ideas," 5.
(b)   Ibid, 61.

neither memory nor trace of their individual, unpersonalized existence. How do we account for this destructiveness of nature, then? Nature, as the scientists present her, uses mere grade and division in her manifestations, only as a working convenience. Below conscious individuality, which we call personality, no individuality persists. In other words, nature does not regard nor prize mere unconscious individuality as a real advance or gain. If she did, she would not so invariably demolish her work. We do not destroy that which we value. If nature progresses, she does not hold mere individuality to be progress, or she would preserve it. We cannot progress by going back along our own steps. A perishing man on the mountain top has gained nothing.

Altitude, however high, whose material base may at any moment dissolve beneath the feet and destroy him, is no gain. If man can be lifted from off the mountain top, so that he can abide aloft, upheld by 'Everlasting Arms,' whatever may crumble beneath him, then, and not till then, can he be said to have gained in the movements of existence.

Though nature had made individual animals, automatic and intelligent, it had gained nothing until it gained consciousness. Why should the 'necessary, immanent instinct,' of which Bückner and others speak, having progressed so far, and, as they seem to think, have gained so much, not progress further and gain more? Why should it stop at an unconscious animal? We see that it did not. We see that it went on to the conscious man. Above conscious man there may yet be evolved an order

as much brighter than conscious man as conscious
man is above the unconscious horse. It is not impossible in this system for impersonal force to be used
over again as personal in a personal organization.
Or, why, having lifted the animal upward along the
terraces of phenomena, and placed his feet in the
frozen dust on the mountain top, not lift his feet still
higher, and endow him with power to move like the
stars, in individual and perpetual glory, above
matter?

It is said that an atom is matter, but the force of
gravitation in an atom pulls from the centre of the
atom. In imagination peel off the outside of that
atom until you have got down to the centre. You
have got down to force, have you not? But where
is your matter? You have your force which must
transcend matter, but your atom, which was matter,
is gone. Let us not confound matter and force.
They may be associated, but cannot be identical.
The man in the saddle is not the same thing as the
horse beneath him, which he guides with a bit and
bridle. Force guides matter, but is not matter, unless
a thing can be said to guide itself, when it is not itself,
but something else. What is there so attractive in
matter, or what in it so necessary to personality, that
man must be chained to it forever? Blind nature, or
'immanent necessary instinct,' knows no reason for
beginning at matter more than at mind, or for stopping at matter or at mere mind. Why should it not
rise and progress forever, and gain forever? If
nature began at matter, why should it not go on to
mind as we see it did; and if it began in mind, why

should it sink back into mere matter? The force that has brought it on from the past is neither exhausted nor bewildered, and can carry it on in the future. This rather proves that all matter is only manifestations of mind, as so many ancient and modern philosophers have contended. For if matter is force and force is mind, then matter is mind, and so it is no longer. Individual phenomena are then only special and changing thoughts.

We prove by admitted principles that men are more than a race of animals. It is contended that nature ever progresses and gains. Now, the mere animal must, according to this theory, be improved upon, and so on to the summit of being. If blind nature found its way from nothing to a conscious, reasoning man, we can be quite sure that it knows its way to an omniscient God. If a Personal Being did not create nature, nature has, in man, created a personal being. As said before, there is a God at one end or the other of progress. The more unconscious things are at the beginning, the more conscious they must be in the end. Development cannot be stopped. If out of nihilism nature evolves life, why should it not out of life evolve immortality? When nature begins, what is to stop it? If it creates many things both in kind and number, it is seen, in all that we observe, to preserve the best. As between individuals and types and forces, is it not according to its most evident way of working that conscious mind-force, as the utilizer of all manifestations of force, should survive as the fittest of all? Whatever else may cease, we cannot suppose that consciousness as the supreme fact in the universe can cease. Nature never inverts the pyramid. Why should conscious, personal mind-force perish, and unconscious, impersonal matter-force survive? In what is the immortal power of the one, and in what is the mortal weakness of the other? Is impersonality superior to personality, or unconscious-ness to consciousness? Does the universal thinking of mankind put a *thing* above or on the same level with a *person?* Is a stone superior or equal in the order of nature to Shakspeare, or a vial of electric-ity to David and Isaiah? Is blindness the honor or the fact of nature? Is a mole nearer the summit of her glory than is an eagle? Is the idiot more the perfection of nature than Socrates? Such a prefer-ence on the part of nature, if it were possible, were the choice of a fool. When the impersonal force de-fines itself by leaping up into personal or will force, or unconsciousness awakens into consciousness, there would seem to be a gain indeed worth preserving, if anything is. In every sense and for every movement of nature, the personal, the conscious, the coherent, the definite, the moral would be the fittest, both for worth and for struggle. .

But it is insisted that the doctrine of the conserva-tion or persistence of force does not prove the immortality of the individual soul. Herbert Spencer says:[a] 'By the persistence of force, we really mean some power which transcends our knowledge and conception. The manifestations, as occurring either in ourselves or outside of us, do not persist; but that which persists is the unknown cause of these manifes-

---

(a)   First Principles, chap. vi., § 60.

tations. In other words, asserting the persistence of force is but another mode of asserting an unconditional reality, without beginning or end.'

This must refer to the manifestation of blind, unintelligent, impersonal force, such as heat, electricity, and gravitation ; but as a force, mind and its work, or manifestation, are one and the same. The mind is conscious that it is a power, force, or cause, unto itself ; and, of course, takes no knowledge of itself as a mere manifestation, from any cause whatever, known or unknown. In reasoning upon the immortality of the soul, from the law of the persistence of type, the persistence of consciousness, and the persistence of force, three independent, if not conflicting lines of argument are pursued ; and we might give up either, if the sufficiency of the others is admitted. These arguments are either all true or all false ; or one is true and the others false. That all three are true, some will deny. If one be true, it matters not if the others be false. If all are false, as is assumed, the dilemma of the scientist is greatest of all. Because, as we know the soul to exist now as a supreme fact, if we fail by either or all of these, the best scientific arguments, to prove the immortality which we affirm, then they must prove the mortality which they affirm. To prove that anything exists, raises the presumption of its perpetual continuance, under any and every possible change. If any deny the presumption, they must prove their denial. The failure to prove the immortality of the soul does not establish its mortality. The existence of the soul in life is admitted to be the most exalted force in the universe. If any

22

admit that the unconscious, impersonal force, such as electricity or heat, persists, though its presence may be concealed, *a fortiori* they must admit that the greater, more intelligent force of the conscious, personal soul must persist, though its presence may be concealed. Disappearance, in neither case, is destruction. The affirmation that it ceases to exist after death must be proved as an independent proposition, by the one who makes it. To say that we have no knowledge of it after death, is no proof that it has ceased to be. Change is not annihilation. Force does not cease because it changes its manifestations, or conceals its presence. When heat is changed into electricity, no force is destroyed. The traveler is not dead because he is out of sight. Existence does not depend on manifestation. Light reveals this world, but it conceals all others. What death is, no one can tell another. It is a secret for each. But science proclaims that everywhere within its searching vision life is triumphant. Reason eagerly explores the field of our own future probabilities, and revelation certifies and glorifies the fact of human immortality. Life is omnipresent. No part of this universe is dead. Life is triumphant. It must be the master, or all things would end. Life is continuous. The one living grain of wheat expands itself into a hundred lives. Death is the last enemy, and life the last friend, in the eternal economy.

But, it is objected, admitting a brute to be a mere impersonal individual, and man to be distinguished by having his individuality lifted into what is understood as personal consciousness, and admitting that the soul of man, as mind-force, cannot be annihilated, it is still contended that death obliterates its individuality and personality, and reduces both the mind of the impersonal brute and the mind of the personal man to the same impersonal level of the one universal force. It is contended that both are manifestations of force, and are reabsorbed into the totality of all force. This doctrine of emanation and reabsorption was taught by Aristotle three hundred and fifty years before, and reproduced by Averroes, an Arabian Philosopher of Spain, one thousand two hundred years after Christ, and has been held by the Hindoos in all ages. Is it not Herbert Spencer's theory, too? With Aristotle, Constructive Reason,[a] as distinguished from Passive Reason,[b] which receives the impression of external things, and perishes with the body, transcends the body, and is capable of separation from it. This Constructive Reason is one individual substance, or universal soul, being one in Socrates, Plato, and other individuals.[c] Each has a part of the whole, whence it follows, according to this theory, that individuality consists only in bodily sensations, which are perishable: so that nothing which is individual, such as sensations, can be immortal, and nothing which is immortal, as the universal soul, can be individual.

(a) Herbert Spencer calls this 'Absolute Being,' 'Unknown Cause,' 'Power,' 'Force,' 'Unconditioned Reality. without Beginning or End.' The Athenians call it ' The Unknown God.'

(b) Herbert Spencer calls this ' Manifestations of force which perish.'

(c) What is this but the idea of One God, who breathed in the body of man the breath of life, and he became a living soul, as taught in the Scriptures? Gen. ii., 7.

This will answer as well as any other speculation to account for the perishableness of *impersonal* individuality; it is not satisfactory as to the future of *personal* individuality. Vast is the difference upward from an individual *thing* to an individual *person*. Any way, the theory of Aristotle, as reproduced by Averroes, proves too much. It admits that this Constructive Reason is one indivisible substance. But that indivisable substance is joined, in man, with individual sensations. The individual sensations die, but the indivisible substance is reabsorbed into the eternal Pleroma called Nirvana. This indivisible substance is individualized by being identified with human sensations. That part of the Universal Soul which is in man is all in man that can have sensations, and therefore in these sensations is individual. But how, according to this theory, can it be immortal, if it be individual? If individuality destroys immortality, and immortality destroys individuality, then the constructive reason of Aristotle, and even the lauded Nirvana, of the Buddhist, cannot be, because it is both one and immortal.

The derived cannot emanate from the underived in the sense of separation, as the Buddhists teach, for that would diminish the infinite; nor can it be reabsorbed into the underived as they teach, for that would increase the infinite. A square is still a square, whether you draw diagonals or circles within it. So the infinite as to *itself* is only the infinite; its manifestations are finite only as to *themselves*. The infinite circumference focalizes in itself as a finite centre; supernature centripetalizes into natural, and inconceivable Power is pictured in perceivable manifestations.

The error of both Aristotle and Averroes, was in antagonizing immortality and personal individuality. It may be conceded that their theory was plausible as to impersonal individuality ; but the soul is immortal, according to science, not because it is an individual, but because it is a force, and so, supreme over matter. Above all other force, it has both individuality and conscious personality, and apart from these grand distinctions we know nothing of it.

But let us go a little further, and see where this extinction of all individuality and personality would land us. Suppose a soul—a part of the universal soul—steeped in all possible wickedness, to die in the midst of all its vileness, and with the loss of its individual sensations and personal identity, is reabsorbed in the great abyss of Soul. The Buddhists call this abyss Nirvana. Now this part of the Universal Soul must be reabsorbed as it is, bad ; not as it is not, good. Ink, if you keep on dropping it long enough, will finally blacken the ocean, and kill all life contained in its illimitable depths. Suppose this absorption to go on for countless ages, bad spirits after bad spirits taken into its very essence ; what must Nirvana itself become after feeding so long upon such food, in spite of the good spirits, if any, that may go there too ? Its eternal accretions of evil make Nirvana a hell. Conscious individuals cannot emanate from an unconscious Nirvana, nor can an unconscious Nirvana reabsorb conscious individuality. The less cannot produce the greater, or absorb the greater.

In the soul's loss of its individuality and its absorption into the Infinite, consists its horror. For, instead of a finite consciousness which it has lost, it acquires an infinite consciousness which is ever reabsorbing evil. Every soul that it engorges brings in its evil, and makes Nirvana the cess-pool of the universe.

In the philosophy of nature, *vestigia nulla retrorsum* —nature takes no steps backward. Heterogeneity never returns to homogeneity; the effect never returns to its cause; the stream never returns to its fountain.

> As life that is, is from all life before;
> So life that is, is life for evermore.
> Of life the whole, a part is all we know:
> From life, a part, to life, the whole, we go.

www.ingramcontent.com/pod-product-compliance
Lightning Source LLC
Chambersburg PA
CBHW021112270326
41929CB00009B/849